"Yes—let's break the grip of Stars and Hits. Music could change the world. Read this book."

**Pete Seeger**

*The Trouble with Music* isn't anything like most books about music. Those other books start by assuming that today's music world looked just the same yesterday and will be the same tomorrow. Mat Callahan understands that today's music world is a product of the past, struggling to bear the future. His story begins with reexamining what all music fundamentally shares, then sets about showing the ways in which those fundamentals have been distorted, all the while insisting we can free the music—and ourselves—to achieve a future worth celebrating. This isn't just a theory: Callahan, a working musician, crams his book with as much detail as ideas—and there's a LOT of ideas.

Making music is a process as old as the human species, which means that if the music's in trouble it's because humanity as a whole is in trouble. *The Trouble with Music* speaks to those troubles and it maps a way out. It's invaluable."

**Dave Marsh, *Rock & Rap Confidential***

This book is music to my eyes. The words are deft, melodic and insightful. Mat Callahan denounces the pipers who call the tunes in a commercial music world where most of what gets touted as creativity is akin to muzak—assaulting us every day, washed-out and conformist, deadening instead of enlivening. *The Trouble With Music* is a vibrant crescendo of protest against the corporate murder of music. While Callahan grieves, he also breathes life into hope for the resuscitation of music as wondrous means of sound rather than stagnant pools of commerce."

**Norman Solomon, *War Made Easy: How Presidents and Pundits Keep Spinning Us to Death***

"As a member of the Looters and one of the founders of Komotion, Mat Callahan has inspired many of us who have been both musicians and activists. *The Trouble With Music,* raises fundamental questions about the role music can play in our troubled world and the struggle each of us go through to bring about change. This book is must reading for music lovers and makers alike."

**Michael Franti, Spearhead**

"This is a thorough look at the absence of soul in all facets of music. Callahan's insight is astonishing. Few who work with music on a daily basis have been able to come close to [the author's] in-depth knowledge of the subject. Kudos to Callahan for bringing us an innovative approach to understanding the negative aspects of music. This book should be compulsory reading for all those those involved in music."

**John Smith, Music Director, KBCS Community Radio, Bellevue/Seattle, WA**

"*The Trouble With Music* is a brilliant, much-needed book. Drowning in the white noise of modern life, 'the trouble with music' is the trouble with life in general. Callahan's passionate prose dissects with surgical precision the dynamics by which our common wealth, in this case our innate ability to share joy and community through making music, is turned into a product to be purchased, diminishing our basic humanity in the process. His years in all sides of the 'business' of music qualifies him like few others to reveal the inner workings of both the creative passion that produces good music, how we might come to a new understanding of what 'good music' actually is, and how banal commodification has flooded our world with 'anti-music.' For musicians and listeners, rockers and rappers, clerks and toe-tappers, *The Trouble With Music* will widen your view, deepen your pleasure and reinforce your justified rage."

**Chris Carlsson, *Processed World* magazine, *The Political Edge, After The Deluge***

# THE TROUBLE
# WITH MUSIC

# THE TROUBLE
# WITH MUSIC

## MAT CALLAHAN

### WITH A FOREWORD
### BY BOFF WHALLEY

EDINBURGH · OAKLAND · WEST VIRGINIA

*The Trouble with Music*
by Mat Callahan

ISBN 1-904859-14-3

Copyright 2005 by Mat Callahan

AK Press
674-A 23rd Street
Oakland, CA 94612
USA
(510) 208-1700
www.akpress.org
akpress@akpress.org

AK Press UK
PO Box 12766
Edinburgh, EH8 9YE
Scotland
(0131) 555-5165
www.akuk.com
ak@akedin.demon.co.uk

The addresses above would be delighted to provide you with the latest complete AK catalog, featuring several thousand books, pamphlets, zines, audio and video products and stylish apparel published and distributed by AK Press. Alternatively, visit our websites for the complete catalog, latest news and secure ordering.

Library of Congress Control Number: 2004105042

Library of Congress Cataloging-in-Publication data.
A catalog record for this title is available from the Library of Congress.

Cover design by John Yates (www.stealworks.com)
Layout provided by Josh Macphee (www.justseeds.org)

Printed in Canada

## DEDICATION

For my Mother, who danced me into the world of music.

## MUSIC ALONE SHALL LIVE
(traditional German round)

Himmel und Erde mussen vergehn;
Aber die musici, aber die musici
Aber die musici, bleiben bestehn.

All things shall vanish from under the sky.
Music alone shall live, music alone shall live,
Music alone shall live, never to die.

# TABLE OF CONTENTS

# Acknowledgements

I owe my gratitude to many friends and colleagues whose experiences and insights guided me throughout the writing of this book. Without the passionate discussions, the heated arguments, and the heartfelt convictions of dedicated music lovers I would never have undertaken this project. Not only do I thank you all but I sincerely hope that I have done justice to the concerns we share.

Building on this foundation several individuals made special contributions I could not have done without. First and foremost is Thomas Powell, an artist, educator and lifelong friend, who undertook the reading of the manuscript as it was being written. Tom's criticisms and suggestions were indispensable. His grasp of the subject's scope and his attention to detail helped maintain my focus while developing a strategy for the presentation of complex material. Furthermore, Tom brought to my attention "What is Art?" Tolstoy's essay was an invaluable aid in organizing my own thinking and providing historical perspective. Indeed, it plays a central role in my argument.

Secondly, writer and activist Chris Carlsson made a decisive contribution at a critical juncture. Just when I was most uncertain about the worthiness of the project and, even, whether to continue, Chris' enthusiastic support coupled with much practical advice kept me on track. Specifically, Chris argued persuasively that many beyond those directly involved in music making would have a strong interest in the subject matter.

Thirdly, the works of Alain Badiou and Slavoj Zizek were vitally important in clarifying basic questions of philosophy and politics that had dogged my research from the beginning. With precision and erudition, each has made radical critiques of prevailing thought, particularly in regard to music and politics in the 20th century. These proved essential to establishing the context for my own thoughts as well as providing useful tools for effective struggle.

Last, but not least, I wish to acknowledge the contribution of my life partner and fellow musician, Yvonne Moore. Not only did she put up with my "one track mind" for months at a time, listening patiently as I rattled on about some problem I was facing, she constantly reminded me of the urgency of this book for musicians like us. Even more importantly, her own commitment to music was the living embodiment of all I was trying to say. Hearing her study, rehearse and perform soulful music kept me rooted in the rich soil of my theme and inspired me to see it through to its conclusion.

Thank you all.

# FOREWORD

I never did like Bruce Springsteen. Something about him just never rang true with me (and if you're touted as the blue-collar poet, then you'd better ring true). And all that common man album imagery, the pristine blue jeans and carefully-rumpled white shirts—I don't know, it just made me wince.

I know that it's really just the music I don't like. But I try to justify this dislike by picking on the context, the album sleeves, the corny neckerchiefs, and those bloody shirts and jeans.

There are a thousand bands and musicians I do like whose cultural contradictions, stylistic failings, political ignorance and all the rest are gently eased to one side, just out of my sight, in a place where I can enjoy the music. Without all that baggage getting in the way.

And here seems to lie the inherent trouble with music criticism.

I'm a sucker for looking at context. Because what makes a good band great, what turns a "musician" into a "genius" is, for me, context. Relevance. The "something other." The ideas, the looks, the quotes, the haircuts. That's what turns a Jewish folkie poet into Bob Dylan, what makes four ranting speed-freaks in tight trousers become The Clash.

I'm in danger of contradicting myself already here (which is fine, since that's how I've always operated).

Let me break it down:

Top of my Pops, number one = music I like that has a cultural and political context.

Second on the list = music I like that just sounds bloody good.

Third down, second from bottom = music I don't like that at least has some worthwhile trappings and debate-starting factors, including corny neckerchiefs.

Fourth, and last = Crap music with no relevance whatsoever. Anti-music.

And so continues the opinionated and rambling stumble into a book, this book, *The Trouble With Music*. Maybe, like me, you'll read Mat's introduction and immediately formulate your own little Music Criticism Top of the Pops, like I just did. I think it helped me to get a lot out of the book. Sometimes I think I've read far too many books on music criticism, but...I can't stop. I love a book that slays me with its brilliance, and I love a book that makes me exclaim "That's crap!" out loud. I love a music book that challenges my notions of good and bad, or that shores up my staid old views. A book which makes me smile with the comfort of agreement or which burns me up with disgust. Happily for the people who asked me to write this, *The Trouble With Music* kept me nodding approvingly along, got me thinking, wondering, disagreeing, arguing.

Because yes, there *is* a problem with music. Mat will call the problem "Anti-music", the flooding of a historically vibrant and creative culture with a pale and bloodless doppelganger.

Put another nickel in the Nickelodeon; all I ever want is you, and music, music, music. Adolf Hitler said that "without the loudspeaker" he would "never have conquered Germany." But while Hollywood likes to remind us that the US Army went to Vietnam listening to Hendrix, the troops in today's Iraq conflict are entertained by the winners of TV's Pop Idol competitions. As Joe Strummer pointed out, "the battle is getting harder."

I was standing with the rest of the members of our band, sometime in 1980-something, at the side of a busy dual carriageway in Dover, England. Four hours earlier we'd been attacked by French punks for "selling out". Sniffer dogs were snaking around our legs and customs officers were shining torches under the van's wheel arches and into our retinas. Six hours later, strip-searched and sneered at and sent on our way, I could only marvel at this thing called rock n' roll that we'd ended up giving our lives to. What was it about our band that seemed to get us into trouble all the time? The whipping boys for both sides of the political spectrum (oh how we loved that!), Chumbawamba was always about more than music, was always about upsetting apple carts and trying to work out the trouble with music. Which is presumably why I was asked to write this piece.

People everywhere are making and selling music that has never been stopped at the border and had a gloved finger up its arse. And as Matt would say, in capitals, it's FAKE. Music with a fake, redundant context. Music made only to be sold, soulless and insipid. Anti-music.

And this band had the good fortune to do the whole rock n' roll thing, from transit-van tour-slogging to the David Letterman show and back again, and all the while with an agenda built on our own personal history of politics in pop, our own personal battle against this anti-music.

Along the way, battles won and/or lost, we got a good hard look at the world we inhabit, the music industry with its working-class heroes and their rambling workaday imagery, pristine blue jeans and carefully-rumpled white shirts. The music industry with its hip young marketing men, white fresh-faced suits selling hip-hop, A&R execs making love to the fat chairmen who run the radio stations.

Tell you what, though: seeing all that greasy crap up close makes you appreciate the good stuff even more. But what do I know?

I do know that if I started in this whole music/artist business afresh, if I was sitting down to write a song for the first time (instead of an introduction to this book), I'd like to bring with me Mat's gorgeous and timeless rant:

> "Who gives a fuck? Who doesn't? The song hurls back a challenge and an invitation. Into the babel of tongues, the vast multiplicity, humanity speaks of humanity. There is a Great Divide. Haves and have nots. Masters and Slaves. But it confronts its nemesis in the bard and the balladeer. The audience gathers to hear what it has known all along. The Message announcing the possibility: All this must change."

There you go. The Trouble with music, blah blah blah... all this must change. I still don't like Springsteen. But Mat's right: all this must change.

**Boff Whalley**
**Chumbawamba**
**2004**

# INTRODUCTION:
# THE CRISIS FACING MUSIC TODAY

**M**usic is everywhere. All the time. Every millimeter of public space is saturated with music no one chooses to hear yet nonetheless is subjected to. Call your dentist and you hear music while you wait. Go shopping and throughout the store or mall you hear mesmerizing melodies. In offices and factories, peppy tunes are pumped in to stimulate production. On the streets, at the cinema, in playgrounds and in restaurants, music is being played, whether you like it or not. At best, a pleasant "aroma," at worst, a nuisance. Constantly present in the background, it is mostly ignored. Music is everywhere and nowhere.

Music is enormously popular. It occupies an important place in many people's lives. A large segment of the general public seeks a relationship to music, through particular composers, performers and genres, in order to satisfy a deep need. This raises a peculiar question. On the one hand, we are bombarded with music from which we cannot escape. On the other, many of us devote a substantial amount of time and effort in seeking out music that moves us.

Music is a battleground. From the saturation of all public space by tuneful trivia to the hue and cry over digital downloading. From the controversy surrounding lyrics in rock and hip-hop songs to the political tumult unleashed by performers criticizing the government. From the articles, interviews, top-ten lists and awards shows that flood every outlet of mass communication to the dizzying array of radio, television and internet sites, all proclaiming the "Next Big Thing" that will change music forever.

Claims and counterclaims, threats and promises, social inclusion and ostracism, clamorous, contentious, and all about music! Regardless of one's position, music's importance is assumed. Whatever one's actual agenda, music is a banner to which troops can be rallied. It is both a target and a prize of political battle.

Yet, few, if any, are actually talking about music itself; how it comes into being and what it does. Most arguments are about lyrics and the costumes or lifestyles with which performers adorn themselves. The message contained in it may be controversial but in and of itself, there's just more music.

. The sheer quantity is staggering. One cannot live in a city anywhere in the world and escape this simple fact. Even devoted fans are overwhelmed by all there is to listen to, let alone appreciate. Yet quantity, by itself, is not what makes this a crisis. Buried under this deluge is a howling absence, a yawning abyss into which the entire edifice of music production is staring.

There are no critical standards by which to evaluate quality. Not only are the standards gone, they have been replaced by another: how many units have been sold. The only criteria that matters.

Exploiting this condition and intensifying its effects is the systematic manufacture and distribution of a phony substitute with which to replace real music. Over the last 20 years, this has had considerable success. Similar to the replacement of essential nutriment by junk food (and for similar reasons) a counterfeit substance is being foisted on an unsuspecting public. I call this "Anti-music" and it is everywhere. Music lovers are being asked to surrender their own critical faculties, their own judgment, in order to more readily consume the McMusic which can be more effectively controlled and more profitably sold than the genuine article.

## ANTI-MUSIC

More than one hundred years ago Leo Tolstoy published an essay called, "What is Art?" In this impassioned argument, Tolstoy bitterly denounced "counterfeit art" and championed its opposite, "true art," while attempting a useful definition of both. In the intervening century the world has been rocked by wars and revolutions unparalleled in their ferocity and scope. The last revolutionary upsurge reached its apex in 1968 with the events in Paris, Beijing, Vietnam, the US and elsewhere. Throughout the Sixties*, music, particularly popular music, enjoyed a renaissance that Tolstoy likely would have applauded. Even in the mainstream of "pop" culture, already a big business, the criteria for what was played on the radio and what was supported by the populace was substantially different than it is today. Furthermore, it was obviously and directly linked to events in society at large, inspired by, and in turn inspiring, the resistance to suffering and injustice that seemed to be on the verge of changing the world. Indeed, the popular or folk culture Tolstoy celebrated as often worthier than its highbrow competitor "true art," had, in an upsurge of populist revolt, swept the bourgeois arts from center stage, utterly demolishing the distinctions between high and low in the process.

---

*Whenever reference is made to the chronological, i.e.: 1960s it will be written numerically. Reference to the political and cultural event that has come to be known as the "Sixties" will be written in letters.

For music, the Sixties didn't end in 1970. In some ways, they didn't end at all. From the formation of small bands to the predominance of electric guitar, from the iconoclastic stance of many artists to the ongoing development of rock and roll, what originated in that period continues today. But with the end of the Cold War, "triumphant" capitalism has intensified its pursuit of the commodification of everything. Your life, your experience, must be made into an object for which you can be forced to pay. This is impossible, but it is nonetheless capital's inexorable logic. And many obstacles must be overcome. Among them is the role that music began to play for millions of people in recent times. Now, music has long been a commodity and a lot of money is made by selling it. That is not what makes it an obstacle.

The problem is that real music has two characteristics that make it unsuitable to capital's long term purpose. First, it is unpredictable. It is never quite certain what it will do. Second, it has at its core the absolutely uncommodifiable component of shared experience—joy, sadness, anger, love, solidarity, thoughtfulness, connection, etc.—shared by music makers and audiences in a completely open exchange. Without these components, music lacks the social and spiritual drive that make it so vital to human life. With them music subverts. The possibility it contains and announces is defiant for the simple reason that the market needs music, but music does not need the market.

Capital does what it must without regard to the consequences. Its representatives have learned a great many lessons from their brush with extinction in the Sixties. So a course of action was set in motion to, as a minimum objective, defang music, render it harmless. Several tactics were employed:

1. Replace quality with celebrity.
2. Place music into every conceivable public and private space, making its prevalent use sonic adornment.
3. Produce enormous quantities of music and flood the world with it.
4. Consolidate control of all distribution and promotion.
5. Simplify and repeat.

These tactics all work in concert, mutually dependent. Celebrity replaces quality when there is so much quantity that no other means of measuring quality exists. They may not be famous because they are good, but they must be good because they are famous. It also depends on the massive promotion essential for manufacturing celebrity, which, in turn, shifts authority from the maker of quality to the maker of celebrity. Then ensure that the most common, most frequent, experience people have with music is being lulled by it to enable the substitution of "ease" for other experiences music is capable of producing. This, in turn, reinforces celebrity because when the music itself produces no emotional charge, it is the fame and glamour of the "star" that inspires awe and reverence. Then clog the channels of distribution with a continuous flow of "new" releases so that every day, every week, there is more to consume, until all aesthetic judgment is short-circuited and one buys sound on the basis of sight; one chooses what one hears on the basis of what it looks like! Together these tactics ensure that there is little room left, only a small social space, for authentic music, the experiences it offers and the feelings it proclaims.

It is the purpose of this book to examine some of the dimensions of this problem. And to offer some possible solutions. It should be clear from the outset that the author is partisan. I am a musician, composer, engineer and producer. I have spent the last 40 years making music and I hope to continue for the rest of my life. I love music and that is part of the reason I write this. But it should be obvious from what's been said so far that it is not only for myself that this task has been undertaken: I am determined that the concerns and passions of my peers, my colleagues, my brothers and sisters in this field of human endeavor be represented. Much of what I have said and will say is a product of years of discussions and arguments among us; our pleasures and our discontents, our joys and our deep frustration. This is not the writing of a critic or promoter. Much less is it the writing of a "consumer." I make music and, to be honest, rarely buy it. Yet I am moved to speak out because the urgency of our situation demands it, and because I am convinced serious thought and conscious resistance can make a difference.

What might this difference be? To begin with, the political and philosophical aspects are complex while the musical ones are less so. Music originates in the human body. I sing, clap my hands, stamp my feet. This is literally universal in an even more fundamental way than speech. All children sing, clap and dance unless otherwise instructed not to and usually before they can utter a word. Music making is rooted in these simple acts that bring delight to the one doing them which is then increased when one is joined by others. Any difference I hope to contribute to making is based on this capacity and this joyous experience. Continually returning for verification and inspiration to this source is one small part of what should be in every child's milieu—not only their education in the institutional sense, but in their general life, all the time, everywhere. This kind of relationship to music could abolish the sonic adornment; simply wipe it out with the lived experience of people making music themselves. People can make their own music wherever they want to, wherever they are. They don't need to have it provided for them by anyone. They only need to be encouraged and, in the longer term given better and better musical tools.

A second part would be reinforcing the connection between music and dance. It is not a limitation to the many diverse forms music may ultimately take to say that its roots and its nourishment reside in physical movement. The musician may ultimately never dance nor the dancer play music but, in the beginning, as children, the link is the healthiest for music, dance and child. These then combine in the social environment, which encourages joining, participation and experience of self-made and shared joy. Playing in the sense of a game *and* playing in the sense of making music.

Based on this foundation is the contemplative activity of listening. With people already musical in their earliest experience, learning to listen is a next step and new horizon of experience. Educating oneself in the breadth and depth of musical expression is a lifelong process, but it must begin! Children must share with each other and with their parents and teachers the wonders that music can do. By learning to appreciate, people can learn to critically judge; to evaluate and compare what it is that makes them experience certain feelings, certain thoughts. This forms the basis for an organic, lived relationship with music that includes being moved both emotionally and intellectually. To learn the effectiveness of devoting one's attention, fully, to a work of mastery by other human beings is to share a spiritual connection with them and enables the envisioning of past, present and future in a dynamic combination. This also takes conscious effort and is not instantly gratified; nevertheless, my own experience emboldens me to say that it is worth it, and moreover that it is an essential part of human life.

So what's the problem? Why isn't this being done? It sounds like something everyone would support. It sounds "harmless," "neutral," unambiguously good. Well, so does the concept of "human rights." So does "universal health care." So does "world peace." The problem lies in the political and philosophical battles raging today that are both complex and, literally, life-and-death matters for us all. Here again, music plays an important part. It is precisely because it does so that so much wealth and power has been directed towards trying to suppress its liberatory potential. It is precisely because music *can* play a vital role in freeing people and challenging the forces of oppression that confusion is being sown and the false is being substituted for the genuine article. It is also why identifying more accurately and defending more resolutely these very attributes of music is so important. What music can do is always connected to the struggles and aspirations of humanity in all their diverse manifestations. It is a universal activity that can unite and inspire. Music is, thus, an activity that gives expression to the universality of the struggle against suffering and injustice.

## THE TROUBLE WITH MUSIC

The trouble with music is that we're in trouble without it; not only are musicians routinely screwed by a viciously exploitative industry, not only are gross injustices done when entire musical legacies are expropriated to be sold like trinkets to tourists; most important is to recognize that without a deep, living connection between people and music there can be no community. Without a love and respect shared by musicians and audiences alike for this wondrous human activity, we are lost.

With it, however, we're not the ones in trouble. Then the trouble with music is that it is out of control. It provides a human connection to the cosmos that defies domination of any kind. It militates against the very forces that would turn everything from the water we drink and the air we breathe into products for consumption and profit.

Music can be made by everyone. People learn that making music as well as listening to it frees them from the toil and tedium of a life dominated by the privileged and the powerful. Music means trouble for those who would own and control it as they perpetuate injustice and suffering. When we forge an intimate bond with this timeless expression of our own feelings and experiences, we can begin imagining a world far different than the one we are told is the best of all possible.

Music is not an object. It is not a thing to be held and stockpiled. It is an experience. It moves us. The enrichment it provides diminishes no one. It is not a *quantity* at all, but a *quality* of feeling and being that, by its very nature, is one shared by many and possessed by none. Rhythm alone demonstrates this in its simple evocation of physical movement according to a beat. What happens when this process is developed beyond its most basic expression is, ultimately, the timeless music we revere as great art. The awe and wonder evoked by such works and performances escapes control by anyone. We know it exists and can be attained by masters but it is, nonetheless, boundless, infinite, unnamable.

This too, is the trouble with music. It laughs at our attempts to grasp it. It invites us in only to disappear as we reach out to clutch at its substance. No matter how hard we try, we cannot explain it. Nevertheless, when we take part in it, we participate in a marvel. Music is, after all, a spirit and a discovery. When we grasp this, we can begin to understand what mastery is. Not domination over others; instead, a disciplined quest. Not the conquest of territory; rather, the liberation of our being.

I have been a musician most of my life. From the very beginning this sparked controversy. Divisions opened up in my family when, at 13, I asked for a guitar. My mother supported me. My stepfather insisted I would grow long hair, take drugs and turn into a vagabond. My mother prevailed, but my stepfather was right. I did grow long hair, take drugs and become a vagabond. I also raised quite a din. But within all the racket my friends and I made was the kernel of truth that is music. This grew stronger, finally bursting through the extraneous trappings of style and youth that had been so much a part of what attracted me in the first place. Music constantly asserted itself as a force more powerful and enduring than getting high, getting laid and getting over.

In the 40 years since I got my first guitar I've been engaged with literally thousands of musicians and technicians from many parts of the world. Questions about work, skill, survival, politics and philosophy continually arise in virtually all conversations with anyone pursuing this occupation. The difficulties are common, the struggles similar. Differences of age, ethnicity, class background or taste may seem significant, but they tend to disappear when discussion reaches, as it usually does, the underlying theme of being a musician.

In the past few years such discussions have become more frustrated and embittered. They have gone beyond the usual complaints and annoyances one always encounters at work. There is a widely shared dismay over the "state" of music today. For virtually all music makers, the enemy appears to have won. Record company hacks and corporate radio programmers decide what will be heard without having the slightest idea what music is about. Advertisers and journalists, hucksters and conmen decide our future without caring about the consequences for real people, let alone the music itself. Our fate is in the hands of cretins and sychophants doing the bidding of bean counters.

This is what compelled me to put down the guitar and pick up the pen. I wanted to defend what I love against what I hate. I wanted to better understand the source of my joy as well as unearth the cause of my sorrow. Most of all, I wanted to do battle against the enemies of music, to find a way to fight and win. Since I am continuously talking about these issues in the course of my work, I decided it was necessary to break the impasse such discussion has reached. On the one hand, to express the concerns and bring to bear the experiences of the great tribe of musicians everywhere. On the other, to add some new perspectives that might help all of us who love music become better equipped to advance our cause. This means anyone and everyone who listens, dances, sings, claps their hands, taps their toes, plays a mean air guitar in the bedroom, whistles in the street, sings in the shower; in a word, shares in the joy music can bring. This means dispelling the mystique of the music industry and thoroughly exposing the disease at its core. But even more important, it means inspiring debate that strengthens all of us who make and love music.

This is what I've learned through 40 years of music making, schlepping from rehearsals to gigs to recording sessions. This is the struggle we share and the solidarity we need to build.

# Too Much Is Not Enough

## Superabundance and the Absence of Critical Thought

Alain Levy, the music industry executive drafted last year to turn around EMI's battered reputation, said that within the next three years he wants the EMI roster to contain two or three superstars artists, selling more than 10m albums each and a further five artists each selling 5m.

EMI says the industry's growth over the next two years is likely to be between a 2% fall in sales and a 2% increase. Mr Levy believes the company can outperform its peers by developing more artists like the top-selling Kylie Minogue and Robbie Williams, rather than gambling large sums on buying-in established stars such as Mariah Carey.

Earlier this year EMI was forced to pay £19.6m to terminate a multi-album deal with the pop diva.

Underlining the stricter approach to expenditure, 400 artists deemed to be under-performers will have their contracts terminated. "We discovered we had 49 artists in Finland. I don't think there are 49 Finns that can sing," he said.

**JOHN CASSY, *THE GUARDIAN*[1]**

I was on tour in Finland a couple years back. My band played a concert in Helsinki. On the bill with us was a young man who sang very well. In fact, he was trained in Scandinavian and Russian folkloric music, was an expert mouth harp player and Tuvan throat singer. We missed his set as we were backstage preparing for our own. When he had finished he rushed into the dressing room almost in tears so thoroughly frustrated was he at the inattentiveness of the audience to his entirely a capella performance. We consoled him with musicians' tales of shared woe. In return, he gave us a private 30 minute concert that was astonishing for its passion and virtuosity. Inquiring about his background, this young man told us he'd started out his musical career as a guitarist in a heavy metal band but fell in love with the sounds and melodies of an older time.

A few days later it was my good fortune to be given a CD made by none other than the booking agent who organized our tour. He is also a musician (like most of us, he couldn't make a living with his music alone). With great trepidation, I put it on expecting it to be mediocre at best and probably really bad. To my surprise it was a brilliant synthesis of modern instruments and rhythms combined with Finnish-inspired melodies and harmonizations. It was an excellent recording of fine musicians playing fresh, original music. Only the Finnish texts limited my appreciation (and the potential audience).

I have this to say to Mr. Levy and his chauvinistic remarks: "You, Sir, are a thief and a boor. You are personally responsible for the demeaning of people and music. You have attained your wealth by viciously exploiting musicians and their audiences and depriving untold numbers of us the opportunity to hear and be heard. Your offenses, however, go beyond your remarks so obviously outrageous to Finns and to me. They include a regime of your own design that would flood the world with tedium produced by a tiny handful of musicians at the expense of both the great variety available and any critical standard. Cynically, you substitute celebrity for quality, thereby making yourself richer and the world poorer. You are the enemy of music and musicians everywhere."

This, then, is the future: Each of us (at least 10 million) will have one Robbie Williams CD to satisfy our musical needs. All other musicians in the world will have to perform our own music to each other, backstage, while preparing to go out and perform covers of Robbie Williams songs to the audience, who now only wants to hear those songs over and over again! Perhaps every two months we will get another CD that 10 or 20 million others will also have and that we want because we hear the songs over and over, on the radio, in supermarkets, at the dentist, on the telephone, in endless copies designed to use the same melodies in every conceivable style from classical to reggae so that everyone will have a version of Robbie Williams' songs that they like.

Now that we are sufficiently globalized, privatized, anesthetized and sterilized, we are ready to enter the music store and make our free choice! Of course, we don't have to make a decision; the decisions have all been made for us by the good people in the music industry who really know what good music is. How do we know they know? Because they are rich and famous. They must have made the right decisions to become rich and famous so the decisions they make for us...now, wait a minute! This could be a problem. The decisions they make for us don't have to be what's best for us! Uh, somebody call security. We've got a radical thought on the loose. Security! Security! We have a radical thought threatening a riot in the pop music section of HMV. Play Brittany immediately and send a couple of gift certificates. We can contain this. The suspect looks confused. She's walking around aimlessly. Heading for the exit. No, she's not buying anything. Right! Quick, apprehend her before she leaves. Make sure she has the announcement of our Supersaver Special on Madonna's *Greatest Hits Volume 10*. Whew! That was close.

I'm joking, aren't I?

Superabundance means:

1. Too much. More than enough.

2. Waste. Resources that could otherwise be usefully, healthfully employed squandered in the making of something disposable, unnecessary; already garbage.

3. Replacement. Taking the place, occupying the physical and social space of something else actually needed or wanted.

Critical Thought means:

1. Differentiation. Having the capacity to tell the difference between not only amounts or quantities but kinds or qualities.

2. Comparison. Having the capacity to weigh, measure, test the relative qualities of differentiated things. This includes comparing things that have weight and measure and others that are beyond measure, are magical, miraculous, timeless, awe inspiring, etc.

3. Decision. The capacity to decide, enabling an act that is not a reflex or reaction to coercion or subterfuge. The commitment to follow differentiation and comparison with exploration, discovery, experience and responsibility to what one has learned and to the world within which one lives.

## IS THERE TOO MUCH MUSIC IN THE WORLD?

How can such a question be asked? How can such a question even make sense? We do not usually think of music in terms of quantity—how much. Usually, we think of it in terms of quality—how good or how bad. Ask anyone involved in making music what their chances of being heard really are, and the question takes on a different, more urgent meaning.

In the year 2000 in the territory of the US, 288,591 albums were released, generating total sales of 784.8 million units. Of that number, 246,000 sold less than 1,000 units. That's 85.2% of the albums released selling less than 1,000 units. 88 albums sold more than 1 million units. Eighty eight. This disparity suggests many things about marketing, popular taste, population growth, and so on, but it also says something else: there is a lot of music being made that has no market value. In fact, according to the quantity/quality equivalence, the vast majority of music being made has no quality either. It might as well be given or thrown away. Conversely, the profit generated by those 88 albums that sell more than one million units each is so great that it masks the underlying contradiction expressed in the title of this chapter.

There is too much music *and* there is not enough. More must be continuously made and thrown away, because music has been made disposable. It is a remnant of human history that we associate with living but have forgotten why. A small number of musical products generate enormous profit, while the vast majority cost more than they earn—all of them more or less quickly become residue, waste. Since there is no place for the "timeless" moments music is capable of producing, there are only the limited, measured moments of shallow enjoyment that must continuously be replaced by new versions of the same shallow enjoyment-producing units. The immortality of a Bach or Coltrane is impossible to conceive of. The "forever" of flamenco or blues or sacred music is even more incomprehensible to this order of things. The endless proliferation of supposedly "new" music obscures and perpetuates the profound lack of the endless or eternal in one truly great piece.

Furthermore, the physical space required to house and broadcast this ever-increasing plenitude squeezes out, marginalizes and overwhelms the authentic. Perhaps more importantly, it renders meaningless the very terms in which music can be understood and most deeply appreciated. Quantity is quality. What we will hear is what we are hearing, what we are hearing is what everyone else is hearing. It must therfore define "good" by virtue of everyone hearing it, and only it! Where can timelessness be found in this universe of three minute ditties? Where can feeling be experienced in this overload of sensation that clogs the very channels by which genuine, illuminating experience is attained?

## A VISIT TO THE RECORD STORE

The record stores are full of music. But what they are actually selling is something else. First of all they offer convenience. When was discovery ever convenient? Second, they offer abundance. But how can something special be abundant? Third, they offer selection. How absurd. If you go into a store to get something you already know you want, there is no selection to be made. If, on the other hand, you are just going in to buy some music, it is you who are being selected as are all consumers. The selection process begins with the producer/marketer of the product designating your demographic niche and producing something likely to appeal to you, thereby separating you from your money. The illusion that you are making a choice is carefully maintained by a vast array of devices. These include critics (actually, consumer guides), radio programmers, promoters and market analysts who work around the clock to ensure that the most profitable "choices" are made. The whole concept of "free choice" is questionable on its face, but in the case of music it is ultimately meaningless. One must listen and reflect if one is to find what truly moves them. In other words, music lovers are "devotees"—they devote large amounts of energy and time to the discovery of moving and profound musical expressions that will provide timeless, measureless moments in real life experience and thus are beyond value. There can be no price for this.

Where does this leave a young person who loves music but doesn't need or want to think about it? Am I only speaking about an elite group of aficionados? The answer is that it leaves young people caught in the middle. Trapped between a capacity for appreciation and the conditioning they are undergoing to become lifelong consumers. So there is much contradiction among young people reflected in the plethora of styles and attitudes about music specifically. Some covet their marginal, exclusivist scenes that identify with a particular genre or sub-genre appreciated only by the enlightened or "hip." Some abandon themselves to that which is most popular with their peers; what is most easily consumed. The former category tends to contain more discerning listeners and more people who will grow up to want an enduring relationship with authentic musical experience. But the fact is that the majority of young people will end up, like their parents, being gently or forcibly coerced into acquiescing to the prevailing attitudes about many things—music included.

In an unintentionally ironic twist, the data reported above was compiled by a company called SoundScan. "SoundScan is an electronic network that collects weekly retail figures from over 17,000 music stores in the U.S., including chains like Tower, Wherehouse, and BestBuy. It's owned and operated by a company based in White Plains, New York, called VNU Marketing Information. This company sells their information to corporate subscribers like record labels and concert promoters for lots of money."[2] Thus, it is by scanning sound that the consumer is shaped into a "sound scanner." One who, in the definition provided by *The Oxford English Dictionary*, "look[s] at quickly in order to identify relevant features or information." In other words, the exact opposite of devoting one's full attention to the "in depth" study or appreciation of a musical work.

Several questions arise in connection to these numbers and comparisons. One is, how can a numeric value be placed on the aesthetic or spiritual value one gives to music? Why does it matter whether a song that brings tears to your eyes has sold 40 or 40 million copies? Does this make you part of some community? Does this validate your perception and opinion? Does it make it right to feel the way you do? Does it make your personal, unique experience a numbered unit indistinguishable from other numbered units? Different implications can be drawn from posing the question in its opposite form: Could it be that no song can bring tears to your eyes (or evoke any strong emotion) because there are too many songs to listen to? That no song moves you because there are so many that you hear none?

## SO YOU WANT TO BE A ROCK N' ROLL STAR?

This is not idle speculation. It is what music makers face on a continuous, daily basis. When considering the effort and expense of making a recording for public release, an underlying question is always present even if no one dares to pose it openly: "Does the world need another CD?" Everyone involved with music production is affected by this musical glut and things have gotten worse, quantitatively and qualitatively, over the last 20 years.

The answers most often given now to such questions are: "The world may not need another CD but I want to make one" or, "I estimate we'll be able to sell _____ number of CDs" or, in the case of the technicians, "I'm glad to have the work." Each of these answers connects to the manufacture of superabundance in a "vicious circle" of self-reinforcement. On the one hand, there is the naive wish to experience making music, recording it, having it released. On the other, the vain illusion that "I" may be the next great genius who will be "discovered" and become rich and famous for sharing my divine gifts with the world. Then there is the "realistic" supply and demand argument—people want this product; that's why we have to make it. Which is, in my experience, usually just as much an illusion but is covered with the "reasonableness" of business talk. In other words, someone gives the impression of certainty when, at best, the enterprise is a gamble with very poor odds.

At the end of the chain there is the technician glad to work at his/her craft and make enough to live on. The only one involved in the entire process who actually views what they do as work. The only one who actually works whether there is success or not. The technicians, the engineers, the studios that were kept afloat making all 246,000 CDs that didn't sell; they are a basic component of the cost of production of the product.

This scenario is played out over and over again with different actors at different levels. (Mariah Carey only sold 2 million CDs—someone asked the question: Does the world need another Mariah Carey album? and answered "No it does not. Or at least we're not going to pay to make it." In fact, they paid her $28 million not to make it.) I can think of several significant artists who are very likely to have more to contribute but who, at one time or another, went for extended periods without anyone thinking they should make another CD (Merle Haggard, Jimmy Cliff and George Clinton—these are just a few well known artists who have been without record deals, and maybe still are for all I know). And, at the same time, vast sums are expended on the "next big thing," dozens of young performers parading their glamorous youth to be purchased not by the public, but by the industry. This is the process by which the raw material is purchased, packaged and resold by record companies. Prince once said, "In Mozart's time, word of mouth built an audience. People found him and heard him play. Then someone came along and said, 'We can sell this experience.' Right there, you've got trouble. Music comes from the spirit, but where does the guy selling the music come from?" Now, Prince is not a failure crying sour grapes. He is both a commercial success of major proportions and, that rarest of "stars," one who is actually a great musician by any measure. So, when he makes this statement we are not dealing with the whining of losers but the perception that pervades the musical "world," although most would not dare to say it for fear of reprisal.

## THE WORLD "R" US

These problems are compounded by other distortions and disparities when one considers the global dimensions. Look beyond the limits of pop music in the US, UK and the rest of the industrialized "North," and include musics from India, Trinidad, Brazil, Bali, etc., or traditional or ancient music made within societies the world over, and superabundance takes on another aspect. There is such variety and quantity that it would take many lifetimes to listen to representative samples of it all. This is not an exaggeration. It is also the point. With the intense concentration of resources in the hands of a few major corporations that generate enormous profits from the sale of millions of units of a tiny number of musical artists, there is an inevitable warping of the entire culture within which music is created and received. A few are heard over and over, ad nauseam, and many are not heard at all. This is not unique to music, of course. Agriculture and other necessary human production are similarly dominated and deformed, and the parallels are not simply metaphoric. They are essentially the same: commodities controlled by the same dominant entities in the capitalist framework of production and consumption. An example of the perversity this leads to is a report issued by the RIAA measuring the economic value of the CD. Among the comparisons it makes is the price per minute of music. In 1983, the report claims, music was worth 51.7 cents a minute. In 2002 music was worth 15 cents a minute. This represents a 71% drop in the cost of music per minute—what a deal! And this was actually the point they were trying to make with these stats?! What a good investment buying a CD is, compared to concert tickets, DVDs and other forms of music delivery.[3]

Was this always so? In the particular form of the music industry, what is relatively new is the monopolization of music which has transpired in the last 15 years. "If you go back to the Sixties, we had bubble gum pop acts then. But we were developing long-term acts too. We had labels like Island and Chrysalis and hundreds of independent record labels driven by entrepreneurs who wanted to break new acts. Then consolidation came and the major record companies bought up the independents. But they squashed the entrepreneurialism by putting it in the structure of a conglomerate. They were still required to show growth, though, so the easiest thing to do was produce short-term products that would drive short-term growth. That's why acts started being broken by in-your-face marketing.

'It's become like the Christmas toy market.'" These are the words of Andy Taylor, head of the Sanctuary Group, which represents a number of major acts. Obviously, Taylor is no anti-capitalist. Yet even within the framework of this system there are many who recognize that the mechanisms by which Sony, EMI, Universal, BMG and Time Warner extract maximum profit out of any product or service they sell militate against the long term interests of music production itself. Furthermore, Taylor exposes hypocritical claims made by many of the top brass of the Big Five,

> He denies piracy is a serious problem and says the music majors are using it to hide a more structural issue: lack of decent material by artists with long-term futures. 'I do think it's an excuse. My view is that the reasons (for falling music sales) are economic downturn and lower quality product.'[4]

I have heard these laments being voiced at least since the late '80s when Island, A&M and Chrysalis (among others) were being bought up and consolidated. There were many then who predicted the situation we are facing now. Naturally, different people offered different explanations and considered alternative courses to the one that's prevailed. Among those were the young artists who produced hip-hop, punk, grunge and numerous other "alternative" popular music styles. Most were consciously and practically aimed at building audiences in opposition to the Majors and their white bread, mindless drivel. A lot of such music came and went in the same manner that a great performance exists for one moment and then is past; to be savored by its participants (performers and audiences alike) but not to be repeated. In fact, a distinguishing feature of what is "disposable" or "waste" and what is enduring is that unquantifiable quality of connection that arises between audience and music maker. When there is a living bond between those who participate in—as opposed to spectate at—the musical event, it lives on beyond the moment; entering into the lives of all involved. This is precisely what "branding," that favorite buzzword of advertisers, is aimed at replacing. Instead of authentic musical (or other) experience we are to identify with a brand and purchase that experience, or simulation of it, in a neat package to be consumed like soda pop.

## CELEBRITY IS NOT QUALITY

And this is the crux of the problem. Because in order for music to convey such feelings, to build such connections, it cannot be branded. This is not just a linguistic play but an actual experience. Once there is an ulterior motive, whether it be to sell something or promote an idea contrary to the spirit of the music itself, the connection is broken and replaced by another sinister one of manipulation and control. Whether the average listener or musician is conscious of this or not, most, in my experience, do sense this phenomenon as it is taking place. Other words or phrases are substituted to describe the feeling. Some will say "It's not real." Some will say they can't "relate" to it. Others will say, "It's not my scene" or "I'm not into that [name a style]." The point is that the connection is not made, it cannot be, because ultimately, music is based in community building. In the words of Raymond Williams, a structure of feeling is composed and shared by all within this social group. The resonance (or lack thereof) of a particular work or artist depend on the vitality they contribute to the lived experience of the group. This group can be larger or smaller in number, but the process is the same.

Historically and universally, music has come into being this way. It plays its role as the cohesive medium that transcends other forms of expression and elevates the participants into an altered state of being—not only of consciousness in the mental sense but of actual being. The most obvious examples are of social groups singing and dancing where all are actively doing either or both.

The collective act that Anti-music encourages and represents is shopping. The bouncy sound that induces semi-trance, the mass hypnosis of consumption. This perverts the entire inside/outside of community feeling that authentic music generates and, in turn, is generated by. Inside/outside now means inside or outside the music industry. The industry markets the sounds that will control those outside the music industry: the suckers, the dupes, the dumb masses. There can be no authentic community generated around "stars," anyway. This veneration of celebrity is obviously sycophantic and obsequious. It is not awe or wonder at mastery, skill, inspiration or spiritual profundity; it is kneeling at the alter of fame itself. It is also pathetic.

## ONCE UPON A TIME...

In what seems like another era—but was only a short time ago—there was a rough (albeit very rough) equivalence between the best known and the best. The biggest name often meant the highest standard. Few would doubt that Aretha Franklin, Jimi Hendrix, The Beatles, Ray Charles, or Bob Dylan were among the best of their peers. Examples abound from all over the world: Jobim, Nascimiento, Gil from Brazil, The Mighty Sparrow or Shadow from Trinidad, Bob Marley, Peter Tosh from Jamaica, Fela Kuti, Sunny Ade from Nigeria (not to mention all those outside the popular field). In other words, artists from many cultures, many lands were brought to the world's attention on records, on the radio and in concert and were, at least, among the best musicians/performers playing the finest compositions. It is important to note that simultaneously there was both a lot of crap being sold as well as many great artists who went unnoticed outside of small, loyal followings. And there are many tragic stories of some of music's finest practitioners dying impoverished, forgotten and alone. Nevertheless, there was some substance to the notion that acclaim and merit were coefficient. This cannot be said anymore. In fact, it is safe to say the opposite. Among the big names in music now there are few who could be considered "the best." On the contrary, it can be assumed that the big names are mediocre or downright awful. "The best" is irrelevant in the quantity/quality equivalence. There is only one standard now: who sold the most units. It's a combination of Championship Wrestling and McDonalds. Phony competition to sell the most burgers.

The problem is not that there is too much music in the world, but that there is too little of the world in music. Or the music we're forced to listen to, that is. There is too little because what is vital and revelatory about the lived experience that informs the best music is absorbed into the machinery of profitability, its soul sucked out of it and its shell returned to the public for their consumption as music. How is this operation accomplished? In a discussion about Fascism, Slavoj Zizek describes the process by which the organic substance of people's feelings are a necessary component of any domination over them:

> ... the ruling ideology, in order to be operative, has to incorporate a series of features in which the exploited/dominated majority will be able to recognize its authentic longings....Of course, Fascist ideology 'manipulates' authentic popular longing for a true community and social solidarity against fierce competition and exploitation; of course it "distorts" the expression of this longing in order to legitimize the continuation of the relations of social domination and exploitation. In order to achieve this effect, however, it nonetheless has to incorporate authentic popular longing.[5]

This describes what the music business has been perfecting with greater and greater efficiency for many years. Before the Sixties they could substitute Pat Boone for Little Richard singing "Tutti Frutti." There was an entire category of substitution of white singers "covering" black singers and their songs. Blacks and whites were literally segregated in large parts of the USA, and black and white musicians were not allowed to perform together anywhere (and there were separate black and white record charts, of course). Obviously, the political and historical aspects of this example are more important and clearer than the musical ones. Indeed, there have been many "covers" of all kinds of music that on their musical merits alone could be considered excellent. Furthermore, in today's world, the once easily-recognized markers of political oppression have been blurred. The oppression is still there, but it is much more cleverly concealed, making such non-musical criteria harder to apply in a useful manner when trying to discern the authentic from the fake in music.

Nevertheless, we can identify the means by which this substitution is achieved and also its ends. We can thus better understand the sources of the authentic in the real lives of real people, our struggles and aspirations, including to be participants in the making of good music. We can also begin to understand the reasons for and the techniques employed in appropriating this vital substance to produce its opposite. A prime example is how numerous big "stars" will seek out and hire young, hip musicians or producers to create the background tracks for their next big hit. "Street credibility" is common parlance in the pop music field, suggesting the necessity for credentials of authenticity that make the musicians/producers believable by the masses who are the target of marketing. If this sounds cynical, it is. Worse, it is sinister. The road to fame is littered with the carcasses, literal and figurative, of talented young people who were used up and thrown away when their moment had passed. (They're in good company, of course. The same was done to Mozart, to mention only one notorious case.)

The result of this process is being shoved at us in a continuous barrage that seeks to destroy the connections between people that cannot be turned into profit for the Big Five music companies to be replaced by ones that can. In doing this they attack not only authentic music but the tools we need to distinguish it from its antithesis, its simulation. The destruction of critical thought and the sensitivity to appreciate shared feeling are primary targets of marketing in general and the marketing of music in particular.

An analogous situation is that of food: there are people starving in the world because there is *too much* food. Food must be destroyed (all the time, every year) because it cannot be sold profitably. The populations that are starving are too poor to constitute a market; they are merely people. Their capacity to feed themselves has been obliterated, in part, by the cheapness of imported foodstuffs making their own produce worthless in monetary terms. All of us must, therefore, be desensitized to the obvious insanity of this predicament. Any critical thought must be suspended, or Monsanto loses all justification for its existence.

Or, to take the analogy one step further: sugar is given away. It costs so little to produce, and such enormous quantities are, that its price must be subsidized by taxpayers. One might say that sugar is like classical music:

without public subsidy, there would be very few symphony halls, opera houses or public concerts of the classics of (mainly) European composers. The music cannot be given away, yet it is at great expense that the entire field is maintained. But the fact is, it has no market value. What might this suggest as to possible alternatives to the prevailing system? Obviously, rich people and their subordinates consider it important to maintain a certain "heritage" or, to put it another way, a certain social ambiance that necessitates the support of such institutions. Civilization requires that "appearances" be maintained, I suppose. Yet one need only think a moment to see that this puts the lie to the whole argument leveled by representatives of the music business.

First of all, anyone suggesting that merit or artistic quality has anything to do with success is either a fool or a charlatan. So much great music cannot be sold, and so much schlock is, that this commonly accepted platitude can be dismissed out of hand. Second, if the CEOs of all the big corporations were genuinely concerned with music, why don't they donate their salaries to music programs in the public schools? Do musicians need corporate fat cats to make music or do children need instruments and education to learn to appreciate the music making experience? Third, if there were simply no music industry at all and only a small tax of, say, the cost of four CDs per year (the number the RIAA claims are the average annual purchase) that was directed to the sustaining of musicians and musical organizations in the manner of universities and libraries, might this not be a better way to ensure the healthy growth and development of musical quality and comprehension? I think so. And what stands in the way? One needs little critical thought to answer that question.

Let's return to the example of Alain Levy head of EMI. As reported in *The Guardian*, "Alain Levy, the executive recruited to turn around EMI's troubled recorded music division, is in line for a $500,000 (£316,800) bonus despite conceding that the group will miss its revenue target for the year and presiding over a sharp drop in the share price."[6] Three days before (November 20, 2002 to be exact), responding to questions as to the cause of the failure to reach the targets he was hired to achieve, Levy said, "When we made that prediction we were expecting the market to be 2.5 per cent down. Now we are expecting a fall of 5 per cent. Piracy is a lot more powerful than we thought and the situation has been worsening month by month."[7] One might be excused for asking who is the pirate here? Indeed, the hue and cry raised about piracy is a smoke screen. The aphorism "capitalism is organized crime" could not be more aptly applied.

# ILLUSIONS OF POWER AND THE POWER OF ILLUSIONS

As one might expect, there is a deep mistrust of the music industry on the part of musicians. Paradoxically, if a record company, particularly a major, approaches an artist, that individual or band is very likely to be thrilled (at least at first). This is explained by a number of factors that in combination produce intense social, psychological and artistic conflict. Most musicians are poor. Record companies are rich. A record deal is employment for musicians, their friends and families. It is social recognition reserved for a privileged few. An illusion of power emanates from this that flatters the ego and gives weight to what this newly important person says and does. It doesn't matter that people at record companies don't know any more about quality or meaning in music than anyone else. They are not trained or prepared to judge what is worthy of support or not. They simply have a job that, in many cases, was acquired through nepotism or personal ties and certainly not on the basis of critical faculties. This job, however, confers upon them enormous social influence. An A&R rep of 18–25 years of age can walk into a nightclub (for free!) and gain immediate access to artists and staff simply on the basis of their status as a record company employee. The fact that an A&R person may never have signed an act let alone had a big success with one they did changes nothing. There are A&R people bouncing around the industry for years, pulling down salaries with lots of perks any musician would be happy with and never actually doing anything productive.

It is very sad that millions of talented, dedicated musicians the world over can be emotionally manipulated to the extremes of euphoria or despair by parasites who contribute nothing to music or to the world. Even though many musicians know well the pitfalls of dealing with the industry, they/we are nonetheless ensnared by a structure of beliefs—more like superstition—that denies reason and lived experience. Musicians that would otherwise be honorably engaged in the making of music can be found groveling at the feet of record company reps, desperately trying to please, to be deemed worthy in the eyes of these "king makers." In an instant, all the criteria of what makes music good—what makes it inspire and uplift, what makes it alive—all of this is discarded, and whatever might make the musician famous becomes the only thing that matters.

The fact that none of this is real; that getting signed rarely ends up in success of any kind for the artist, that even when success is achieved it is often at the expense of the quality of the music and the quality of the life the musician makes; this is of little consequence in a distorted world of vanity and privilege. Indeed, it is part of a larger truth that it has long been this way. If anything, what is going on now is a return to a norm that was well-established centuries ago. The actual deviation from that norm is what transpired during the revolutionary storms of the Sixties. What preceded that period and what has followed in its wake are more similar to the plight of musicians throughout the ages.

The tragedy in this peculiar inversion is that music has real power, which is the object of desire of the non-musician and the object of appropriation of the music business. It is exactly that power that the musician surrenders, willingly, in return for the illusion of success offered in its place. Musicians routinely and as a matter of course bring pleasure and fulfillment to themselves and their audiences (however large or small). But this is viewed as insignificant in a social order that can only market celebrity; that can only profit from that which, by the dominance of capital, it can manufacture and control. EMI cannot make music, but it can make celebrity. It is of no value to EMI that a group is playing for a packed house of excited concert-goers, or that a particular songwriter has a loyal following. These audiences do not constitute a market. They are the "clients" of the artists themselves. Until that group or songwriter is transformed into a media phenomenon—a "name"—they can never sell the numbers of units (tickets, CDs or T-Shirts) that is profitable. Until that audience is transformed into a market for a product—not just people with intelligence and feelings—that can then be manipulated by the record company, it is not worth the investment. And by virtue of having the capital to invest, anyone without that capital is automatically excluded (estimates of 250,000–1 million dollars being required to "launch" an act are common these days). This is one reason mainstream media (which includes the major record companies) carefully maintains the lie that while theirs is the taste that rules, they, like all despots, insist that they are only the humble representatives of the popular will. In other words, it's not Alain Levy forcing us to like what he likes, oh no. It is Alain Levy insisting that he knows what is good because he knows what the public thinks is good. He is only serving our interests!

As a result, there is no musical or aesthetic criteria of quality. There is not even an authentic experiential one (as in, it makes me feel strong emotions, it moves me). "He's really BIG!" is more important and more likely to be trusted than, "She's really GOOD!" What is being said here is that BIG is a measurable, incontestable fact. It has social weight. It is objective and therefore "real." But GOOD is not. It is ephemeral. Not measurable, certainly contestable, not real. This is not unlike the marketing fiction: "there's coffee and there's STARBUCKS." Jane is a musician. Yeah, but Sandra is on a Major Label!!! Wow! Seriousness is Major Label. Not important is everything else.

Who, then, will decide what the aesthetic or technical criteria for quality will be? Well, for starters, I will. I will establish the criteria and I will struggle for my views openly and without recourse to numbers or references to "conventional wisdom." I will grapple with those elements in music that I find objectionable (Anti-music) and I will seek to better identify those that resonate in my heart. Hopefully, others will join me in this process, particularly other music makers. This will require two operations: 1) a lot of listening and, 2) a lot of thought. This necessarily means conflicting viewpoints and challenging cherished beliefs. The process thus begun takes a lot of time and no time. A lot since there is so much music, no time because it must become the process by which one lives one's life. If I am to truly appreciate the skill and wisdom contained in the music-making process and the life-affirming and revitalizing nature of its product, music must become a part of my life, and I a part of the life and well being of music.

For most people, this may not seem like such a big deal. As stated in the introduction to this book, music is everywhere all the time. The point, however, is to turn phony music off. Stop listening to it. Start rejecting what is being advertised. Challenge the assumption that what is famous is good. Doubt the quality of that which is already well known and seek to make your own discoveries of hidden treasures that are, in fact, all over the place but need to be sought out. Of course, there are many great artists among the famous. Of course, there are classic works in all genres that require our attention if, for no other reason, the comparison necessary to decide what we think is truly worthy of our love and respect. But make the time to devote your full attention to listening and feeling and you will discover the passions at play and the mastery at work in glorious sound.

Fundamentally, we need to effectively combat the appearance of legitimate authority that has been usurped by the music industry and reassert the truly legitimate authority of the music maker and the audience. This includes critics who seriously undertake the task of informing their readers through lively debate as opposed to simply telling people what to buy. This means that responsibility be taken by musicians, technicians, instrument builders and others involved with making music to inspire and inform each other and their audiences directly, at every opportunity, as a supplement to making music in its own right. This requires effort that may not be rewarded by immediate results. In fact, it is a constant struggle in a world dominated by the Owners Of Everything. But turning off the soundtrack of idiocy will enable, and is enabled by, the turning on of the joy music provides. Of this there can never be too much. Always just enough.

Most of what has been spoken of so far concerns the world since 1983 when the first commercially released CDs entered the marketplace. But what about the many millions of vinyl records made before that time? Between 80 and 90% of that music has not been re-released on CD! There is an enormous amount of wonderful music—compositions, performances, exquisite moments—that are only available to those who have them or trouble themselves to seek them out. Furthermore, much that was recorded to vinyl was made under the guidance of producers and engineers who were, first and foremost, music lovers themselves. Many of the classic—and best—recordings made between 1950 and 1983 were made by people who genuinely believed they were capturing for posterity and public enlightenment what were among the highest achievements of musicians and composers. Of course, there was tons of crap then, too. Of course, there was a music industry that deliberately exploited musicians and wantonly plundered the legacies of oppressed and struggling people throughout the world. But the whole enterprise was relatively small time back then. The numbers of people with record players was growing but it was small until the early 1960s. The big money was in television and movies, and music was most profitable in association with these media. Thus, relative to today, a disproportionate share of what was recorded and released was actually chosen by the likes of John Hammond, Jerry Wexler, Ahmet Ertegun, Teo Macero, Bob Van Gelder and others of their caliber; who had a wide knowledge of music and its history as well as a genuine, altruistic devotion to serving it in the public interest. This does not mean these men were saints or that there were not others at the same time, who were consciously and systematically ripping off impoverished musicians for their publishing and performance royalties and claiming credit for writing music they had nothing to do with except profiting from its sale. But these men, and numerous others, were leaders in the field and could successfully battle the parasites and profiteers who have subsequently come to dominate it. To their credit, they sought out and recorded representative samplings of what music is all about.

It is no wonder that there is a thriving network of collectors and aficionados—including young samplers and DJs—who convene at record fairs taking place regularly throughout Europe, North America and other parts of the world. It is exciting to me to witness the unbridled enthusiasm and deep respect, even awe, these folks express at finding and savoring music. It is just one example of music inspiring the quest to find it and rewarding that search with unparalleled satisfaction. There is much more to be said about this phenomenon. But here and now it is important to note that it stands in stark contrast to the predominant way music is bought and sold.

## FOOTNOTES

1    Cassy, John. "1800 jobs go as EMI cuts £100m." *The Guardian*. March 21, 2002.

2    http://ask.yahoo.com/ask/20020215.html/
Soundscan uses the barcode to count sales. It is the basis for the Billboard Charts that are referred to when anyone says: "Number One in the charts." Ostensibly, the data is objective; untainted by self-interested manipulation. The fact that charts—particularly in the US—have long been tampered with to manufacture "hits" and do not accurately reflect actual sales to customers is another of the hidden mechanisms by which the Music Industry has maintained its dubious claims to representing the interests or tastes of the populace. Soundscan does provide more reliable data. Nevertheless, this is still manipulated in the same way poll data in elections is. One rarely hears, for example, about the millions of people who buy Gospel music, or music from various Middle Eastern and South Asian countries that have thriving music industries of their own. Indeed, the "objectivity" of Soundscan data gathering is used to disguise its role in maintaining the imperial dominance of the US culture industry. This dominance is an ideological and political construction, not a neutral, uncontested reality born of spontaneous wishes on the part of the populace. While rock and roll and its derivatives enjoy enormous popularity and influence world wide, they are by no means monolithic, uniform, or even universally popular. Language alone prevents this from ever being totally achievable. English is not the most spoken language in the world; Mandarin is. Popular song, in particular, will always be intimately connected to the dialects and idioms of popular speech.

3    Wechsler, Andrew R. and George R. Schink. "CDs: A Better Value than Ever." May 21, 2002.
A report prepared for the Recording Industry Association of America, Inc. by LECG, Inc. 1600 M Street, N.W., Suite 700, Washington, D.C. 20036.

4    Cope, Nigel. "Business Profile: The head of Sanctuary Group says music industry is as much about touring and merchandise as it is about record sales." *The Independent*. December 2, 2002.

5    Zizek, Slavoj. *The Ticklish Subject*. Verso Press, 1999, p. 184–185.

6    Cassy, John. "EMI find bonus for recruit." *The Guardian*. November 23, 2002.

7    Cope, Nigel. "Business Profile: The head of Sanctuary Group says music industry is as much about touring and merchandise as it is about record sales." *The Independent*. December 2, 2002.

# SPEAKING
# OF MUSIC

## CRITICS, EXPERTS
## AND THE EDUCATION
## OF AUDIENCES

Writing about music is like dancing about architecture—it's really a stupid thing to want to do.

**ELVIS COSTELLO**

Most rock journalism is people who can't write interviewing people who can't talk for people who can't read.

**FRANK ZAPPA**

I say this with fear and trembling, seeing that I am expressing a judgement about a man, and man is not a bad animal, indeed, but a changeable one.

**PLATO, *PARMENIDES***

Speaking of music arouses passion. There is much at stake, since group identity, place in the social hierarchy and even one's view of the world are symbolized by the music one listens to. Critics, musicians and the general public all weigh in with contradictory claims. The one measure none dispute is sales. Disappearing in the fog is another measure: quality. Even though many notice the widening chasm between what sells and what is good, few seriously consider the consequences for music. A peculiar impasse has been reached, where ideals of freedom and justice are totally confused with how quality is to be judged, and by whom.

## POP DOES NOT MEAN POPULAR

There are two meanings, often used interchangeably, of the word popular. The first is: "liked by many". The second is: "originating in The Many". At one time, popular music meant the latter and contrasted to the fine arts of the cultivated elites. Now, however, popular music means that which sells or is intended to sell to the populace regardless of its origins. In practice, this means that a large quantity of music is produced according to formulas, more or less rationally designed, and promoted for sale amongst the populace as a replacement for that which organically arises from amongst them. This is what I call Anti-music. It is the sonic equivalent of fast food. To a certain extent it imitates what is genuinely popular, or folk art, but it is basically false, since it lacks the essential characteristics that have defined music of the populace since time immemorial. These characteristics are the musical expression of three conditions of life: suffering, struggling and rejoicing.

Music gives expression to the feelings that arise from the people's experience of these conditions. It arises everywhere spontaneously, like spoken language, and it has always and everywhere served one fundamental purpose: to unite the community in alleviating its suffering, strengthening the struggle against it and rejoicing in the wonder of rejuvenating life. Music can therefore be spoken of in a critical process. How well or how poorly a particular piece, performance or artist does in achieving the desired result can be evaluated according to these timeless elements of which all popular music is composed.

The substitution of Anti-music for the authentic is done by extracting certain physical characteristics—rhythm, melody, harmony and timbre—from the authentic and using them to construct a mold. This mold is then used to shape the energies and talents of individual musical artists for sale. Eliminated in the process is any reference to suffering, struggling or rejoicing. In their place is put diversion, narcissism and escape; time-killing in place of timelessness.

While there are many critics who sincerely engage in explorations of these problems, most fail for three reasons. First, they do not differentiate between the two meanings of popular, making them equivalent. Second, they know too little of the history of the people from which true popular music originates. Third, they fail to grasp the actual ways music itself has evolved in connection to the suffering, struggling and rejoicing of the populace; the specific practices musicians develop to give expression to the feelings arising therefrom.

Finally, music critics are too often unwilling to take responsibility for the effects their words might have on music and musicians, or, more importantly, are unwilling to evaluate the effect of the popular on the populace. In other words, critics abdicate any responsibility for having to determine whether something that is popular, meaning it sells a lot, is in the interests of the populace, meaning what will further the people's struggle against suffering and injustice.

## A CHANGE IS GONNA COME

The quintessential example of this is the history and music of the African diaspora, particularly that which developed in the United States. Since it burst on the world stage with jazz in the early decades of the 20th century, this music has been the subject of much analysis and debate. Its origins in work songs, field hollers, religious music and blues are widely known. Its connections to African roots have been explored and commented on in depth. Its vitally important role in the development of popular music in the late 20th century is universally recognized. But black people are still oppressed.

Herein lies the great contradiction faced by critics: how can they write knowledgeably about the most important influence in what is called popular music and disconnect it from the lives of the actual people who gave it birth and nourishment? How can one speak of the popular being what sells the most CDs in the face of this obvious and ever-present example of the popular in its more fundamental and creative sense? A brief look at history illustrates the problem and its ramifications. At the very moment of triumph of the American and French Revolutions and the declaration of the Rights of Man, black slaves were rising to claim these universal rights in Haiti. The threat this posed to the slave owners was so great that they immediately attacked the Haitians, imprisoning their leader, Toussaint L'Overture, leaving him to rot in a French prison. While unsuccessful in preventing the establishment of the country of Haiti, they spent the next two hundred years (down to the present day) isolating, invading, bullying and generally oppressing the Haitian people.[1]

Of course, the same was done in the US. For a brief period following the Civil War, freed slaves laid claim to many of the rights to which they were entitled by the US Constitution. The elites of North and South engineered the legal changes, enforced by the likes of the KKK, to restore blacks to semi-slavery, a position they occupied until the 1960s. This is the soil from which sprang the music of black people, which subsequently took the world by storm, influencing every musician who has come into contact with it.

It is useful to follow the example of black music precisely because it is exemplary, rather than exclusive. In other words, as a particular genre of popular art it has much in common with all popular art from whatever place, time or culture it comes. Thus Irish music and flamenco, Arabic and Russian music all share the characteristics that identify music as originating from among the people. But black music does have particular relevance in that it has been carried by an expansionist US to the world at large. Simultaneously, it remains rooted in the culture of a people who continue to suffer oppression inside the US. Thus, black music continues to display all the attributes of its origins even as it continues to evolve.

The crucial distinction between the noble words of the Constitution and the actions taken by the government legitimized by that document must be made. The ways in which the populace is manipulated by the "popular" are refinements on an old theme whereby brute force and public relations are combined to "manufacture consent".[2] The role music critics play in this process is that of maintaining the appearance of "free speech." This expression of "independent" thinking provides the gloss that conceals the actual social relations in cultural production, in particular, and society in general.

## CRITICS WITHOUT CRITERIA

Art criticism began with bourgeois critics writing about bourgeois music. This was a mutually reinforcing function necessary to the establishment of the bourgeois arts. In fact, it was a component of the political struggle against monarchy, the church and all vestiges of a dying social order. This model continued to be used, even as the popular arts were ascendant. The explosion of the Sixties brought forth music critics from amongst the rebellious youth of that period, who could authentically speak about a counterculture of which they were an active part. That culture was a direct result of the struggle of black people and the music it produced being taken up by white youth. The combination of influences brought about rock and roll as is widely known.

Now, however, the essential linkage has been broken. Following the end of the revolutionary storms of the Sixties, criticism of all kinds has been cut adrift from the very source that gives it a reason for being. Indeed, an antagonistic divide has opened up—one that more closely resembles the classic, 19th century image of the pompous art critic lording it over the starving artist. Everyone can imagine it: music critic dismisses work of a composer who dies in poverty only to have his work become world famous after his death. During the Sixties, this relationship was completely reversed: musicians became gods and the journalists became acolytes or disciples. Put more prosaically, musicians shook off the judgments of an old way of thinking and established new criteria for music making and journalists followed this direction in their writing. This temporary disorder has been readjusted. Now musicians are to a large extent at the mercy of critics and the media outlets they work for. Substituting for criteria are the particular tastes of the critic. These tastes are themselves shaped by the promotion that goes into making music popular. What serves the interests of the music industry, and in turn employs the critics, is, of course, what the music critic likes!

With the replacement of the authentically popular by pop, the most basic criteria for the evaluation of quality are eliminated. Everyone is an expert, everyone's opinion is equally valid and no one knows anything except what is most popular! THE ONLY CRITERION IS HOW MANY PEOPLE BUY THE PRODUCT.

I recently asked my son, who is both a lover of hip-hop and a teacher of 11-year-old children, to explain the popularity of Eminem. He led a class discussion on the subject. Here are the results:

1. Obviously, he has cool beats (compliments of Dr. Dre).
2. Videos:
    a.) He has more of them.
    b.) They are funny, cool, he wears cool costumes (i.e. Osama waving a white flag, Elvis, Rapmobile, etc.).
3. He puts down everything. Nothing is sacred.
4. He blames parents for the problems of kids. They love this one.

5. He says tons of bad words.

6. He jacks (robs) his mother.

7. He says the craziest/silliest/stupidest lyrics.

8. THEY CAN IDENTIFY WITH HIS ANGER (They really felt this one!!!).

9. Finally, they think he has a cool style of dress.

Now, if 11 year-old children are as aware as this survey clearly demonstrates, then what do they need critics for? Asked another way: what do we have to teach our children?

Might there not be useful discussion of how this artist's statement affects the lives of the listener? Might there not be an examination of the sources of these children's anger, their relationships with their parents and the reasons bad words have the effect they do? What kind of a world produces such music?

It is worthy to note that only one of the points the children mentioned concerns music. Admittedly, it is the first, the word "obviously" stating the presumption that the music (cool beats) must be good. But this assumption is precisely the one no one should make. It is at this crucial juncture that we must begin establishing criteria.

There is a vocabulary of sounds, rhythms and melodies that define the musical language of hip-hop. Dr. Dre is not only a talented musician, he is among the originators of this vocabulary. This is an example of how all music develops. There is a correlation between certain sounds and their emotional content within a broader social framework. History, of society and of music within it, can be studied and understood. It is possible to develop a deeper appreciation of the inventiveness of Dr. Dre (and any creative artist) by learning:

what choices he made,

what sources he drew upon,

what effects he was seeking to achieve and

what he discarded or ruled out in this process.

This is not only for the aspiring young musician, it is also for the education of an audience. It is preparation for a closer, more intimate relationship with music than that which is being encouraged by society today. Today, audiences are to be thought of as markets. The listener is a consumer. This is not merely word substitution. It is the destruction of an organic, uncommodifiable relationship between people and their creative expressions, and the construction of an exploitative one in its place. It is necessarily an exploitative one (as opposed to equal exchange of goods or services) because a profit must be derived from it and profit means someone is getting ripped off.

There have been numerous critiques of Eminem that have clearly situated the music in its social context. This is useful, to be sure. But deeper problems exist about which music journalism is generally silent. Partly, this is the dual and contradictory uses of the word "popular" already discussed. But beyond that distinction lies the even larger question of what is in the interests of the populace. Not only who will judge music, but who will rule. And music always, everywhere is asking, "might there be an end to rule?"

## SOVEREIGNTY OF THE PEOPLE AND THE RISE OF THE POPULAR

The current situation can trace its origins to the French and American revolutions and the enthronement of the People as sovereign. This concept of the social body comprised (in theory) of all humans and subservient to no other power, terrestrial or divine, forms the philosophical, political and social basis for the dominance of popular culture in the world today. Of course, in practice, the People thus constituted actually meant propertied white males (as what happened to Haiti clearly demonstrates). Correspondence in the realm of music to that actual political state of affairs should be no surprise. Throughout the 19th century, the bourgeois arts predominated. While a great deal was written about them, very little was written about what the laboring majorities listened to or created themselves, and it was a lot. As the political category of the People approached inclusion of all people, the culture of the populace assumed a corresponding position of preeminence in society. The enfranchisement of women corresponded with the rise of popular culture and its rapid dissemination by means of new technologies leading toward the dominant place it took after World War II. Enfranchisement of African-Americans in the 1960s corresponded to the international expansion of the influence of black culture in general and in music especially. These developments were by no means steady, cumulative acquisitions of territory for the People. On the contrary, they were intense, revolutionary and counterrevolutionary wars fought almost without pause until 1991 with the collapse of the Soviet Union. Furthermore, in no place did the legal recognition of the People automatically mean that the People ruled (democracy). Nevertheless, it is quite clear that prior to the First World War and the Russian revolution, popular culture, particularly popular music, was seldom written about. For several thousand years, while music was being seriously discussed, the music of the slaves or the laboring classes was consciously dismissed. The actualization, at least in law, of the sovereignty of the People, meaning everyone, meant the music made by the populace had to be talked about.

## PHASES AND STAGES

There are three important phases of this development that we need to examine in order to better grasp the role that art criticism has actually played. The first is the period when art criticism became a mass phenomenon in its own right, establishing itself as a legitimate field of endeavor. This, for our purposes, is the 19th and early 20th centuries. The second is what followed the Russian revolution of 1917: the rise of working class and anti-colonial struggles and the corresponding ascendancy of popular culture. This culminated in the world-wide revolution of the Sixties during and through which popular culture and above all, music assumed pre-eminence. Phase two includes the rapid spread and systematic deployment of music in service of revolution and counterrevolution. It is a period full of contentious debate surrounding the role of art in society, the relative position of art to politics (subservient to or independent of) and who will be the judge: political commissars, art critics or artists themselves. The last phase, the present, is characterized by the confused attempt to disavow any higher purpose art might serve than its own expression and the pleasure that it brings, while at the same time trying to fill the void this leaves. This void is the absence of a higher purpose, be it spiritual, political or some other. Virtually all art criticism today (especially music criticism) is a desperate attempt to evade this contradiction. Most criticism employs one of two postures: passion or detachment of the writer. This is to obscure the fact that they have nothing more to say than how a work of art affects them as individuals. It is only their opinion. They cannot legitimately criticize it because they have no criteria or training that can lay any claim to either principle or expertise. All must sooner or later resort to either the numbers game (how many units sold) or the social effects of the work. The latter cannot be judged by commercial criteria alone. Thus, music critics are inexorably led back into the realms of politics and philosophy, without being equipped to deal intelligently with these subjects!

## PHASE ONE: ART AND THE BROTHERHOOD OF MAN

Leo Tolstoy wrote "What Is Art?" in 1898[3], at the end of the first phase mentioned above. It is to his enduring credit that Tolstoy boldly asserts that most art, including much produced by those we would call great masters, was really counterfeit and bad. Furthermore, after a quick but comprehensive survey of what had been written about beauty, truth and aesthetics in general, he remorselessly dismisses the whole pile of verbiage as completely missing the point. The point, with which I heartily concur, is that art is a condition of human life and its function is community building. All the abstract speculation about beauty was, at best, an attempt to impose scientific or rational criteria on a social practice whose role was, precisely, to convey and inspire feeling, not reason. The authenticity or veracity of such feeling lies in the actual experience the artist making the work is drawing on as subject matter and the sincerity and truthfulness with which the artist carries out his or her task. This cannot be commissioned by a Duke or a Queen. This cannot be produced on command like a dressmaker might make a suit of clothes. Indeed, as Tolstoy correctly states, the vast majority of musical, literary and artistic works since the Renaissance were made to suit the purposes of those who ordered them made. Though among these there is some inspired, true art, the great bulk of them are merely technically proficient exercises in formula, devoid of the lived experience or sincerity of the artist.

In place of actual experience-based emotions and an honest aspiration to connect with one's fellow human beings, the art Tolstoy is discussing is preoccupied with three themes: vanity, tedium of living and above all, sexual love or lust. These are what entertain and divert the bourgeois and the idle rich. Since these classes have long since renounced religion and no longer pursue Christian ideals except as it serves their political purposes, it is not fashionable, nor is it sufficiently diverting, to deal with anything that does not bring immediate sensual pleasure and relieve boredom. Since these classes are also the financiers or patrons of artists, it is to their order that artists produce. It is certainly arguable that Tolstoy's blade cuts too wide a swath; that there is more to Shakespeare and Beethoven than pandering to the rich. Furthermore, in our eyes, the Symbolist poets Tolstoy summarily dismissed had a great deal more to offer than incomprehensibility and bad form. But these excesses do not undermine Tolstoy's basic position. His determination to overthrow an entire way of thinking about art is genuine, well informed and draws strong, clear lines where there were only smoke and mirrors. Furthermore, Tolstoy exposes accepted norms as far from self-evidently legitimate when he says: "Three conditions contribute to the production in our society of objects of counterfeit art. These conditions are: 1. the considerable remuneration of artists for their works and the resultant establishing of the artist as a professional, 2. art criticism, and 3. art schools."[4] This is shocking stuff and was intended to be, particularly as Tolstoy was himself an aristocrat, a world famous novelist widely popular in exactly the manner he attacks, and he includes himself among those guilty of betraying the true purpose of art! As Tolstoy states in his conclusion, "The purpose of art in our time consists in transferring from the realm of reason to the realm of feeling the truth that people's well-being lies in being united among themselves and in establishing, in place of the violence that now reigns, that Kingdom of God—that is, of love—which we all regard as the highest aim of human life."[5] Tolstoy was a Christian in a very peculiar way, so it is important to let him clarify what he means by such nomenclature. "The expression, the union of men with God and with each other, may appear vague to people accustomed to hearing these words so often abused, and yet the words have a very clear meaning. These words mean that the Christian union of people, contrary to the partial, exclusive union of some people, is one that unites all people without exception."[6]

A few more points about Tolstoy are in order. Integral to his spiritual quest was championing the liberation of the serfs of Russia along with all laboring people. His efforts drew him into the revolutionary debates of his time, in which he developed a radical critique of capitalism and the state, identifying himself as a Christian Anarchist. Among those inspired by his ideas was Mahatma Gandhi, with whom Tolstoy maintained a lively correspondence. While his politics may be debated, there is no doubt that he was speaking of the same general principles originally brought to center stage in human affairs by the French and American revolutions; in a word, the community of all humans. He names this the "religious consciousness of the age." Whether or not one accepts such terms, the underlying substance is the same. This powerful aspiration has been battered and beaten down but it remains, undaunted, as the single most important question facing all people, everywhere. Thus there is a deep resonance with us living today when Tolstoy says, "The religious consciousness of our time does not single out any 'one' society of people, but, on the contrary, demands the union of all, absolutely all people, without exception, and places brotherly love for all people above all other virtues, and therefore the feelings conveyed by the art of our time not only cannot coincide with the feelings conveyed by former art, but must be opposed to them."[7]

It is important to keep in mind, however, that Tolstoy's book appeared just before the rise of popular culture, at a time when the popular arts were still considered unworthy of attention. We will return to examine Tolstoy's ideas in light of subsequent historical developments later in this chapter.

## PHASE TWO: ART AND THE REVOLUTION

Tolstoy's arguments resemble those that were raised during the decades following the Russian revolution, what I call Phase two, except that instead of the term "religious" consciousness, class consciousness or revolutionary consciousness was used. While there is far more involved than merely substituting words, the contours of the discussion, the criteria advanced and many of the specific ideas Tolstoy raised were taken up in a new context. Indeed, it can be said that this period was a triumph for Tolstoy's position in some important ways. Not only was bourgeois art knocked off its pedestal but the global struggle for revolution elevated the popular arts above it. As the world faced the unprecedented carnage of World War I, the only way out of the doom it spelled for civilization, and the despair felt by many artists and intellectuals, lay in the spirit of the people united against imperialism and war. The three institutional pillars of counterfeit art production were shaken to their foundations. Professionals were challenged by "cultural workers" or amateurs. Art criticism was turned into a battlefield of ideology and politics. Art schools continued to function, but from this period onward would be compelled to justify their purpose since so many from the ranks of the uneducated were producing the most relevant, innovative and influential art. The world stage was stormed by avowedly proletarian literature and art. Critics such as Theodoro Adorno, Max Horkheimer and Walter Benjamin made penetrating critiques of the ways modern capitalism, particularly in its fascist form, was using culture to mold the consciousness of the masses. These were joined by artist/theoreticians such as Bertolt Brecht, John Heartfield, Luis Bunuel, Jean Renoir; dadaist and surrealist movements, workers' theater projects and factory choruses. In Russia and China there were effusions of theory and practical expression based in revolutionary experience. Notable among these were Sergei Eisenstein and Vladimir Mayakovsky, the constructivist movement in graphic design along with virtual armies of musicians and dancers, while, in China, literary movements brought forth writers such as Hu Shih and Lu Hsun. It is impossible to mention more than a tiny sample of contributors to these debates since they were legion and came from many countries of the world. The point is that these subjects were at least a major theme if not the dominant one in virtually all discussion of art and music in the period between World Wars I and II.

Surprising as it might seem to some readers today, nowhere was this more prevalent than in the United States. It might be hard to believe given the present state of affairs, but in his brilliant book, *The Cultural Front*, Michael Denning demonstrates that what is today considered "American Culture" was largely shaped by just these forces. What the world has come to know as representative of this country was forged in the struggles of the decades between 1935 and 1955—what Denning calls the "Age of the CIO" (Congress of Industrial Organizations). Some of the greatest popular music and literature was made during this period, quintessentially American and yet proletarian and internationalist. Paul Robeson, Woody Guthrie, Billie Holiday, Pete Seeger, Leadbelly, Duke Ellington—the list is endless and it is most enlightening. The body and soul of what America purveys to the world as its legacy was made by artists whose work was dedicated to the "popular" in the artistic sense, to the People as a political category, and against racism, fascism, imperialism and war. Orson Welles, Dashiell Hammett, Richard Wright, John Steinbeck, Langston Hughes— again, the list is endless. In the light of history, it is somewhat ironic that at opposite ends of the Cold War between the USSR and the US were parallel constructions of a popular culture characterized by its conscious championing of the People, albeit with different rhetoric attached, and different ruling groups manipulating and using it for their own political agendas. It cannot be emphasized enough that in terms of Tolstoy's critique of counterfeit art and the underlying question of service to a greater social good, the period described in Denning's book witnessed an evanescent flowering of popular work and the criticism that accompanied its production throughout the world.

It must be noted, of course, that in both the US and the USSR there was massive repression specifically directed at artists. There are many examples of how art was criticized by the bullet, not only by the pen. Suicide, imprisonment, blacklisting and exile were the fates of many of the greatest artists in the world at that time. But it needs to be made clear that this was not confined to the Nazis or the Communists. In fact, there are many among the American artists I listed above who were punished for their political and social views, some grievously, never to recover. In fact, the period known as the McCarthy era, was "art criticism" at its most vicious. The entire field of popular culture in the United States was under attack of the most brutal kind. Exemplified by the case of the "Hollywood Ten", a great purge was undertaken to wipe out any vestige of resistance to the ruling elites. As the Cold War got underway in earnest, all reference to social themes that were in any way critical of the US, the American Way of Life, and the Free Enterprise System were forbidden. Mention the working class, internationalism or revolution, and you were likely to be threatened with arrest, denied permits to perform, physically attacked and publicly ridiculed. (Films such as *The Front*, starring Woody Allen, tell part of this story.)

## PHASE WITHIN A PHASE: THE SIXTIES

While McCarthyism dealt a serious blow to art and artists in the US, it was soon overwhelmed by the next wave of revolutionary struggle. This began almost immediately after W.W.II with the anti-colonial movements, above all the Chinese revolution. This was followed by the Vietnamese struggle for independence and the Civil Rights movement in the US. By the early Sixties these struggles had been joined by a new generation of young people in most countries of the world. Radicalized by the rising tide of resistance to the old order shaken so profoundly by W.W.II and subsequent revolutions, the youth demanded, among other things, the fulfillment of the promises made by the French and American revolutions. This initially took the form of Free Speech Movements, Civil Rights and anti-Apartheid movements, National Liberation movements and a general demand for equality and justice. Simultaneously, and in direct connection, the rise of popular music, and especially rock and roll, announced the coming of a generation intent on changing the world. It was at this moment in history that much of what we today call music journalism began.

Throughout Europe and North America (and soon after, Latin America as well) magazines and periodicals sprang up dedicated to popular music, which initially made no distinction between political and artistic matters. Writers commonly discussed issues of music, drugs, the police, the Vietnam war and Civil Rights all in the same breath. There was an intimate link between the journalists and the music and politics they were writing about since they had to be involved to speak knowledgeably to their audience, who were the very ones being drafted, experimenting with drugs, demonstrating for civil rights and attending rock and roll concerts. Some among the older generation of critics, such as Ralph Gleason in San Francisco, championed the work of artists as diverse as Miles Davis and Bob Dylan. But by and large, art criticism, and music journalism especially, underwent a transformation directly corresponding to the final conquest by the popular arts of preeminent position in cultural production. Tolstoy's demands were being met in spades. Not only did Jimi Hendrix and the Beatles have to be "taken seriously", nobody cared much about what "serious" art critics had to say. The irrelevance of bourgeois art and its claims to superiority in aesthetic or social terms had become an established fact.

To a large extent this was due to the vitality of the struggles for liberation and the arrival of new musical technologies combined with the unleashing of long repressed energies amongst young people. The role of African-American music is of special importance, since it was both the basic component of rock and roll and was directly connected to the Civil Rights movement. Moreover, it most clearly embodied the whole concept of the "popular" in its broadest dimensions, expressing as it did, all aspects of social life breaking free of 400 years of slavery and repression.

The period was characterized by an organic bond between art and revolution, between the triumph of the popular and defeat of the bourgeois in culture and above all in music. This was expressed in many different ways, from many conflicting viewpoints in the music journalism of that time. But regardless of the position taken by any particular writer, it is difficult to conceive of talk about music not including such discussion, since it had to deal with what was the subject of much of the music being made and what was on the lips of the masses of young people throughout the world.

## PHASE THREE: ART AND THE
## MARKET (OR POP VS. THE POPULAR)

As the revolutionary waves of the Sixties receded, they left in their wake structures that were to be inhabited by subsequent generations. These were mostly shells, emptied of the spirit that gave them life and purpose. There had been an explosion of music and writing about it that established networks of concert venues, record companies, radio stations and magazines that have continued to develop to the present day. But taking the place of a world-changing, radical attitude were stylistic fads, adolescence as an end, and, increasingly, the unalloyed pursuit of fame and gain. Irreverence and rebellion became fashionable poses aimed at achieving notoriety rather than challenging the outmoded ideas of a corrupt social order. Career replaced Life. I recall vividly the first time I heard the word "market" applied to the people I was performing music for. This seemed weird to me at the time. In fact, it was sinister. A linguistic turn signaled the re-conquest of social space by the enemies of music and the ideals that had inspired it for several decades. The one thing that was irreversible, the one thing that was left, was that popular music was firmly established as the dominant form.

This has made for a complicated inversion of the arguments Tolstoy advanced regarding the criteria for judging art. The popular is now supreme, but by and large it demonstrates many of the worst traits of bourgeois art Tolstoy so accurately described. Clearly, vanity, boredom and sex are by far the most common themes in pop music. Clearly, the function of this is to divert attention, to provide escape and to encourage narcissism. "Turning rebellion into money", as Joe Strummer sang, was a basic strategy of record companies that enlisted the active support of journalists with ease. But it was more than that. Steadily, "pop" replaced the popular.

By the early '90s most music critics were consumer guides. With some notable exceptions, music magazines and daily newspapers reported the latest concert or CD release, frequently copying the press releases of the artists or record companies verbatim and pawning this off on the unsuspecting readers as "journalism." Even in supposedly "serious" music magazines, there was less and less discussion of music itself or the role it was playing in society and more and more about technology, sports, fashion (clothing), lifestyles of stars and advice columns for the coolness impaired. The best writing was often the frustration and anger of the journalist about this state of affairs; not actual music criticism so much as op-ed pieces lambasting the powers that be in the music industry or society at large.

Of course, this is grossly oversimplified. Specific musical genres such as punk rock and hip-hop spawned their own writers and critics who, in many cases, continue to champion the social purposes that these musics were born to serve. Indeed, recent political developments have intensified debate around just these subjects within the broad and loosely defined legions of hip-hop fans. Nevertheless, this is not characteristic of music journalism, much less art criticism, in general. It would be no exaggeration to say that an abyss has opened up between "pop" culture (some call it "soda-pop culture" because of its links to Pepsi and other purveyors of soft drinks) and all that does not have the massive promotional resources to make it popular.

Once, the populace itself was the ground from which sprang the musical fruits to be commented on and discussed by music critics. "Popular" meant "originating in the populace". Now, the music industry (or, more broadly, Adorno's culture industry[8]) manufactures the products and spends enormous amounts of money making them popular. Popular (or "pop") now means "widely consumed". Thus, even the best intentioned and informed music critic is faced with writing about these manufactured "stars" and "hits" that have virtually nothing to do with genuinely popular, or people's art, or they find themselves irrelevant and, more than likely, out of work!

What Tolstoy's utopian vision implied was the brotherhood of man by way of the elevation of the laboring people and their way of life into the universal culture enjoyed by all. What has happened instead is the bourgeoisification of the popular. The Thatcherite myopia of everyone owning stock and aspiring to acquire the same things the rich have is what guides this development. "There is no society, only individuals", said Thatcher, with the support of countless ideologues and pundits. It is the hopelessly deluded view that everyone wants to be rich and live in privileged luxury. First of all, even if it were possible for 6 billion people to be supported by the labor of robots and the earth could sustain such overconsumption as the wealthy few engage in today, not everyone wants to live this way. Secondly, a carefree existence is exactly the opposite of what has produced timeless art. Even if such an existence were possible, it would not be desirable for musicians or other artists for the simple reason that art making would be boring and dead.

Tolstoy confronted this deception head on. His attack exposes the effect on art that the narcissism and self-aggrandizement of the bourgeois produced. Furthermore, he vigorously opposed this with a resonant alternative: our most profound emotions arise from our aspirations to connect with each other as members of a community and to connect with the universe as our wondrous home. These aspirations have nothing in common with what today's bourgeoisified pop culture offers instead: technical bombast, adolescent naughtiness, glamorous display and the glorification of the trivial. It is ironic that we have arrived at a place where Tolstoy's critique is starkly relevant again but with the transposition of the popular and the bourgeois in art production.

## BEYOND PHASES: TIMELESSNESS IN OUR TIMES

To combat Anti-music (or counterfeit art, to use Tolstoy's terminology) we need to return to the question of criteria. These criteria fall into two categories: social effect and mastery. The first category is fundamental and should be debated by all. The second is more specific to the music maker's practice and, thus, may not be of general interest. The category of social effect deals with three types of experience that make up the human condition: suffering, struggling and rejoicing. Each of these is a site for the ritual or actual conflict between pleasure and the greater good. The category of mastery is where the measurement of time is transformed into timelessness, where the novel and the exotic become "forever" and "everywhere" and where all that is known is systematically turned into miracles.

## SUFFERING, STRUGGLING, REJOICING

People are everywhere, at all times, suffering, struggling and rejoicing. These are also the measures of music. How well does a particular composer or performer capture the spirit of one or more of these experiences? It is not merely to adorn or accompany that music plays its role, it is to express and evoke the feelings of human beings about their own suffering, their own struggling or their own rejoicing. To inspire or conjure up these feelings is why music is made. Its success in doing so is readily apparent to listeners when it is achieved, notably lacking when it is not.

The problem with aesthetic considerations such as beauty or ugliness, symmetry or asymmetry, technically astonishing or childishly simple is that they are completely relative and time bound. They change constantly as innovations, social or technical, outside of music occur. They have relevance to the individual or community at a particular place and time, but tell us only superficial things about the intrinsic qualities of music itself. For these qualities we have to look deeper and examine the way music connects to its ahistoric or timeless purpose, which is to build community while imagining another, better one. Music is named; it is identified as itself, like tree or truck. But what makes it music as opposed to tree or truck is not its name but a quality that can only be experienced by listening to it, interacting with it and appreciating its effect on oneself and on many. Absent this quality, this expression of feeling, it is better to listen to a tree or a truck. A tree blowing in the breeze or a truck chugging along have rhythm and melody that can be turned into music in the imagination. Anti-music destroys this ability. It desensitizes the listener, shutting down the imagination and preventing the effects that authentic music produces. (Muzak, as we'll see in a moment, is the prototype for pop, corresponding to a scientific analysis of the effects of tempo, major and minor keys, timbre of musical instruments and duration of pieces of music. Such formulas are actually used by radio programmers in many parts of the world.)

The music of the African-American church best exemplifies what real music does since it comprehensively embodies suffering, struggling and rejoicing. The effectiveness of the music, its artistic value, will be apparent beyond its technical virtuosity or the refinement of its performance. Its intrinsic spiritual qualities will be exhibited and can be judged by an intense interactive process engaged in by the participants in the church service or by an observer listening outside.

The same is true of flamenco, Arabic, European classical, Chinese or any music one can think of. These styles are different vessels for the same contents. Interestingly, it is the music of the slave or the laboring masses that has taught the world what it needs most from music and illuminates Tolstoy's critique.

## PLEASURE VS. THE GOOD

From the earliest writings about music, which date back at least 5,000 years, its role in society has been a subject of great debate. In all the cultures that wrote about music, the necessity of harnessing this powerful force in the service of social ends was never in doubt. In every case the essential question was contention between the sacred and the profane, pleasure and moral goodness, spiritual degeneracy or uplift. Since all writing about music has been done in hierarchical societies, the interests of the rulers or dominant groups are usually those represented. In the present, this question of who will be the dominant group, who will rule and, therefore, be the judge remains the most important question facing society.

In *The Republic*, Plato wrote that in an ideal society music had to be carefully monitored, lest it undermine the Good to which all should be encouraged to aspire. He dismissed the music of the slave and the laborer as not worthy of consideration or a danger if allowed to influence the youth. Innovation or change were not desirable except as corrections to flaws discovered in existing pieces. Pleasure was not evil, but it was a lower order of consciousness and distracting to the pursuit of wisdom which was how Goodness was defined. Later, in *Philebus*, Plato argues for the Mixture which includes both Thought and Pleasure, and is better than either alone. This was not a compromise but a recognition that between the polarity of the Limit and the Unlimited lay the harmony, the attunement, that brought about health and happiness. These may seem hopelessly antiquated views to the modern critic, but as we shall see, they remain part of any discussion of music today. In any case, Plato gave music paramount importance along with the study of arithmetic, geometry and astronomy.[9]

For most music critics the question of the greater good never arises. There is good music and there is bad. There is music that gives pleasure and music that fails to. Pleasure is the measure and the greater good is an obstacle to its enjoyment. Obvious problems such as pleasure turning into pain or that the needs of society might be the responsibility of its members are strictly avoided. In fact, there is a vast, mutually supporting network of denial amongst writers on music to censure any among their ranks who might violate this "Fundamentalism of Fun." When bristling at the charge that they are merely consumer guides, some will raise theoretical arguments citing such thinkers as Nietzsche, Foucault or Derrida.

Nietzsche, music critic par excellence, sought to rid Europe of "the Plato disease" and Christianity's slave morality. There is no God and no God's Eye from which to observe Truth. Appolo (Reason) tyrannizes Dionysis (Passion). It is the poet (or musician) who releases humanity's soaring spirit and banishes the sage to his cave. Now, Nietzsche's views seem to have won out: "truth" itself is no longer thought of. But are the play of passions any more "free"? It seems his piping Pan has been ambushed by a more elusive foe.

The End of Truth arrived and with it the Church of the Free Market. Indeed, in the last decades of the 20th century, we were inundated with Endings. The End of History, the End of Science, the End of Philosophy and so forth. The obsession with finitude corresponds directly to the reduction of the universe and all it contains into cheesy products nicely displayed at WalMart. As a parade of "Big Ideas" came and went, all failing to lead us to the Promised Land, we find ourselves at the mall looking for a parking place. Science, politics and even love abandoned their emancipatory claims. Only the Market could free the People, bringing the good life to all. And the arts? Alas, the arts were the envy of all the rest, their mysteries so coveted that the only agreement possible was to make them subordinate. Yoked oxen. Far from either Plato's philosopher-king or Nietzsche's poet-philosopher, the artist became a whore.

To counteract this malaise it is necessary to reassert the very characteristics of authentic popular music. Its candid sexuality mixes with its awe of the universe. Its comic desacralizing combines with its devotion to the bond that joins people together. Its celebration of folly is joined to the quest for wisdom. The conflict is not resolved once and for all. It is the ongoing, unfolding reason why.

Again, reference to the culture of African-Americans is instructive. The schism between blues and gospel exactly represents the two poles of pleasure vs. the greater good. Blues for the worship of the devil. Gospel for the worship of god. The tavern or the church; the bordello of the damned or the tabernacle of the lord. Of course, all practitioners of the music itself recognized that it was the words that made the main difference, not the musical sounds. Indeed, the lesson this teaches is that beneath the specific and contradictory purposes to which the music was put lay the needs of an embattled, materially impoverished community. To serve the needs of this community, a music was devised that became a balm for deep wounds, a weapon for resistance and a joy for the day to come. That this music has enriched humanity is widely recognized. What is appreciated less is how instructive are its basic components and how they have been put to use. Not only the music itself, but how it is made and how it is judged are valuable critical tools for understanding all music and, particularly, what arises from the populace.

The work of Ray Charles is outstanding in this regard, since it is, on the one hand, emblematic of the popular and, on the other, the music of a true master. Charles pioneered the merger of blues and gospel forms (and much else such as jazz and country and western) and identified this as "Soul." This merger was both a musical one and a celebration of the ongoing struggle between pleasure and the greater good. This does not mean the final resolution or the erection of strict barriers. Quite the contrary, it is a recognition that, through music, a socially constructive expression can be given to this contradiction to enrich the lived lives of the people. Rather than strictly separating two aims, it unites them through rejoicing in the struggle against suffering. And this is done by applying highly developed practices of music making, employing principles handed down through generations.

"Sex, drugs and rock n roll" became a battle-cry of latter day Nietzschean rebellion against White Anglo-Saxon Protestant morality. It has been repeated ad nauseam and accepted as axiomatic by most pop music journalists. Indeed, under the guise of defiance, much pop criticism is a kind of thought control: the fashion police, designed to prohibit anyone from challenging their way of opposing pleasure to the greater good. It is a desperate attempt to protect the "rights" of the hypothetical "individual." In other words, each of us has our opinion, these opinions are equal, no one must impose theirs on anyone else—hence, there can be no criteria for judging quality, let alone truth. Aside from the philosophical problems this poses, it doesn't really satisfy because it rejects the greater good altogether. It denies that real people live in a world larger than the concert hall or record shop, that not everyone is happy to "live fast, die young, and leave a good looking corpse." People work, raise children, seek friendship. For many, the greatest pleasure is serving the greater good. In order to evade such questions, most music journalism simply ignores the necessity of community-forming which is the function music serves and without which, music does not exist.

Opposed to this, Ray Charles' work, and what is universally true of popular art, recognizes the existence of such needs, faces the contradictions squarely and uses them in the celebration of life. Hence his stirring performances of "Lift Every Voice and Sing" and "Let's Go Get Stoned". The texts may be debated outside of the music. But the vitality of the music itself and the relationship to the lived experience of the populace from which it sprang is undeniable. Moreover, it sets a musical standard by which all music can be measured. And, finally, it draws attention to the actual condition of a people who are oppressed and struggling, in this case, African-Americans.

But then, where on earth do the People actually hold Power?*

## MUZAK, ANTI-MUSIC AND CRITERIA

Duke Ellington once said: "There are only two kinds of music. Good music and all the rest." This is true for music, but it does not include a separate category of sound: Anti-music. There is no clearer example than Muzak and their own literature says best why it is not music:

---

*There are two meanings of the word "power." Most European languages have two words for these two different kinds of power—potestas and potentia, pouvoir and puissance, macht and vermögen. English requires qualifiers such as power over vs. power to, or coercive force vs. motive force. To clarify what I want to say in this book I will use the capitalized "Power" to designate coercive force, domination or rule and the uncapitalized "power" to mean potency, vitality, possibility, or creative drive.

Because music is art, but Muzak is science. And when you employ the science of Muzak: in an office, workers tend to get more done, more efficiently, and feel happier. In an industrial plant, people feel better and, with less fatigue and tension, their jobs seem less monotonous. In a store, people seem to shop in a more relaxed and leisurely manner. In a bank, customers are generally more calm, tellers and other personnel are more efficient. In general, people feel better about where they are; whether it's during work or leisure time. Muzak is all this and more. That's why we say Muzak is much more than music.[10]

Like Prozac for depression, Muzak is designed to make the prison seem like a playground, alienation seem like freedom. There is one difference between Muzak and Anti-music generally. Attention. Muzak depends on the inattention of the listener. Anti-music deliberately diverts it. In both cases the purpose is the manipulation of the listener. It is the replacement of the ancient, chosen interaction between musician and audience with the interaction between managers and managed, manipulators and manipulated. In place of an emotional connection between people, we get an involuntary response to sensory stimulation. Replacing honesty is deception.

Muzak proudly markets its "audio architecture," guaranteeing results based on criteria they have established to determine the effectiveness of their product. Now, if such criteria are possible for Anti-music, what is the difficulty in establishing criteria to evaluate the authentic?

## GOOD MUSIC

Good music is that which:

1. Engages the listener's attention, holding it for the duration of the piece—in effect, suspending time.

2. Transports the listener to an imaginary place, without leaving the physical place in which the music is heard (we speak of being "moved.")

3. Evokes emotional response without relying on visceral effect—except as required by the music itself. (this mainly concerns timbre and volume.)

4. Introduces novel elements in one of four ways:

-never before or rarely heard

-unusual, personal expression unlike any or most others

-rare technical virtuosity of performance, arrangement or composition

-infuses the old with new enthusiasm and perspective making it new again

5. Invigorates thought about music either before, during or after the performance in one of three directions:
-wanting to hear more
-wanting to know more
-wanting to do more.

Even these general attributes of good music need to be put in the context of a relationship between musician and audience. Each must teach the other in an ongoing exchange. Music can exhibit all the qualities listed above, be it for large numbers or only for a small, dedicated group that appreciates them—Busta Rhymes or Cecil Taylor, The Streets or John Cage, Gypsy Kings or Karlheinz Stockhausen. Thus, an audience needs to be educated to some degree in order to comprehend any specific music. Conversely, audiences seek to have their genuine needs met and will demand that musicians meet them. This is not easily resolved. Certainly not by government edict or the "rule" of the marketplace. Exploration and discovery (even with many failed attempts) need to be respected and supported by society in order to expand the possibilities of music. On the other hand, musicians need to honor their necessary social role by learning from the public they are attempting to educate. While this is a minefield of ego-battering rejection and nerve-shattering trial and error, the basic principle must be fought for: music makers have to assume responsibility for the maintenance of quality and dedication to the cause of music itself while learning from the public they play for what it is that public needs.

Above all, musicians must aspire to mastery as opposed to fame and gain. This is, after all, how all of us who become musicians are sooner or later inspired to do so. We hear the work of masters.

## TIME AND MUSICAL MASTERY

Much philosophy has been taken up with the question of Being and Time. Much musical practice is taken up with Being in Time. In another of the curious double meanings of important words that have run through this chapter, Time has a particular meaning in music that comments, in a constructive way, on the questions of philosophy. Keeping time, having good time, being in time are all commonly used phrases that describe two key elements of music. The first of these is rhythm, which is a way of measuring time in order to create and unite the performances of numbers of players. The second is duration, which is closely connected to rhythm but has more to do with how long or how short notes or sounds last, up to and including the duration of an entire piece of music. Rhythm is the heartbeat and the blood flow that is internal to and the "life force" of the musical event as a unique and unifying time maker. Duration is the relationship between this universe of "timeless" time and the real time by which the musician and musical event are connected to the rest of the universe. Mastering this is the most basic component of good musicianship. This leads to something flowing directly from it, which is also the first of four qualities of mastery in music.

1. Timelessness. This, of course, does not mean bad rhythm. This means that the master seeks to produce the timeless quality that enables a composition or performance to expand the temporal limits of the moment that it enters and exits existence. This makes two things happen. First, the music lasts as an ongoing infusion of quality into the vast body of music made at any moment anywhere by its example and the standard it sets (we constantly refer to great musical pieces when comparing them to others). Second, it joins with the other timeless music produced before or after the actual composition and its performance (it is living proof of the existence of this category and these standards which are everlasting). This is accomplished by producing at the moment of performance a suspension of time (in the chronological sense) by musicians playing in time (in the musical sense). When an audience loses all awareness of how long a piece of music is, how much time has passed since the performance began, it is a great performance indeed. In this sense, the duration of a piece takes its own time by making it itself. This is not easily accomplished, and most attempts fail.

2. Production of the Same through the novel. The Same, in this sense, is not the replica or copy of an object. Rather, it is a quality of experience. The novel, new or original is essential because it is one key component in the highest quality of experience that is, then, the Same. It serves to reinvigorate and renew, and it connects the Timeless to the lived present. However, music does not progress. It is not better now than it was fifty, five hundred or five thousand years ago. A great piece of music is always new sounding while a new piece that is not of this caliber will lose its novelty very quickly and soon become "dated" or boring. It will be incapable of producing the Same in the sense of the way it makes the musician and audience feel. The reason this category is important is that novelty, "the latest style," "the hippest trend," is constantly used to suppress the Timeless. The truly new is so because of its immediacy, its urgent connection to the Same, right now. While technology and music are constantly changing and are stylistically diverse, there are in every genre, style or tradition representative masterpieces or bodies of work that produce this quality of feeling and are not bound by history. It is recognizable as such

by music makers, and must be a measurement against that which all new work is judged.

3. The invention and discovery of truth. Invention in the sense of linking the creative imagination to the tools at hand. Discovery, in the sense of the exploration of spontaneity, the play of technique on previously untried paths, the use of accidental combinations (of people, instruments, sound sources, notes and rhythm), of the extrapolation of inspiration, seizing the intuitive thought and following it. Social effect will be determined by the process of invention and discovery within a particular historical time, but aims to produce that which will be Timeless. Timelessness rejects "Taste" and "Talent"—ambiguous categories that serve to confuse. Musical truth faces its enemy, Opinion, which says there can be no certainty. Against opinion, music demonstrates these certainties: 1) Music is, above all, an activity. It exists because we make it. 2) Music making is a collective process that produces collectivities. "We" above "I". 3) Music exceeds knowledge. We use what we know to make it, but the result amazes us. 4) Music uses measures, frequencies, ratios to produce the immeasurable, the unquantifiable, the unlimited: the True.

4. Principle maintains itself through struggle with the illusion, the lie, the possessive and the exception. Illusion is that which appears to be real, commonsense, obvious or easy, but is distinguished by its frustration and defeat of genuine effort. The Lie is the deliberately false statement intended to capture the energy of the creative act and replace it with the lifeless object. The possessive is the doomed attempt to identify one's life with ownership. Life cannot be owned, lived experience least of all. The exception is the harbinger of illusion, as well as the basis for transformation. Principle struggles with exception, knowing that the truly exceptional is necessary and desirable. In the present historical context, the "exception" has been made the rule. Everyone and everything is exceptional, great, fantastic, ad infinitum. Such hyperbole has been propagated precisely to destroy principle and its ruthless denunciation of mediocrity.

This is, above all, a practical question. It is part of an ongoing dialogue between participants in the music making process and all other musicians who have ever lived or ever will live. It is uncompromising and cannot be adjudicated by rule or decree, but must be created through active, continuous construction and destruction.

## SUMMARY

Music can be judged by its social effect and in comparison to its own history, to itself. Musicians, audiences and critics need to educate each other in an ongoing and contentious debate aimed at sharpening these criteria and using them to combat Anti-music. Opinion and aesthetics are of limited value—they are not useless, but cannot substitute for analysis, training and practice. Expertise must be measured in the same manner. It matters little to music and its appreciation how famous an artist is. In fact, it is the duty of music makers to make the best possible music they can, while actively engaging with audiences in debate about the criteria they are using to do this. Simultaneously, audiences must challenge the authority of the "experts" by demanding from them the authentic representation of their own feelings. Musicians must challenge audiences to support genuine exploration and discovery (which includes failing at times). Musicians need to carefully distinguish between pandering to "popular taste" in order to get rich and famous, as opposed to expressing their real thoughts and feelings to an audience. Critics have a role to play in furthering this ongoing debate by sharpening fundamental questions about social effect, as well as encouraging their readers to better understand the questions of mastery.

After "The Century of the Common Man" we have returned to the basic questions raised by Tolstoy. His simple criteria remain useful today. While he paid too little attention to important differences that could prevent the people of one culture from understanding the music/art of another, he was basically correct in stating that there are recognizable attributes to true music (and art) that will connect it pan-culturally. The century was, in fact, the century of war and revolution. What Tolstoy could not have known is that the popular would rise to predominate art production without the populace effectively controlling the State—or doing away with it. There would remain a gap between the democratic ideal and the oligarchic reality. In this context, the popular was twisted so that it appeared to originate from the people but, in fact, originated in much the same way the bourgeois arts of the previous three centuries did—on commission by the privileged. Furthermore, in the ongoing struggle for political Power the role of the judge has been thoroughly confused. Music and public alike have suffered from overt political control of art by culture commissars on the one hand, and by the more devious manipulations of the free market and its pundits, on the other.

What this demands, then, is a reassertion of the authority of music makers and their allegiance to mastery of their craft in service of both pleasure and the greater good.

1    James, CLR. *The Black Jacobins*. Vintage Books, 1989.

This book is essential reading for anyone interested in the history of Haiti, in particular, and the African diaspora, in general.

2    Walter Lippman coined the phrase "manufacture consent." Stuart Ewen, a professor of Media Studies at Hunter College in New York and author of a number of books on the media and public relations, most notably *PR: A Social History of Spin*, talks about Lippman: "What Lippman lays out in *Public Opinion* and in a subsequent book called *The Phantom Public* are the basic rules of behavior of those people who are interested in influencing public opinion. While some of the technologies have changed, the basic strategies that Lippman lays out are there from the beginning, and what is clear is, Never talk to people about real ideas. Never try to inform people about what issues are at play. Go to the gut. Symbols are more powerful than ideas. If you give people ideas they're going to argue with each other. They're going to debate things. But if you hit them with symbols, particularly symbols that have been separated from ideas and which have a kind of universal poignancy, you can turn a heterogeneous mass of opinion into a homogenous perception, a homogenous will. What Lippman says in the 1920s is that the key to persuasion is to intensify feeling and to degrade signification. This is his terminology. Politicians and steering committees and corporate boards have been behaving along those terms ever since." Barsamian, David. "Public Relations: Corporate Spin and Propaganda. An Interview with Stuart Ewen." *Z Magazine*. May, 2000.

http://www.zmag.org/zmag/articlesbarsamian/ewenmay2000.htm

3    Tolstoy, Leo. *What Is Art?* Penguin Books, 1995.

4    Ibid. p. 93

5    Ibid. p. 167

6    Ibid. p. 129

7    Ibid. p. 128

8    "Interested parties explain the culture industry in technological terms. It is alleged that because millions participate in it, certain reproduction processes are necessary that inevitably require identical needs in innumerable places to be satisfied with identical goods. The technical contrast between the few production centers and the large number of widely dispersed consumption points is said to demand organization and planning by management. Furthermore, it is claimed that standards were based in the first place on consumers' needs, and for that reason were accepted with so little resistance. The result is the circle of manipulation and retroactive need in which the unity of the system grows ever stronger. No mention is made of the fact that the basis on which technology acquires power over society is the power of those whose economic hold over society is greatest. A technological rationale is the rationale of domination itself. It is the coercive nature of society alienated from itself. Automobiles, bombs, and movies keep the whole thing together until their leveling element shows its strength in the very wrong which it furthered. It has made the technology of the culture industry no more than the achievement of standardization and mass production, sacrificing whatever involved a distinction between the logic of the work and that of the social system." Adorno, Theodore and Max Horkheimer. "Dialectic of Enlightenment." *The Culture Industry: Enlightenment as Mass Deception.*. 1944.

http://www.marxists.org/reference/subject/philosophy/index.htm.

9    The terms Mixture, Thought, Pleasure, Limit and Unlimited are capitalized because they are used in Plato's writings to designate specifically defined categories of thinking.

What this calls attention to is the antagonism between Plato's position and those of his opponents. Among these were the Sophists who, though differing with each other, shared one thing in common: denial of the category of thinking called truth, thereby deeply wounding philosophy itself. This closely resembles positions that currently prevail in academia, politics and, of course, art/music criticism.

10  Mike [sic]. "Muzak." http://media.hyperreal.org/zines/est/articles/muzak.html. Additional materials came from: Muzak, 915 Yale Avenue North, Seattle, WA 98109, USA.

"Muzak was the invention of General George Owen Squier, who had invented both a high-speed telegraph and telephone-line multiplexing during his rise to the command of the United States Army Signal Corps. He took his inspiration from *Looking Backward*, Edward Bellamy's utopian novel that featured a 'musical telephone' which would bring music programming—rousing in the morning, soothing in the evening—to every house in a then futuristically posited dawning of the twenty-first century. Squier entered an agreement with the North American Company, an Ohio utilities conglomerate, to produce a service called Wired Radio that would offer subscribers a choice of three program channels over telephone lines to homes or retail shops. Shortly before his death in 1934, Squier's efforts to come up with a catchier name for his company, resulted in the term Muzak, a blend of the word 'music' with the final syllable from George Eastman's universally pronounceable synthetic trade name, Kodak."

—Humez, Nick. "Muzak." *St. James Encyclopedia of Popular Culture*. 2002.
http://findarticles.com/p/articles/mi_g1epc/is_tov/ai_2419100854

# DIRTY WORK

## THE HIDDEN WORLD OF MUSIC PRODUCTION

I n the film version of Tolkien's *Lord of the Rings*, we get the perfect example of the way in which production is imagined today. Particularly memorable are numerous scenes of Saruman's giant factory. Talk about "dark satanic mills"! Hideous creatures toil without respite, producing even more hideous creatures, the Orks. Giant machines and blazing furnaces grind and spit in a dirty, dangerous underground complex. This is where labor is done. Above is the world of heroic battle and romantic love, of vision quests and high adventure. Work is dark, sinister and hidden. Life is something and somewhere else.

Of course, in the "real world" work goes on. But as one commentator recently wrote: "The big theme is employee well-being; this is exactly the sort of cozy euphemism beloved of employers. Forget workers' rights, let's talk aromatherapy. Forget the power relationship between boss and employee, let's talk about flat organizations, fun, creativity and play in the knowledge economy. No other area of national life generates quite such a level of Orwellian gobbledegook as management." Which, nevertheless fails to address the underlying problem: "By a neat twist of fate, we are now losing more working days to stress than we did to industrial action in the late '70s. A generation of political battle, legislation and public policy to destroy the trade union movement and suppress industrial conflict, has been spectacularly subverted. This punctures the Thatcher mythology's triumphalism. Most of us don't join picket lines; instead we take duvet days, or go off sick when we are simply not willing or capable of coping with the pressures of the job."[1]

What does this have to do with music? Fundamentally, music making is labor. Work is required and skills are needed. All the magical, miraculous, awe-inspiring, spiritually-uplifting effects that music produces arise from this ground. It is on the basis of craft that the art is made possible. Or, put another way, the art demands that a craft be maintained to ensure its possibility. This presents a number of problems: to begin with, keeping work behind the scenes has always been, in a peculiar way, necessary in the arts, particularly the performing arts. It is important to maintain a distance between the performance seen/heard by the audience and the actual labor that goes into making it. This is fiction but not falsehood; it is a necessary component of the imaginary world art seeks to create. It is part of the framing of a piece that sets it apart from the surrounding environment and society, on which it comments, reflects, and, thereby, affects. An ambiance, an aura, is thus both real and unreal simultaneously. It exists or is created, and yet it functions as illusion. It is most effective and impressive precisely when the participants know what is happening, fully partake in it, and yet are "somewhere else" by way of the performance. It is not charlatanry, but rather a device by which, in the best cases, art can serve to enlighten and inspire.

This technique is being exploited in an attempt to persuade us that we are all happy consumers, that no production is going on, or at least it's only going on in some dark corner of the world we need not concern ourselves with. That which entertains and gives us pleasure cannot be work and does not require work to be produced (work that we enjoy is a hobby). This logic has specific features in the popular arts, particularly music, where developments over the last two decades have reached a point of crisis. A tension that has been present for two centuries, in Europe and America, at least, has begun to mutate into an unrecognizable "organism" in which the virus becomes the body it has invaded. An example of this is that the glamour and glitz of advertising has become the performance itself. Long associated with the promotion of events, concerts, album releases and so forth, Hype has taken on a life of its own and is now more important than the musical event it is promoting. Advertising is advertising advertisement. "Selling is what selling sells," to quote the late Joe Strummer. We have the bizarre situation in which music is a soundtrack to a video, which is an advertisement for the music!

The erasure of work from this equation is necessary for two key reasons: work is a social activity people do while being constantly urged to forget, and it is where society gets divided into Haves and Have Nots, Boss and Worker, Master and Slave. In a word: it spoils the party. What concerns us here, however, is the specific way this manifests itself among musicians. There is scant reference anywhere to long years of practice and rehearsal, stress-filled recording sessions, tedious and tortuous touring not to mention the anxieties of survival in an intensely competitive environment where "success" is ephemeral and "failure" is concrete. Because music remains an essential component of the advertisement, it is imperative that those required to make it—especially those who make it!—be focused on the glitz and glamour in order that their own, actual experience in the production process be effaced.

Suddenly, it becomes necessary to the appreciation and experience of music to close the gap between the labor-intensive production process and the audience. Suddenly, it is urgent that people be made aware of what is actually involved in making music in order to create (or re-create) the distance necessary for music to do its most useful and effective duty.

A small anecdote might shed some light on this. In 1968, when I was 17, I joined the Musician's Union Local #6 in San Francisco. I was required to at that time, because I wanted to perform publicly in night clubs and dance halls. When I had paid my initiation fee and had been sworn in, I was handed the Union's newspaper. On the back page was a long list of musicians and groups who were in arrears (non-payment of dues). On this list were the names of some of the soon to become legendary groups of the San Francisco Sound. The Grateful Dead, Quicksilver Messenger Service, Jefferson Airplane, Big Brother and the Holding Company, among others. A worldwide revolution was in progress, music was the oracle of truth. Who needs a corrupt and conservative Trade Union? We're artists! Never explicitly said, but obviously implied was: "We're not workers." I have lived to see the shortcomings of that position.

## PRACTICE

To begin with, musicians must practice and rehearse. This is work. Countless hours are spent over the course of many years, even a lifetime, devoted to acquiring technique, learning particular compositions, preparing for performance with other musicians and so on. Furthermore, most musicians practice in dingy, dank rehearsal rooms. These may be the garages of their parents' home, the basements of their apartments or some semi-isolated warehouse or abandoned factory. Sound is forever a problem because, to all but the musicians themselves, it is noise and a nuisance. In most cases, years are spent in such conditions. Only the very successful can afford well-equipped studios that ensure good sound and a semblance of comfort. But regardless of the conditions, all of this is labor intensive. It is undeniably a craft—10% inspiration and 90% perspiration. An enormous amount of free labor goes into the music making process. Vast quantities of time and effort are invested by, mainly, young musicians and technicians, without compensation. It is not unreasonable to suggest that the entire music industry would collapse without this foundation of unpaid labor.

Then, there is getting to the gig.

Most working musicians spend more time loading and unloading equipment than actually performing. Aside from the back injuries and other physical effects of this manual labor, there is the basic fact that in order to perform, this other completely non-musical aspect of work must be done. When a group or an artist has a road crew they have really "made it." That is real, measurable success! Add to this the endless hours of sound checking and waiting around in usually cramped or crumbling backstage areas, and you begin to get the picture of what this life is really like. Of course, it is not only the musicians who endure this. It is also the technicians. The sound and lighting people who are essential to any show. The maintenance of equipment and the organization of material goes on continuously before, during and after the performance. Often, the technical people work in close proximity with the musicians, and their lot is more or less the same. The big difference is that the technicians are always in demand and the musician's fortunes rise and fall with the popularity of their music.

## TOURING

If a group or individual achieves a certain level of popularity, there is touring. From single vehicles to cargo vans to Silver Eagles and planes, musicians travel all over the world to get to their audiences. Some do it constantly, literally living on the road. Others only do it occasionally and for relatively short distances. But the process is largely the same in any case. Many hours of driving for an hour or two on stage. Staying in hotels (usually the cheapest flea-bag available), eating lousy food and sleeping in short, broken chunks of time. After a few weeks on the road, sleep-deprevation is a serious question for any band. And the compensation? Most musicians make enough to survive on the road with maybe enough left over to pay their rent back home (if they have some place they call home) Of course, this is relative to the size of the audience that supports the artist and differs from style to style. In classical and jazz, for example, conditions are generally a bit better than for all other forms of music (they are also among the only ones still unionized). If a group is playing a particular form of ethnic music that is getting the "star treatment" in the country they're visiting, things tend to be better. For example, if African musicians tour Europe or the States, they're likely to get decent accommodations and meals (if their dietary requirements can be met). But in every genre, the level of comfort is directly related to the level of ticket sales (nowadays you can add merchandising and direct concert sales of CDs). If you live in any big city in any part of a wealthy country, open a newspaper and see how many musical performances are happening on every night of every week of every year. You should get some idea how many musicians are on tour at any given time. And this is constant. Consider that the vast majority of them, and this includes some that are quite well known, are traveling in RVs and small passenger vans pulling trailers of equipment and staying at the cheapest hotel their agents can find.

When one goes into the recording studio the scene changes, but it is not much different. Most recording studios are fairly clean, well-lit places, although many are not! The owner's investment has to be, first of all, on the recording room(s) and equipment. As one would expect, the fancier, better-off studios have lounges and facilities for cooking, showering and sometimes sleeping, that provide a modicum of comfort for the people working in them—although, again, many do not. But from the poorest hovel to the best-equipped, most luxurious studio there is, one device more important than all others without which nothing could be accomplished: the coffee machine. Why? Because anyone with any experience recording knows that without caffeine, the long hours and intense pressures involved could not be attempted, much less maintained. Sex, drugs and rock and roll? Sex will be porn flicks on the lounge TV, drugs will be coffee and lots of it, rock and roll will usually come at the end of the process of recording when the band is listening to rough mixes while packing their gear. And there will be hours and hours and hours of waiting.

Before returning to the particular stresses and strains of the recording studio, it is worth pausing on this issue of waiting. On the Rolling Stones' 30th Anniversary someone hailed Charlie Watts with the greeting: "30 years of rock and roll!" Charlie's reply? "More like 5 years of rock and roll and 25 years of waiting." This is a relatively accurate equation; the amount of time musicians spend waiting is enormous. Anyone who fails to recognize this basic reality cannot know what music making is all about. It certainly has to be calculated into any measurement of the labor time necessary to make music.

The endless hours of waiting in the recording studio are a new phenomenon born of the multi-track tape recorder. There was a time not so long ago when recording was relatively fast for the musicians. Most of the work was done by a few technicians. The artists would come in together, set up and play. This might be tedious and slow, and there would still be plenty of waiting, but the basic purpose was to record an actual performance of music under studio conditions (as opposed to a live concert). This is still done today. But more often, the musical components are recorded one by one, in isolation from each other and layered in such a way that they will result in a complete performance. This means that, for example, once the drummer has finished his/her tracks, the rest of the band will each perform their parts, alone or in pairs, up to the lead vocalist or soloist. This often means that while each individual is performing the rest of the musicians are sitting around, on-call in case they are needed but essentially just waiting.

# IF YOU CAN'T DAZZLE 'EM WITH
# BRILLIANCE, BAFFLE 'EM WITH BULLSHIT

Now, none of this is a criticism or complaint. It is just the way it is. But that's the point: there is nothing glamorous about the life of a musician or technician. The demands of the craft alone make it essential that an enormous amount of time and energy are spent outside the spotlight. Stephen Gould's Punctuated Equilibrium theory comes to mind as an appropriate metaphor. His description of how evolution actually proceeds over eons of apparently changeless time to be abruptly interrupted by large bursts of new life forms is roughly equivalent to the way musicians function: long stretches of seemingly inconsequential effort, punctuated by the dazzling moment of performance, whether it's live or in the studio. What seems to matter most is that hour on stage. In fact, that hour could not exist without the thousands of others that accumulate before and after, preparing the music and musician for it. Why does this matter more now than it ever did? It has always required labor and skill and tedium and sacrifice to produce music.

What has changed in recent years is more apparent when we look at where music is performed and the relationship between performer and audience. It is obvious that music is likely to be best when performed in a situation conducive to its reception, be that a coffee house or Carnegie Hall. If the environment is not suitable, then the music, the musician and the audience suffer. We might call this a real distance or separation between performer and audience; between inside and outside the performance vis-à-vis the world at large. This is the stage or performing space we enter or approach to experience the performance. Even when a musician is performing on the street, for free, gathering an audience and playing to whomever might amble by, there is an imaginary theater created that encompasses the performer and audience (at least if the musician is good!).

Now, however, the very dynamic by which performance is set up to ensure its most effective delivery is being twisted into a theme park parody of real life, or, put another way, a real life tragedy in a theme park— something like a murder in Disneyland. Instead of a distance between performer and audience within a theater or performance space, a distance is manufactured between the musician as a person and other people as people. This is not merely the ages old elevation of the gifted or the star. This is the vast expansion of a distance of another type entirely; that between superior and inferior beings. Super heroes and the cretinous humanoids they condescendingly save. And this operates in real life! The performance space disappears, or rather begins to appear in all media, all the time.

Completely non-musical elements dominate the music that is ostensibly the end product in the chain of hype and hoopla. More money and other resources are spent promoting music than making it. "Music" videos are an obvious example. Headlines about drugs, weapons charges, sex lives and death have become an important part of marketing, and certainly more important than the musical abilities of the artist (dead rock stars are a highly profitable enterprise, incidentally). The clothing and everyday appearance of the artist is more important than how they sound. I'm not talking about the stage costumes; everything is designed to separate the musician from the public. Their glory is a result of some divine gift visited on a person of humble origins, just like everybody else, but somehow completely different! It's like the winner of the lottery or the guy who scores big in Vegas. Miraculously lifted out of the mass of "regular" people and placed among a pantheon of gods.

The distance being created is fake. It produces a false basis for the appreciation of what is most important anyway, the music itself. In fact it militates against the real, necessary, distance which itself requires an understanding that the musician is a human being and, however specially gifted, a member of the same species as the audience. Fantasy is one thing music can create or might aspire to. But fantasy on the basis of lies is what? Paranoia? Psychosis? Hysteria? Go ask a shrink. The end result is neither good music nor healthy, productive relationships between musician and audience. There is reverence enough for those whose work we most admire. Turning them into icons is detrimental to the contribution they make. Indeed, what is most admirable, and a key component of the proximity/distance effect necessary to the production of the best music, is the underlying sense of human connection. It is not the "I can do that" that is most important, but that a human being can do that. It is also true that young people are inspired to take up music by the great performances of others and, in this sense, "I can do that" is vital. But when we participate in a sublime musical event it is precisely not because we can "do that" that makes it what it is. It is that the feeling that "WE are doing that", participating in an extraordinary act, that pervades and sweeps us away. Of course, one knows that one is the audience for whom a master is performing. But immanent in any great performance is the potential of being transported to another state of being, and this is done with the performer—not by the performer alone.

Such cannot be accomplished by the likes of Madonna or the Broadway musicals she borrowed from to disguise her musical vacuousness. All one can hope for is to stand in awe of bombast and technical virtuosity; the gymnastics (I hesitate to call it dance) and special effects. What is on display is mastery over people, not mastery by people. The audience cannot be included in this as participant, let alone community member. It's like the advertisement for THX Sound that begins every movie with the slogan: "The audience is listening." Who is speaking to whom, here? What kind of "audience" needs to be told what it is doing?! There is another message being sent which excludes the audience from anything except passive, cow-like, cud chewing. In other words, "We've got your money, now shut up and eat your popcorn!" We are being told to substitute this alienating procedure which must include viscerally stimulating light and sound effects for the real connection of real music which relies on emotional and intellectual stimulation to achieve its result. Almost all television, most movies and now, more and more, music are overwhelmed by the presence of this soul-sucking, jive-ass, goo. It is the real filth from which we must disconnect in order for the connection between artist and audience to be made.

## DIRTY WORK

This brings us back to the relevance of the "dirty work" which is production of any kind in present day society. Escape is the purpose of entertainment. Transformation is the purpose of production. The former seeks to evade the consequences of an oppressive, unjust social order by pacifying the populace and sanitizing their thought. The latter is necessitated by life itself. In order for anything to happen labor is necessary. But since most labor is ripped off by some corporation or government, it has to be removed from the public mind, its very existence hidden in the manner that defecating or leprosy is. Work is dirty. It is something "clean" people don't do. The dirt on the faces of our stars comes from battle or adventure, not work. This is one reason there was such an anti-aesthetic at the beginning of punk and hip-hop. The kids knew what they were hearing and seeing in life and art was bullshit. They rebelled against the goo and made dirty, noisy music and wore dirty, noisy clothes. Of course, this rapidly became a formulaic sound and a predictable fashion statement. Nevertheless, the need for transformative, life affirming experience, untainted by the manipulations of Power inevitably led (and continues to lead) to the trashing and destruction of symbolic representations of cleanliness and order. While this is not often a consciously political statement or one relating directly to work, per se, it is in fact related to both politics and work by virtue of the realities of social life for most people, musicians included.

Music is produced by the labor of the musician. This is not to say that talent and inspiration are anything less than crucial elements. In fact, these immeasureable, intangible qualities are essential but are, themselves made manifest by "dirty work". First, because they too need labor to fulfill their potential and second, because the labor of untold numbers of people with varying degrees of music making ability is required as the foundation of the language through which talent and inspiration speak.

It is important to note that the problem addressed here is not economic. It is a favorite ploy of the music industry to reduce everything to numbers when dealing with musicians: numbers of units or tickets sold, etc. This is an effective tactic in diverting musicians' attention away from the very process that is their own source of inspiration and productive use of their talents. It is a means of devaluing and rendering socially impotent the very strength musicians have as creators of music. This is crucial since the delusion of musicians is necessary for the perpetuation of the entire music industry. We need to see the actual connections between the "dirty work" of music making in order to better appreciate both the producer and his/her product. At least musicians do, if only to protect themselves, their livelihoods and their sanity.

But it goes beyond this obvious, direct connection to the shifting, changing relations amongst the audience, the musician, and society at large.

## WORK, SKILL, TALENT AND MASTERY

The world is not one undifferentiated mass of matter in motion. Difference exists. Indeed, existence means difference. This is not often measurable except in sports or mathematics—how fast someone runs or how high one jumps is an obvious measure of difference. These exceptions notwithstanding, it is something immeasureable that we use the word "talent" to describe. We also use the word "inspiration" to describe an idea that seems to miraculously spring to mind; the kernel from which develops all the work that follows. The qualities some humans display more than others are both central to the creation of music and devilishly misleading at the same time. They are part of what makes music magical and vulnerable to fakery. Before exploring the important role of talent and inspiration, however, it is necessary to grasp the equally important, and integrally linked, relationship of work and skill.

No matter how it is gained, there is always a component of technical knowledge required to compose or perform music, let alone to do these tasks well. This does not require formal, institutional training. Sometimes, it does not even require training in the sense most often used when applied to acquired skill. There are examples of great musicianship developing very early and without apparent outside influence (Mozart is the classic example of the child prodigy). In fact, the two fields of human endeavor where children and people with crippling mental disorders can, on rare occasions, outperform adults are music and mathematics. For reasons that are a matter of speculation, the brains of certain people are capable of making the necessary computations and, in the case of music, combining these with the manual dexterity required to perform feats that astonish. But, for the most part, such examples only dramatize the technical facility required while raising the questions of talent and inspiration. After all, one may be astonished by a three year old performing complex music, but one cannot acquire these skills themselves by waiting to be reborn or otherwise transformed by a bolt from the blue. On the contrary, whatever methods are employed, a large amount of data must be internalized and then combined with the physical skills required to make devices make sound, even if the device in question is the human voice.

Initially, this takes the shape of imitation. As in the learning of a spoken language, music triggers responses in all people that make them more or less capable of singing, dancing and clapping their hands. This process becomes more refined when one attempts to replicate a song they have heard or a particular rhythm they like to move to. Beyond that, the specific skills required by specific instruments mean both an increased data load and higher levels of manual dexterity (in the case of drummers and organists, it includes pedal dexterity as well).

A problem arises, however, when the question of mastery, or great accomplishment, is removed from the realm of human effort and placed in the realm of God or fortune. What is divine in music, what is spiritually uplifting, is in the end a product of a combination of factors, which should become clearer as this inquiry proceeds. But when mastery is thought to be unattainable by human effort, then it cannot be taught or learned, and what actually exists in the world cannot be explained. This is precisely the hook on which the music industry hangs its justification of the star system. According to their logic "A Star Is Born," not made. They simply discover them and bring them to the public's attention. In practice, however, they do exactly the opposite, while fostering an illusion by which the rest of us are bamboozled. They manufacture stars, and have for a long time. Of course, among these stars are talented musicians, but it is not musical talent that is the key ingredient of stardom. This is more fully discussed in other chapters. What concerns us here is the falsehood being propagated that fools many into believing that mastery either does not exist or is solely a gift of God or good fortune.

In fact, mastery is attainable through human effort. If it were not, then there would be no passage of music from generation to generation, no passing on of particular songs or techniques, no productive sharing of ideas or experiences, no means by which a particular ethnic culture would develop distinct from any other in fact, very little music at all. Indeed, the world is full of music schools based on the presumption that this is self evident. Yet all education, music education in particular, must struggle against the twin incubi of "talent" and "luck". The gifted are used against the gift. Pursuit of goods replaces pursuit of the Good. Shared, experienced wonder becomes the possession of the few graced by divine light. What is moving and uplifting is subverted by the crass acquisition of privilege and property. This opposition is maintained at considerable cost by the music industry, in particular, and the techniques of Public Relations in general. In the words of Edward Bernays (father of PR): "If we understand the mechanism and motives of the group mind, it is now possible to control and regiment the masses according to our will without their knowing it."[2] This has worked marvelously well over the last century, doing great harm to education.

Some might argue (as friends of mine who teach music often do) that there is no way to teach certain crucial elements of what it takes to make good music. Some children simply don't demonstrate the capacity and others do. And, those that do seem to acquire or absorb musical skills with little assistance. This brings us back to difference. Obviously there are differences between people's capabilities, whether this is a product of genetic or cultural makeup. Natural or "nurtural," so to speak. In any case, the large quantity of fine music played by fine musicians the world over suggests that there is no lack of talent or inspiration in the world. In fact, talent and inspiration are not rare, they are fairly common. The difficulties of providing the most effective nourishment for these human qualities are increased, however, by the mystification surrounding them. In any community or sufficiently large group of people, talent and inspiration inevitably emerge, unless they are suppressed by an authority that does not want them expressed. The fact that their exact manifestation is unpredictable does not prevent us from predicting that they will arise given the basic condition of sufficient numbers of people. Looked at another way, unless there are widespread and systematically employed educational tools, then the talent and inspiration that emerges operates in a vacuum, without means of sustenance and encouragement. It is a squandered resource.

In fact, what prevails in music and among technicians is a *de facto* apprenticeship system not unlike that of the medieval guilds, whereby young aspirants are accepted by masters on the basis of their devotion and demonstrated potential. This only underscores the practical need for mastery. To this day, almost everyone engaged in music making (composer, musician, instrument builder, sound technician) learns their craft and develops into a professional in this manner. Schools for classical music or jazz are actually the exception and, even there, the "best and brightest" always need to study individually with a mentor who can impart the lessons of experience and the criteria of judgment, without which quality evaporates as an achievable aim. Therefore, mastery is only attainable through human effort.

## MASTERS AND MASTERS

A master is a person that has consummate knowledge of a particular activity that goes beyond technical virtuosity to express a deeper, timeless wisdom that connects that person to any great musician, anywhere at any time. In this sense, music is ahistoric. It is not only of the now on this day in history; it is of the great Now of eternity (or at least the very long time people have been and, hopefully, will be making music). The master is one who grasps that and can convey it to others, be they many (an audience) or one (a student). It is a dialogue going on between great musicians who have lived, now live and will yet live. This is mastery.

However, mastery has been taken out of the hands of masters of this kind and placed in the hands of masters of another kind. The slave master. The gang boss. The corporate executive. The confusion sown by this distorts our understanding of work and life, effort and skill. This is a world where the power of thought, experience, dedication and hard work are nothing compared to the Power of money, political influence, military might and narcissism; where Power as coercive force is dominant over power as the liberation of potential. In such a world we are compelled to fight for the kind of mastery and power that serves those who do the work in opposition to the mastery and Power of those who enslave and oppress. This may seem far removed from the question of music and musician, yet it is at the heart of the problem. This problem cannot be solved other than by going to the roots of these words, their contradictory signification and, ultimately, to the practices that are essential to life and the production of music.

Part of the solution resides in using mastery as the goal towards which the hard work and sacrifice musicians make is directed, as opposed to riches and fame. After all the tedious rehearsing, hauling equipment, waiting and anxiety, what do musicians have to show for it? How is one to measure one's achievement? I suggest that the measurement be made not by how much money or how much media attention one acquires, but rather according to the timeless qualities of mastery itself. This may begin with the excitement, the awe and wonder that one feels upon hearing great musicians play great music. But soon enough it must develop into a profound respect for both process and product. To participate in this is an honor and responsibility. It means seeking connection with all those who came before and will come after by devoting one's heart and soul to making a small contribution. Whether or not one actually becomes great in comparison to the standards set by the very best is not as significant as the dogged pursuit of the qualities that live within high quality. In other words, the prize is not acclaim or notoriety. The prize is knowing that all of the creative power one has to offer has been unleashed. This is the source of the genuine satisfaction one attains each time a step is taken in the right direction. It is going to be shared by one's peers and close associates. It will be confirmed through collective experience and discussion. In fact, collective experience and discussion are essential to achieving the result. No matter how many solitary hours one spends practicing, composing or listening to music, the end result is always social and collective.

This is another part of the solution. It lies precisely in collectivity. Against the narcissism of the star system must be put the singular fact that virtually all music is made by groups of people and not alone. Even great soloists or singer-songwriters know how closely their work is bound to that of others like them and, of course, to the audience. The chemistry of a band, the groove of a rhythm section, the total unity of an orchestra, the dialogue between soloists, the harmonizations of vocalists, the interlocking lines of a fugue, the list is endless and the goal is the same. Even if you attain it only once out of every thousand times you perform, you know the feeling and will settle for nothing less.

The recognition of our mutual interdependence should lead to the demand for mutual commitment and common standards among musicians. It may be pleasing to have a group feeling or collective spirit, but it is essential that all contribute what is necessary for the music to be its best. Equality in the legal or political sense is irrelevant and counterproductive in this case. Everyone's contribution, however small, must be necessary, or it does not belong in the performance at all. This is an important distinction, because what may be an admirable goal in social organization is often confusing in the musical situation.

## DEMOCRACY AND MASTERY

In discussions and preparations, egalitarianism and mutual respect are desirable and usually the most practical route to getting the work done. But in the musical situation, in the actual practice of composition, performance, recording or mixing, it is another matter entirely. Under these conditions, what must lead is the composition, however that is defined (by written score, by a sonic concept, by an intuitively defined "sound", etc.). This precludes voting and compromise. It requires the dedication of each participant to whatever will make the whole sound best. If this means one instrument is in the foreground and others are barely heard, then so be it. If one musician only beats the tambourine three times in the whole piece while another is constantly playing, so be it. The only criteria should be musical and, to repeat, all parts however large or small must be necessary or should not be played in the first place. It must be recognized that most music requires many hours of rehearsal, and pieces will have to be performed dozens, even hundreds, of times before they sound their best. Even in the case of totally improvised music this is true, insofar as the preparation of the individual musicians, which often means years of practice and performance on their instruments, is required as the basis for the success of what appears as a spontaneous, once in a lifetime moment.

The damage caused by the confusion of democratic and aesthetic criteria is considerable. If this contradiction is not resolved carefully and well, then either the music or the musicians suffer, usually both. "Carefully" means respecting the sensitivities of individuals while firmly establishing the goals and methods of the project. "Well" means thoroughly rooting out all possible sources of misunderstanding through hard struggle and uncompromising adherence to principle. If musicians are not properly equipped with all the tools of their trade, including those of creative vision and devotion to music, they are not likely to produce the best possible result, at least not consistently.

It is commonly thought that the burning nova of brilliance flashes and is gone. This oft celebrated aspect of the creative spirit or individual does exist, but is greatly exaggerated, to the detriment of the more important quality of consistency. Consistency is one of the measures of mastery. Continuity, dependability, regenerativity and nourishment are among the properties of this facet of music making. One important standard by which all serious musicians gauge their performance is that their worst is still good. Every show will be different; even within one show there will be differences. But consistency of performance is the bedrock of extraordinary performance. All musicians and composers strive for those incredible, unpredictable moments when it all comes together; the moments that exceed all others, reaching the heights of passion and intensity. It is possible then to view consistency as the steady, determined effort to attain these heights that are beyond measure or prediction; and yet can only be attained through steady, determined effort.

I'm emphasizing mastery because it is vital to music making in its own right and it has particular importance now in the struggle to defend and reinvigorate music. Deployed against the trivializing, dehumanizing forces of the Culture Industry, it is among the most effective weapons musicians and music lovers can wield.

# FOOTNOTES

1    Bunting, Madeleine. "New year, same grind." *The Guardian.* January 6, 2003.
2    Bernays, Edward. "The Engineering of Consent." *The Annals of the American Academy of Political and Social Science.* March, 1947.

# Leo Fender, Gottfried Silbermann, Ambrose Fleming and Digidesign

## Technology and Music

No human pursuit achieves dignity until it can be called work, and when you can experience a physical loneliness for the tools of your trade, you see that the other things—the experiments, the irrelevant vocations, the vanities you used to hold—were false to you.

Beryl Markham, *West With the Night*

**R**ecently, Quincy Jones was asked what, in his long career as a producer, was the most significant technological innovation for music making. His answer: "The Fender bass."

Jones was born in 1933. 28 years previously, in 1905, Ambrose Fleming had developed the first diode, or valve, which shortly thereafter became the vacuum tube, the basis of electrical amplification. This enabled the harnessing of electricity in the making of music.

By way of comparison, nothing had had as wide an influence since the development by Gottfried Silbermann of an instrument first built by Bartolomeo Cristofori called the pianoforte (the soft-loud). And for similar reasons.

For centuries horns, pipes and drums were by far the loudest music making devices. Stringed instruments, whether plucked or bowed, were always softer and needed many players to "amplify" them. The human voice needed similar multiplication and the construction of great amplification chambers: amphitheaters, churches and concert halls. Furthermore the keyboard, which for centuries had demonstrated its usefulness in enabling one musician to perform many notes over a wide frequency range, was only employed by the harpsichord and the clavichord and was barely audible when performed with other instruments. The only loud member of the keyboard family was the church organ; each one, of necessity, being unique and non-transportable. The pianoforte solved these problems of strings and keyboards; it combined these advantages in an instrument that could be manufactured in large quantities, disseminated far and wide and played anywhere in more or less the same manner by anyone. In fact the keyboard itself, separate from the piano, remains the basic tool of much contemporary music making as a result of this virtually universal dissemination. Thus, the pianoforte elevated the keyboard and a stringed instrument to a volume level where it could be played in orchestras.

The combination of the vacuum tube and the electro-magnetic pickup attached to a guitar had this kind of impact in the 20th century.

There are specific reasons Quincy Jones said Fender bass, as opposed to the electric guitar which I'll get into later but Leo Fender's design of an inexpensive, dependable instrument that could be as loud as drums and horns transformed music as it was conceived, performed and heard. To be accurate, Fender was not the first. There were others, such as Adolph Rickenbacker, whose contributions should not be overlooked, but for our purposes Fender is exemplary.

There were many other inventions and modifications of existing instruments over the same time period. The saxophone and the steel drum (or pan) are among the most important, but when we speak of certain events marking a change from one period to another, electrical amplification and the electric guitar (and bass) were pivotal shifts from all that had come before. Developments in amplification meant that by the last third of the twentieth century, the first generation of people was born who may have never heard music performed without it being amplified and transmitted through loudspeakers! Furthermore, a cheap, portable and relatively easy-to-play instrument exploded into the forefront of popular culture, pushing aside the horns and pianos that had dominated previously. Even the synthesizer, another late twentieth century electronic innovation, did not have so large an effect as the amplified electric guitar (although it comes close, particularly as it again expanded the use of the keyboard and the multitimbral capabilities of one musician).

Within a generation, bands got louder and smaller. Popular song writing shifted from being largely piano based to more and more guitar based—a guitar solo was possible for the first time! The coincidence of these innovations with great migrations and social upheavals throughout large parts of the world channeled the creativity in a generally populist and urban direction, first and foremost in the US, but very rapidly in Europe, Africa, Latin America and Asia as well.

The ubiquity not only of the technology but the uses to which it is put has been the basis of great controversy inside and outside of the profession of music. Certainly the way music sounded changed. While previously existing instruments did not disappear, they were no longer alone at center stage. Whole genres emerged, based on the uses of the old instruments in combination with the new. The particular importance Quincy Jones ascribed to the Fender bass is part of this development. In the classical or jazz orchestra, using their conventional instruments, bass frequencies and the bass instrument itself were difficult to hear clearly, if at all. When it came to recording it was even worse. The limitations of the recording machines made capturing the sounds of the bass a real challenge. With the Fender bass, an instrument was made that could cut through the band without overpowering it and be clearly recorded. Suddenly, the low frequencies so important to African-American music of which Jones is a major practitioner, were possible to hear and feel (physically feel, as anyone who has stood next to a contrabass player knows, your body is vibrated by these low frequencies).

Of course, the onslaught of the "popular" took the shape of the transmission of "folk" forms such as blues, jazz and country music (in the US) into the cities to which their practitioners were moving in ever larger numbers. The needs of these musicians were being met at the same time the audiences for their music were growing. It was not the first time in history there had been an open conflict between high and low art, but it may be the first time that a new group of instruments and technologies were so perfectly suited to the purposes of the lower classes. They were cheap, they were portable and they were loud!

Older instruments and genres are rarely replaced completely; rather they are displaced and added to. Thus there was a vast proliferation of divergent types or categories. While the electric guitar may be said to symbolize the 20th century, it does so along with the expanded use of the string quartet, the a capella group, the music of the European middle ages, not to mention the growing interest in and practice of music of diverse ethnic or regional traditions. This is important to keep in mind in the arguments to follow.

There are these significant innovations. There are these new possibilities. There are challenges to established customs or traditions of musical performance, entire hierarchies dislodged in the process. But they have not meant the elimination of what has come before. If anything, the opposite is true; at the same time rock and roll seized the world's attention and became the sound of youth rebellion, virtually all other forms and styles of music hitherto performed have enjoyed their own renaissances. The importance of all musical performance has increased.

So has the volume.

## WHY AMPLIFY?

Amplification is necessitated by and, in turn necessitates, a public. As opposed to the private, personal or intimate (imagine a mother singing her baby to sleep), amplification is required to get beyond a close, exclusive connection to one of a different type. While, arguably, there is no difference to music whether it is performed for one person or for one million, there is a great difference when one considers the sound itself. No one but the musician playing and a very small audience can actually hear what an acoustic guitar sounds like. Certainly, none of the nuances and complexities of arrangement and performance can be heard. Once this instrument is amplified, however, it can be heard by many thousands. It is no wonder that prior to electricity, amplification meant drums, cymbals, gongs and horns and lots of people playing them. This characterized public gatherings, whether they were for ritual, festivity, or warfare.

This is not a neutral, unambiguous good, however. To amplify is to extend influence. The construction of a public is to harness its potential in the service of certain aims. The power of an amp, the volume it can produce, has its direct coefficient in another kind of Power: political Power—the Power to dominate and control.

It is never merely an abstract question of the greater the capacity, the better the amplifier. Amplification requires permission from state authorities. It has the same status as weapons like firearms or explosives. It must be regulated. It must be limited and channeled; its use monopolized by the state. Clearly this is because it is a key component of any outburst of popular feeling. This is best exemplified by rock and roll—its volume was, and continues to be, a crucial component of its musical effect. Moreover, it is this potential within the populace that constantly threatens to delegitimize, to overthrow the state authorities.

In *Noise: The Political Economy of Music*, French economist, Jacques Attali explores this question. He enjoins us to listen to the world, as opposed to looking at it. Instead of only viewing the pyramids or the Parthenon, we should consider what sounds were being made there. "Our science has always desired to monitor, measure, abstract, and castrate meaning, forgetting that life is full of noise and that death alone is silent: work noise, noise of man, and noise of beast. Noise bought, sold, or prohibited. Nothing essential happens in the absence of noise."[1] Nothing better exemplifies this than the attention paid by the Greeks to the science of acoustics. Not only how to construct buildings so that people could better see, but in order that they could better hear. Their grasp of mathematics and architecture enabled the construction of the Amphitheater, which remains the best structure for the amplification of sound to large groups of people. In fact, their methods are superior to many commonly employed today. And their purpose was explicit: to mobilize society for work, war and worship.

Listening, then, reveals conflict. Examples abound of this antagonism in amplification, this deployment of decibels.

The Nazis exploited amplification as they banned jazz. As Hitler put it in 1938, "Without the loudspeaker, we would never have conquered Germany." The US army blasted jazz over loudspeakers as they bulldozed the date palms of "uncooperative" Iraqis during the current occupation. And what happened when Bob Dylan strapped on an electric guitar at the Newport Folk Festival in 1965?

Amplification is a battleground on which armies are mobilized and banners unfurled. Music, more than ever, disturbing the peace. "Turn it down!" say the neighbors. "Pump up the volume!" say the kids. It's connected now with loudness in its own right, a quantity of decibels becoming a distinct quality of sound. From the inaudible to the unbearable, whispers to roars.

## TALKING LOUD AND SAYING NOTHING!

Amplification appears to amplify itself. It claims superiority in quantitative, "objective" terms. More watts = more volume = better. We are asked to uncritically accept that this is an improvement. Even more, it is what improvement is! The sales pitch is always loudly announcing: "the biggest, most powerful," offering "unlimited possibilities!" Yet the superiority of greater volume or any technological innovation is limited, not only relatively, as in soft to loud, but absolutely in terms of the purpose it is designed to serve. Thus, for example, all musical instruments were forbidden in certain religious sects (the Shakers are an example). Music was only permissible if it was made by singing and clapping. Technology was viewed as an obstacle to the celebration of the infinite or sacred.

Contrary to the claims of advertising that machines are marvels that magically enable us to perform miracles, it is, indeed, the opposite that they actually do. Technology defines the limit. It quite precisely excludes the infinite or the sacred. Specific tasks must be performed and in a certain amount of time. As every technician knows, machines consume our time in order to be put to use. First, we need to learn how to make them work. We must abide by their discipline, including the time they take to function, if we want them to perform. And, of course, they all break down.

To overcome such objections and ensure its dominance, Technology has been sacralized.

The 20th century ended, as it had begun, with a fanfare for technology. The promise made in 1880 and repeated with even greater gusto in 1980 was the deliverance of humanity from drudgery and want via new machines. Once it was the train and the telegraph. Now it is the computer and the internet. The digital domain, virtual reality, cyber space, world wide web, the internet all announcing a wondrous, ever-expanding universe of possibility. The perpetual motion machine had arrived. There was even a musical genre that celebrated this new era: Techno.[2]

In his *Manifesto For Philosophy*, philosopher Alain Badiou states: "The meditations, calculations and diatribes about technology, widespread though they are, are nonetheless uniformly ridiculous." Furthermore, it is completely inappropriate to present science as belonging to the same register in terms of thought as technology. There is certainly a relation of necessity between science and technology but it does not imply any community of interests...If, for example, we consider a very great theorem from modern mathematics, the one that demonstrates the independence of the Continuum Hypothesis (Paul Cohen, 1963), we find within it a concentration of thought, an inventive beauty, a surprise of the concept, a risky rupture, in a nutshell, an intellectual aesthetic that we can, if we so choose, compare to the greatest poems of our century, to the politico-military audacity of a revolutionary stratagem, or to the most intense emotions of an amorous encounter, but certainly not to an electric coffee grinder or a color television, as useful and ingenious as these objects may be.[3]

Doubtless, there are still those who actually believe as they did a decade ago in the gospel of the gigabyte, the deification of the digit. But more are likely to have arrived at the mundane conclusion that these tools can be useful, but they present as many problems as they solve. While there are advantages, there are also drawbacks. When considering how many times the adjective "revolutionary" was applied to these new gadgets, one has to confront the fact that too little has changed.

Amplification, in fact, provides a stunning example. In spite of all the great improvements that have been made in amplifiers and speakers, one never knows how any concert will sound! It is one of the scandals of our time that from the smallest club to the largest stadium, musicians and audiences are more often than not subjected to really horrible sound. In the majority of public performances, amplification is quite loud but the acoustics of the room and the mix of the instruments subverts the music played and listened to. I must stress that this is not my opinion. This is a fact that every musician or sound technician knows only too well.

As Badiou says: "Gentlemen, Technicians, one more effort if you are truly working towards the planetary reign of technology! Not enough technology, technology that is still very rudimentary—that is the real situation: the reign of Capital bridles and simplifies technology whose 'virtualities' are infinite."[4]

Or, in the words of James Brown, they're just, "Talking loud and saying nothing!"

## SCIENCE VS. TECHNOLOGY

The distinction Badiou makes between science and technology is crucial for music. It is an important means of freeing music making from the mysticism of marketing. Music theory and the craft of instrument building depend on the mathematical presentation of sound as a naturally occurring phenomenon. From the lyre to the diddley-bow, the vibrating string has been the model for a study that is several thousand years old. It is necessary to recall this now since it demonstrates the use of the most powerful tool we have: thought.[5]

Unbeknownst to many, all music makers owe a profound debt to Pythagoras. 2500 years ago his studies of mathematics, medicine and music led to the discovery of truths that guide us today. In an exhaustive review of Greek philosophy, John Burnet wrote, "The purgative function of music was fully recognized in the psychotherapy of these days. It originated in the practice of the Korybantic priests, who treated nervous and hysterical patients by wild pipe music, thus exciting them to the pitch of exhaustion, which was followed in turn by a healthy sleep from which the patient awoke cured....the originality of Pythagoras consisted in this, that he regarded scientific, and especially mathematical, study as the best purge for the soul. We cannot tell whether music or medicine came first, or, in other words, whether the purge of the body was explained by the purge of the soul, or vice versa."[6]

Whatever the sequence, Pythogoras discovered the relationship between number and musical pitch (all musicians know of octaves, thirds, fifths and so on). Furthermore, he made a connection between the tuning of the string and attunement of the human being. The ratios were expressions of an underlying order or harmony. We still use the word "tonic" to describe both the root note of a musical scale and a healing substance. Similarly, we speak of "temperament" in tuning instruments and human personality.

This, in turn, exemplified a crucial contribution Pythagoras made to philosophy: the doctrine of the Limit. While it was commonly known that the universe was Unlimited, or infinite in time and space, it was unclear how differentiation between forces or the objects moved by them could arise. Pythagoras introduced the concept of the Limit in order to explain difference, or how form arises out of undifferentiated matter. He used music and medicine to illustrate the function of the Limit. These were not merely pictures, however. They were mathematically expressed in equations that aimed at establishing precisely what forms were. This, in turn, led to defining what attunement was, whether that was in the perfectly divided string or in the healthy organism. While it appears that Pythagoras associated the Unlimited with evil or chaos and the Limit with good or order, Plato later stated that the critical relationship between these two concepts was their Mixture. Burnet explains, "It is just for that reason that the 'mixed life', which includes both Thought and Pleasure, is found to be superior, not only to the life of Pleasure alone, but also to the life of Thought alone."[7]

The Limit, however, was not a religious concept requiring faith and the placation of gods. On the contrary, its application meant the pursuit of concord or harmony in mathematical, medicinal and musical terms. Suitable solutions to theoretical and practical problems were only those that could be demonstrated, tested, and proved universal. A musical example of this is the "Pythagorean comma". This is the name given to necessary adjustments made in the tuning of keyboard and other stringed instruments to make all their pitches in any sequence and combination sound concordant. The twelve tones (black and white keys) within the octave should produce 12 pure 5ths, or subdivisions of the tonic note of a scale. But it is a phenomenon of nature that only 11 do. The twelfth is called the "wolf 5th" because, without adjustment, it is so out of tune it howls like a wolf. "The wolf 5th is necessary to compensate for the fact that a complete chain of 12 pure 5ths would exceed the equivalent of seven octaves by a small amount known as the Pythagorean comma. Hence the wolf 5th is smaller than pure by a Pythagorean comma to ensure that a complete cycle will produce a perfect unison."[8] The Unlimited enters. The 5ths that eventually never resolve perfectly and circle infinitely without repeating. Thus, adjustments—impurities—had to be made in the numerical calculation in order to make intonation sound right, concordant.

To this day, builders of guitars, pianos and other musical instruments use these ratios, albeit modified by centuries of experiment, so that musicians can play. The Limit defined as precisely as possible so that the artist may explore the Unlimited.

Of course, discordance or concordance is an attitude or choice of the creative imagination. Whether it's a harpsichord or a slide guitar, the plucked string produces sound of variable pitch. What is beautiful or moving? This requires a decision. It requires a subject who will make this decision, and that is what a machine can never be. Information alone does not produce wisdom. Pythagoras is credited with coining the word Philosophy. When asked if he was a divine sage, Pythagoras is purported to have described himself as merely a "lover of wisdom." His study of mathematics, music and medicine produced truths we still use today, which shows that thinking is the most powerful tool of all.

We may be enamored with certain instruments. But being bigger, faster, louder, etc. only more vigorously excites the physical senses, perhaps leaving us exhilarated or exhausted for a moment. But that doesn't mean they satisfy.

## MUSIC IS DYNAMIC

What every musician learns sooner or later is that there is something else, obscured by the brute force of amplification, that is more significant than amplification itself. This is dynamics. Soft-loud. Piano-forte. The electric guitar can be made very loud. This, as has already been stated, was the crucial change in an instrument that was among the softest of all. But its ultimate musical use is not sheer, unchanging loudness. It is the expansion of the dynamic range that enabled the instrument to become so versatile and useful. Likewise with the Fender bass. It is not simply that low frequencies, once so difficult to hear, were now loud. It was that they could take a more prominent place in relation to other instruments.

Most important, music is never a continuous unvarying sound. It is always composed of dynamics. The fluctuation of air pressure, the sound wave, implies this. Music composes itself on the basis of these fluctuations precisely by transforming them, manipulating their intensity and multiplying their variations. Out of unlimited vibrations we invent or discover limits that move us. The emphasis on certain beats and the silences between them is what makes rhythm. Melody is not only a string of notes, but depends on rhythmic placement to be melody. It is not loudness that makes music, but dynamics.

The limit presents itself. Louder is not necessarily better; besides, when everything is at the same volume, it's boring.

## RECORDING AND THE AUTHENTIC

But there was something else going on simultaneously that had an even greater impact than amplification alone. This was the development of the technology of recording. Parallel and in conjunction with the amplification of musical instruments was the means to record and store musical performance. Similar to the relationship between film and theater or books and the oral transmission of words, music was undergoing a process by which a new and in some ways independent form of its expression was being made. By the late '60s recording began to take on a life of its own, and, like film before it, diverged from its parent in essential ways. Up to the period exemplified by the Beatles, virtually all recordings were simply replications of live performance. Musicians would assemble and perform music that would be captured by microphones and stored in various mediums (copper wire, shellac, tape, etc.). With the development of multi-track recorders it was possible to store many different performances made at completely different times and have them coincide in a single performance to be heard over and over again through a loudspeaker. Thus it was that the Beatles stopped performing live because, among other reasons, they could never replicate in concert the compositions they were creating in the recording studio.

In his seminal work, *The Work of Art in the Age of Mechanical Reproduction,* Walter Benjamin made the observation that a significant shift occurs when art is made for reproducibility.[9] From the Renaissance emerged the concept of the original. Individuals of genius produced such original work, and it acquired great value in the simultaneously emerging market for art. Until the photograph, the film and the sound recording, this one was the model. Authenticity was defined on this basis. The god-like genius of a Rembrandt was, over time, extrapolated into the performing arts as well, culminating in music publishing and concert promotion of the works of equivalent god-like geniuses. Authenticity was crucial to price.

As Benjamin pointed out, reproducibility changes all that. The singular, original work is not as important as the multiple. The god-like genius is not as important as the "star" whose original is simply a mold for millions of copies, and the sale of those millions of copies are the measure of the value of the "star." While there continues to be a market for the one, original work—a Van Gogh is worth millions of dollars—it is not the most important. Now it is the mass market that is dominant. The one lingers, but only as a haunting reminder of a time gone by. Now the replica, multiplied millions of times, is coveted above all. Indeed, an original has no value unless millions of copies of it can be sold.

Attali traces these developments. Beginning with sacrificing, or the ritual function of music, he argues that while music always served political Power, it was not a commodity, it had no value. With representation—meaning performance for a fee—music entered the world of commerce. The merchant and the capitalist replaced the aristocrat and the church as the "highest bidder" for the musician's wares. What followed was repetition, or mechanical reproduction, and all that has been discussed above.

Once art was bought and sold, its sacred function was replaced by its economic and political functions. As Marx put it:

> The bourgeoisie, wherever it has got the upper hand, has put an end to all feudal, patriarchal, idyllic relations. It has pitilessly torn asunder the motley feudal bonds that unite man to his "natural superiors" and has left remaining no other bonds between man and man than naked self-interest, than callous "cash payment." It has drowned the most heavenly ecstasies of religious fervor, of chivalrous enthusiasm, of philistine sentimentalism, in the icy water of egotistical calculation.[10]

This has led inexorably to violent antagonisms in the very qualities of experience and belief which arise from opposing purposes. The dollar cannot be holy. The market is not the church. The purchase of commodities can never be the worship of the infinite. No matter how cynical we may have become, we all confront these polarities in practice.

Furthermore, under this regime, sacrifice is differentiated from labor explicitly and conclusively. The latter must be directed at tangible results, whereas the former is directed at intangible ones. All sacrifice aims to please or revere an entity or ideal that does not occupy space and time. All labor is directed at sustaining those who live in space and time. This matters a great deal when one considers the artist or artisan. Once the purpose of art making was no longer principally religious or sacred, the value placed on skill began to diminish. Indeed, as soon as it became feasible to profitably sell art that required less skill to manufacture, the arts that required greater skill also required subsidization. Nowadays, "fine art" often means "without a market" whereas popular art means cheaply manufactured and profitably sold. Certain art forms would cease to exist without subsidy. Ballet and modern dance along with classical and "new" music are obvious examples.

Skill is not simply mechanical. It requires the application of judgment. The ability to judge is acquired by the study of all the experience, in some cases thousands of years worth, concentrated in the task at hand. We differentiate between the years one must dedicate to learning a skill and unskilled labor applied to a machine. We recognize the difference in the objects thus produced, and we admire the unrewarded effort needed to master a craft. We call it a sacrifice, and sacrifice is an appropriate word because, no matter how pleasurable learning might be, acquiring skill is not compensated for. This is certainly true of musicians—one might get paid for a performance but never enough to cover the years spent learning to play. If musicians were to calculate the hours, months, years and decades invested in competent performance and demand payment for them, the music business would collapse. The more time dedicated to the acquisition of skill, the greater this disparity.

One might argue that there are famous virtuosos who are paid splendidly for their performances. Pavarotti is a multi-millionaire. But, it is not the virtuosity for which so much is being paid. It is the fame. The time invested in developing the talent is not part of the equation. Also, for every rich and famous virtuoso there are many others who are relatively or completely unknown. Throughout history, some of the greatest musicians have been utterly ignored by all but a tiny, marginalized community that recognized their gifts. There are simply too many examples of wonderful talent dying broke and alone for us to be deluded by the recognition given a few.

As the saying goes, "Don't quit your day job!"

## SO, WHAT'S NEW?

In the century since mechanical reproduction was introduced, we can see clearly that the overall result is redundancy. Copying. Waste. Nothing is new or original. We live in the age of the redundant, which has only intensified the contradiction between art's ritual and its political or economic functions. As Marx and Engels put it, "All that is solid melts into air, all that is sacred is profaned and man is, at last, forced to face his real conditions of life, and his relations with his kind."

Authenticity today is that which cannot be purchased. You have be young and black to rap (or at least poor and pissed off as in the case of Eminem). You have to express feelings that arise from real experience, real frustration, real pain. And not by a choice you made but by what was thrust upon you; the cards dealt by an unfair world. That which can be bought is fake. It may be envied, but in music, it can never be authentic. People may lust after the trappings of triumph, but everyone knows this is not what makes a great song. Valueless objects or expressions need to be invested with "meaning," "originality," "authenticity," in order to attract a public who will value them. They must be hermetically sealed against the fraudulence of their actual purpose: to be purchased! Indeed, the real experience sought by most people is that which capital has blown away: a deeply emotional connection to the sacred.

What emerges from the rubble of the titanic struggles of the last one hundred years is that the sacred people actually seek is anything that is beyond the clutches of capital. Anything without a dollar value. Anything without a price. For isn't capital the ultimate finite? It is the accumulation of dead labor. All those stocks and bonds, all that gold, all that oil, is nothing but the measurement of what has been made by sweat and blood. The toil goes on but the "stuff" is stored to be bought and sold at a profit. The stockpiling of goods is pitted against the common good.

But there is never enough. This great mountain of objects is always running out, must always be replenished. No matter how much is produced, more is required. The insatiability of this appetite makes every process, every effort limited. The end is always in sight and all ends converge in the pursuit of more, more, more until death.

Infinity is something else, entirely.

"To see a World in a Grain of Sand
And a Heaven in a Wild Flower
Hold Infinity in the palm of your hand
And Eternity in an hour."—William Blake

After all the dust settles, music makers still have to struggle to make a living doing what we love to do. The development and proliferation of new technologies has only made this clearer. It has not resolved anything.

While he gathers together a great deal of historical data and has some startling insights, Attali makes two errors common to many music theorists. First, he is trapped in a progressive mode. Everything about his argument follows a linear, historical development. This is useful as far as the actual development of things go, but it overlooks the more important fact that music itself does not progress. Music cannot be said to be better or worse than it ever was. It has certainly changed. Technology has affected what we hear as music. But music as such is ahistoric. Novelty is important but only within and dependent upon the timelessness that gives music its power.

Secondly, Attali fails to recognize that there are two distinct types of labor involved in the technological developments by which society measures progress. One is drudgery—backbreaking and demoralizing. The other is pleasurable and inspiring—a joy that encompasses the work and the tools with which we do it. I love to work on music. I love to rehearse, write and perform. I love my guitar. I know many engineers and instrument builders who, similarly, love their craft and the tools they employ. This is not limited to wood and leather. Many genuinely enjoy working with computers and samplers, drum machines and other "hi-tech" devices. The point is that, even in a society in which labor is exploited and our time is stolen from us, we still enjoy labor, at least when it involves tasks that intrigue us and fire our imaginations. The technologies we use in this process are not enemies or sources of frustration. They are useful tools that enhance our experience.

This may seem to contradict what I said earlier about sacrifice. The contradiction, however, arises only in relation to the market, to the buying and selling of labor. It is only because it has no market value, it can command no price, that this labor is viewed as sacrifice, and only then by the market, not by the one who enjoys doing it. A "labor of love" is its own reward.

Thus, even though Attali (and others) acknowledge positive aspects of mechanical reproduction, they don't really believe it. They can only see the uses to which capital puts these inventions. They downplay the fact that the artisan coexists with the factory worker. This is perhaps more true about making music than making shoes or automobiles. But that's precisely the point. In tracing the development of technology and music, what emerges most clearly is that it is precisely to escape the factory and the drudgery of exploited labor that people make music and enjoy the technologies that enable them to do so!

To be fair, Attali concludes with a chapter on composition which envisions the making of music for the joy it brings. He presents it as a utopian vision of possibility to come. I would argue that it is not somewhere in the future at all. It is here and now. It is the fundamental basis of making music. The vast majority of musical performance already takes place outside of any market; kids jamming, hobby bands rehearsing, private parties and political benefits happen all the time, everywhere. We must not lose sight (sound?) of this phenomenon. It is, as Attali suggests, an important part of life, and any solution we may hope to find to the problems we face.

## RECORDING: PERFORMANCE AND COMPOSITION

By the last two decades of the twentieth century, the processes of recording had passed through numerous stages, including perfecting the recording machines, improving the storage mediums and increasing the fidelity of the loudspeakers that carried the sound to the listeners' ears ("Fidelity" here means exactly what it did for the engineers who first used the word: the most accurate replication of the sound source. What went into the microphone came out of the speakers sounding as much as possible like the sound that went in). The leap that was made by Digidesign, among others, was that of editing. From the time recording to magnetic tape was made possible, engineers had had the capability of cutting up (literally) pieces of music and recombining them in different ways. But with the digital editing enabled by Pro Tools and other computer based systems, absolutely accurate and infinitely flexible editing came into practical use. This meant errors in a musician's performance could be corrected. It also meant entire performances or parts of performances could be recombined in limitless ways, rendering the original unrecognizable as the source.[11] For the first time, it is legitimate to ask: what constitutes a performance? And who is performing the musician or the editor?

Frank Zappa once remarked that the Synclavier, a forerunner of Pro Tools with similar capabilities, was for him as a composer, a liberating thing. Why? Because he didn't have to deal with musicians any more! He could write his concertos and orchestral works and hear them played exactly as he wrote them not as they were performed by sometimes less-than-stellar humans. With his typical wit, he made biting remarks about the costs of rehearsing an orchestra and the stubborn refusal of certain musicians and organizations to take seriously the effort required to give a genuinely impassioned and technically proficient rendition of his compositions. So, from the perspective of composition the question arises again: what is performance and who is performing?

A simple answer might be: at a concert, the musician performs, on a recording the composer performs. Put another way, live, there is the performance of the composition which takes place immediately and only once. In the recording studio, there is the composition of the performance. This separates performance from where it takes place and where it is heard. It is also endlessly repeatable. Now, a clear divide between two art forms has emerged. That they are deeply intertwined, involving many of the same practitioners and audiences in both does not alter this basic fact.

But confusion persists because of the more contentious issue between the technos and the telos of music and art making in general, the instruments versus the purposes to which they are put, the means and the ends. Great controversies have raged for centuries on this theme, perhaps never more heatedly than in the 20th. To this day, there are those who think the youth who learned to make music with samplers, synthesizers and other computerized devices are not really musicians; they are only pushing buttons and the machines are making the "music." There is no technique required, some say, because the technology does it for you. Worse, it widens the already dangerous divide between the authentic expression of human feeling and the mere toying with diversionary gadgets; between the emotional connections made by real music and the alienation produced by machines.

It is obvious that the use of digital editing, computer programming, auto-tuning and other mechanical devices facilitates the more systematic production and promotion of Anti-music. They are, in many cases, used to reinforce the technological destruction of music. Rhythm, more than any other musical element, has been mechanized and formulized, the antithesis of its ancient sources. At the root of computer-based technology is the correlation between number and music, specifically the counting of beats which can be translated into digital information. Many argue that it is precisely this that enables turning music into numbers and is the very source of the problem.[12]

Nonetheless, all of these objections fail to account for more recent developments. What is most worthy of note is not the latest update of Pro Tools software or some nifty plug-in. These have become utterly commonplace to the point of annoyance! If anything, this technology has already reached its limit. It is useful. It is necessary for certain functions. It has made for new musical possibilities. But surprising doomsayers and techno-gurus alike, has been the re-establishment, on an even firmer basis than ever, of the importance of the unique performance and the imagination in composition. More highly prized than ever is the musicianship required to play "old" instruments well. More deeply respected than ever is the unfettered imagination that can compose music that inspires. Far from being rendered obsolete, more skills for more tasks are more necessary.

There is a widened divide between live performance and recorded music. Novel twists redefine the roles of performer and composer; still, as the very existence of the music industry is called into question by the technology of computers and internet downloading, musicians are becoming more aware to what extent their livelihoods and their lives depend on interaction with real people, not markets. This has led to a renewed emphasis on live concerts and a decreased reliance on recordings to reach one's audiences. Thus, we see a "backwards" trend not predicted by the theorists at all in which more musicians realize they must simply get out and play.[13]

## THE SIGNAL TO NOISE RATIO AND HIGH FIDELITY

There is an equation that all technicians use regarding recorded sound: the signal-to-noise ratio. Literally, and in its most specific sense, this means the range, usually expressed in decibels, between the loudest sound a recording medium can accommodate and its background noise level. Since this phrase was coined it has provoked much social and political criticism about the character of music and the relative value placed on these terms. "One man's music is another man's noise."[14] In fact, at the very time the technology was enabling some of the changes mentioned above, Public Enemy, an influential rap group from New York, made a song called: "Bring the Noise." Attali's *Noise* was also published at this time. And everyone can envision a group of young people moving wildly to what they consider great music while their parents (or the older generation) is holding their ears and fleeing all the racket!

All of this brings us to a place where several different streams converge. Those streams include: music, technology, social conflict, philosophy and religion. They converge in the works of artists. They converge in the instruments invented and manufactured by technicians and builders. They converge in the sounds and arguments we hear around us all the time. They converge at the point of conflict between use value and exchange value, between what most of us need from music (its spiritual and communal purpose) and what capital needs (to extract profit from owning, buying and selling). What is the signal and what is the noise?

For the music maker, be she or he composer, musician, engineer or instrument builder these are the vital questions of everyday existence. How to make a living and how to make a Life. They are the basis on which crucial decisions are made and definitive actions taken. Indeed, these questions become obsessive in the sense that virtually all discussion with one's colleagues sooner or later ends up dissecting and analyzing their most microscopic components, and usually with great passion. There is much at stake.

We are all familiar with "High Fidelity," a term that became popular during the proliferation of recordings and their necessary household appliances in the '50s and early, pre-stereo, '60s. But there is an important connection beyond the popular one to which we must refer. The high fidelity of technical parlance is connected to both the etymology of the word fidelity and the ethical dimensions it implies. The word originates in the Latin, *fidelius*, meaning "faithful." It has two *Oxford English Dictionary* definitions: 1. continuing loyalty to a person, cause or belief. and, 2. the degree of exactness with which something is copied or reproduced. Obviously, technicians used the second definition when they chose the word to describe the functions of their machines. But it is the first definition that is surfacing now as the most important when considering subjects like "performance" or "noise."

It is no digression to refer to the common experience of many in their post-teenage years when they hear the music of their youth. We experience a "fidelity" to the events encapsulated in the songs of those formative years. We feel a love for the lived experiences that music creates. With "Bring the Noise" Public Enemy wasn't claiming that noise was better than music, nor were they engaging in trivial word play or abstract debate—they were calling for a fidelity to the struggle for liberation embodied in the lived experience of black people in America (and, by extension, the oppressed everywhere). As the name of their group states clearly: to be young and black is to be a public enemy, suggesting the questions: who is the public and who are our friends? Fidelity to resistance celebrated in a song is noise to the oppressor but music to the ears of the oppressed.

It has become a point of honor for many young musicians to express themselves in what they know will be considered "noise" by their forebears. Alain Badiou pioneered this idea with his "ethic of truths." He refers to events such as the French revolution or May '68 as the moments in history that "break out" of the constraints of the norm, or the uneventful, and force everyone to reconsider everything. We must pledge our fidelity to these events if we are to have anything like a meaningful ethics by which to guide our judgments and deeds. The source we must look to is not abstract ideas or obscure academic definitions but real events that take place in social life. This is precisely what the battle over signal-to-noise ratios and fidelity implies in terms of our choices and decisions as music makers. This is why for some of us "noisy" is good, distortion is beautiful and "high fidelity" means "true to the moment," not slick, perfectly in tune pabulum.

What could be more of an "event" than performance? Performance takes place at a particular time, in a particular place, and never recurs. No one would become a musician without having heard a performance that was such an event, a moment in time in which life was lived and not merely endured. Recording it so that it can be played over and over does not change the fact that there was a unique performance that did not happen before and will not happen again. Even if it is a composer inputting her ideas into a computer to have them perfectly and repeatedly performed by machines, there is a moment that is the physical act of performing each component of the piece that will ultimately emerge from the machines, in much the same way that multi-track recording did this prior to the emergence of digital technology. There remains this kernel of the performative act whereby a composer must draw the ideas from his or her imagination and combine them in the commands given to machines. Indeed, some would argue that the newest instrument of all is the recording studio in which a composer or mixer performs on this large, complex group of sound-making devices, not unlike the church organist of old.

The illusion fostered by replicability is that the performance never took place or is always taking place. But as everyone who participates in this process knows, decisions are made, actions are carried out and one has to live with the consequences forever. Performance may not be on a stage in front of an audience, but it is performance nonetheless and one will be reminded of this fact, to their pleasure or embarrassment, by the evidence preserved in the recording. Moreover, a recording may be endlessly replicable, but it will not be copied or played at all unless the music is good. This has consequences for deciding what is signal, what is noise and to what music makers owe their fidelity. Far from liquidating creativity, skill and talent, modern technologies have only intensified the contradictions surrounding their application. The most obvious example is that the advent of the drum machine did not render drummers obsolete. On the contrary, it has heightened our awareness of the importance and profundity of actually played rhythm. If anything, drumming by real drummers has become more vital, and its intricacies more in demand than ever before. It has led to a recognition of, in the words of the drummer of The Roots, "the beauty of the human flaw."

Yes, recording has become an art form that owes less and less to its parent, the live performance of music. But the perfectibility, via editing, of the otherwise flawed "actual" event has revealed its opposite side: the ultimately dehumanized, mechanized sound of machines imitating human performance. And what, after the initial novelty wears off, could be more boring than a machine imitating a human? The delight and amazement one might experience seeing a mechanical doll has as much to do with the craft and imagination of its maker as it does with what the doll is doing. Player pianos, music boxes, and other contrivances that performed music "perfectly" and over and over were always so different from the real performance by a human being that no serious comparison could be made between them, anyway. Now, we have reached the point where actual human performance can be made "perfect" and then repeated. More than ever, music makers are faced with the conscious, ethical choice between expanding human possibility and enslaving humans to the machinery of dull repetition. The essential questions are starkly clear. We can aspire to great performance, to the event of the fully lived life, or we can be the raw materials consumed by machines and turned into replicas, digital dummies, forever imitating what some crass entrepreneur wants to sell as lived life.

I remain defiantly optimistic for one simple reason: ultimately, musicians themselves must perform in order to experience performance. No machine can ever replicate that experience. While music is generally made to be heard by an audience, it is fundamentally an experience of the musician that is being shared. The exhilaration I feel doing it is the exhilaration you feel hearing it. This is one reason that along with all the new technology, young people are still buying guitars and drums, basses and pianos, horns and harmonicas, cellos and accordions. People want to play!

Fidelity to that event is what is at stake now in virtually every recording project or live concert. Separating the noise of deception from the signal of a real, lived experience is the battle waged wherever music is made. That technology can now make virtually noise-free recordings, that the signal-to-noise ratio is near zero, has simply revealed more precisely what noise is: an attitude, a point of view, a decision or commitment; it is not about sound at all. Whether it is Public Enemy singing, "Bring the Noise" or Peter Gabriel singing, "Turn up the signal, wipe out the noise!" the principle is the same: what privilege and Power call noise is one thing. What is fake, illusory, sterile, antiseptic and dehumanizing is another and is the real noise opposing music.

Music can make use of all sound. Musicians must make their own decisions and commitments based on the purposes, effects and possibilities of the music making process. It is the ethical and political that define noise. On the one side, the oppressor calls our music noise so we say, "Right. I love noise." On the other, we know what the real noise is and we say: Only living beings make music. Only music being made can bring the maker the joy of making it. It is the event of great performance, to which all musicians aspire, that we owe our fidelity. Everything else is a lie.

# FOOTNOTES

1 "Music is a herald, for change is inscribed in noise faster than it transforms society....Listening to music is listening to all noise, realizing that its appropriation and control is a reflection of power, that it is essentially political."
Attali, Jacques. *Noise: The Political Economy of Music*. University of Minnesota Press, 1985, p. 3.

2 Techno, like all genres has diverse participants and sharply polarized aesthetics. Among the originators of what became Techno are great musicians such as Kraftwerk, Brian Eno and Derrick May, whose influence on many genres are worldwide and profound. Simultaneously, techno's trajectory is a glaring example of how music is transformed into Anti-music. While never approaching the social import of rock or hip-hop, techno has, nonetheless, nearly ubiquitous presence in the urban landscape. Rave culture was once a battleground of technophiles championing diametrically opposing viewpoints towards music, festival and politics. Moreover, closely associated with techno by virtue of the machines employed to make it were sub-genres such as "industrial" where groups like Einstürzende Neubauten, Consolidated, Meat Beat Manifesto and Disposable Heroes of Hiphopracy pioneered raging beats with raging politics to blast a hole in the complacency of "pop" music.

3 Badiou, Alain. *Manifesto For Philosophy*. State University of New York Press, 1989, p. 54.

4 Ibid. p. 54.

5 The diddley-bow is a musical instrument. "One traditional practice which predated the cheap mass-produced mail-order guitar—and in fact survived well into the mid-twentieth century among those for whom even an instrument costing a buck eighty-nine was an inaccessible extravagance—was the trick of nailing a length of wire to a barn wall and using a piece of glass or metal to change the pitch. Known as a 'diddley-bow', such contrivances provided a first experience of plucked-string instruments for many a wannabe guitarist, including the young John Lee Hooker and B.B. King. Under the influence of the slide or the hand-bent string, the rigid, tempered European scale melted to reveal all the hidden places between the notes: the precise, chiming instrument giving forth a liquid African cry."
Shaar Murray, Charles. "Cryin' the Blues." *The Observer*. November 16, 2003.

6 Burnet, John. *Greek Philosophy: Thales to Plato*. St. Martin's Press, 1961, p. 44–45.

7 Ibid. p. 331.

8 "Pythagoras." *The Oxford Companion to Music*. Oxford University Press, 2002.

9 Benjamin, Walter. "The Work of Art In the Age Of Mechanical Reproduction." *Illuminations*. Schocken Books, 1968, p. 217.

10 Marx, Karl and Friedrich Engels. *The Communist Manifesto*. Oxford University Press, 1992,. p. 5.

11 For those of us involved with this technology there are many other capabilities. These include developments of machines/software/plugins for the three fundamental components of recorded sound: reverberation, equalization and compression. Important as these are, they do not significantly alter the work or methods of work that go into recording, programming and mixing music.

12 Skip MacDonald, guitarist with Tackhead and Little Axe and among a group of musicians who played on some of the most influential recordings of the '80s had this to say of this period:

"Musicians were sentenced to death for a long period," he recalls. "DJs could cut records without a band, and it cut costs, so record companies loved it. I can remember a time when Tackhead's drummer, Keith LeBlanc, would walk round with a pitcher of water so he could pour it on the drum machine and the computer, because the drum machine was actually taking his gig!

"If you go back to, like, the 1960s, if you heard a record on the radio, you would know who it was within four bars," agrees MacDonald. "It was only after the advent of the first sequencers and drum machines, when people were just trying to get their heads around the new technology, that everybody started imitating everybody else.

"But there are pockets of resistance, musical rebels that still like the music. I think the way forward is to get live playing with some of the old vibes sampled in: to try to create a situation where all the technology is available, along with the individual talents of the musicians."

Gill, Andy. "Little Axe: Blues for the 21st century." *The Independent.* September 24, 2004.

13    There is an abundance of data demonstrating this. Unprecedented increases in the sales of musical instruments tabulated by industry trade publications, for example. Similarly, increases in attendance at all kinds of musical performance from grand opera to Tuvan throat singing to punk rock are reported in newspapers and periodicals from *The Guardian* to industry rags like *Billboard* or *Pollstar*.

"End of" pronouncements are generally bogus, anyway. End of history, end of science, end of music, etc. Just as theater continues to thrive long after TV and Film promised to kill it, so, too, music's live performance.

14    Callahan, Mat. "Try Communication." (on Yvonne Moore's CD) *Between You And I.* COD Music, 1999.

# The War of
# the World Views

## Radio and Music

In August, 1968 "People Got To Be Free" by The Rascals hits number one in the Charts.

Pop Music Charts Archive

At last it's official: junk pop has taken over the charts.

A new survey proves—once and for all—the dominance of manufactured boy and girl bands and solo stars. A university study of chart hits over the past 20 years shows 2002 is the worst on record—with only three of this year's No 1 singles by living, "real" artists.

James Morrison, *The Independent*

**F**or most people born in the last 100 years, radio and broadcast music have been a fixture of everyday life. Particularly in the US, radio and music were bound together like the double helix of DNA, each extending the range and influence of the other as society was saturated with sound. For many music lovers there is a special affection for radio, a shared enthusiasm for a shared experience. Particular stations, DJs, musical genres and times of day are meeting places that connect people over great distances. For musicians, radio has been a means to reach out and "speak to the world."

Simultaneously, control of the airwaves has been hotly contested. Almost immediately, the commercial potential of the new medium was exploited, and advertising began to dominate radio programming. Still more significant was the use of radio for the shaping of public opinion. From its inception, broadcasting was seen as a means for directing the thought and behavior of the masses, of controlling the "public mind."

Today, it might appear that Big Money and Big Brother control Big Media, end of story. But this ignores two vital forces that challenge such claims. Critical thinking and the turbulent restlessness of the common people always pose a threat to tyranny. The Big Idea and the Great Unwashed are ultimately more important than Big Money, Big Brother and their Big Media in determining the use of any technology, including radio. Moreover, contrary to what ruling elites would have us believe, history is not determined solely by their quest for wealth and Power. In fact, the very period within which radio plays such an important part is characterized by popular revolt.

This is obscured, however, by a pair of widely held misconceptions. One is "there's no accounting for taste" or, expressed by radio programmers, "we're only giving the people what they want to hear." The other is that technology is a force unto itself that controls its creators. Thus technology may either be feared or revered, but humans are its servants, not its masters. Philosophers, scientists, politicians and businessmen have promoted these ideas to the detriment of music makers and their audiences.[1] Instead of liberating people and their imaginations, they encourage fatalistic acceptance of the status quo. Yet both are false and, as we shall see, the history of radio and music demonstrates this better than any abstract argument. Moreover, what we will find is that the potential that music and radio share is that of the open public space to which all are invited, but not coerced, to participate. The message may be political, philosophical, religious, scientific or amorous. It may be festive, sorrowful, sexy or thought provoking. But it is essentially social. It is public in the broadest and best sense of the word.

## THE WAR OF THE WORLDS IN A WORLD OF WARS

Orson Welles' "War of the Worlds" radio show was broadcast October 30, 1938. The panic it caused and the controversy it stirred announced the importance of a medium barely 20 years old. Already, the outlines of all subsequent conflicts in the field of telecommunications were clearly drawn. Welle's production of H.G. Wells' popular novel of a Martian attack on Earth might be viewed as part of a very real "war of the world-views" in the contentious arena of broadcast media: first in radio, then television and now the internet. In 1927, expressing a commonly repeated theme, H.G. Wells himself attacked radio as being for "very sedentary persons living in badly lighted houses or otherwise unable to read...and who have no capacity for thought or conversation." "War of the Worlds" was produced by the Columbia Workshop, sponsored by the fledgling Columbia Broadcasting Network, in part, to compete with the erstwhile monopoly of NBC the world's first commercial radio network. In fact, so dominant had NBC already become that Columbia was willing to try adventuresome programming by new and decidedly literary figures in an effort to productively fill the time when 40 million Americans were listening to "Amos 'n Andy".

Already, music was the mainstay of radio programming, punctuated by comedy and news. Ratings and advertising were strengthening their grip in opposition to "The Public Interest." By 1930, Crossley, Inc. was publishing formal ratings that showed that "Amos 'n Andy" was four times more popular than any CBS show, thereby establishing the basis by which advertisers could determine the value of airtime. Regulatory battles between various government agencies, corporate lobbyists and public interest groups were shaping up. Herbert Hoover, Commerce Department Secretary in 1923, said: "It is inconceivable that we should allow so great a possibility for service to be drowned in advertising chatter." In 1927, the Federal Radio Commission was created by Congress with the power to license and regulate stations. This was the forerunner of the Federal Communications Commission which, in a precursor to the Microsoft monopolization battles of today, forced NBC in 1943 to divest itself of one of its networks in the interests of competition.

Note how clearly the basic irreconcilability of the public interest and the business interest were defined. There was a presumption, at the time radio broadcasting began, that these interests were diametrically opposed and in open conflict. The pretense that there is an identity of interests, that, in the words of Margaret Thatcher, "there is no such thing as society,"[2] was the battlecry of post-Sixties reactionaries. More recently, this view has foundered on its own internal contradictions, clearly manifested in the great financial scandals of the opening years of the 21st century. Public and private remain bitterly contested sites. Indeed, private property, particularly the ownership of the rights to broadcast over the airwaves, faces an obvious predicament. How can it justify its claims to own the air? From a juridical, not to mention logical, point of view there is greater legitimacy to the claim that only a government that derives its authority from the consent of the governed, and represents their interests, has the right to determine how air is used and in what way the governed will benefit. Pirate radio raises these issues in a particularly acute way.

In any case, radio penetrates every corner of society and plays a major role in the manipulation of public opinion. It is no accident that its birth coincides with that of the Public Relations industry and the early "scientific" uses of propaganda to shape the popular will.[3] Behind the "advertising chatter" were the theories of social engineers whose aim was political Power. The purposes to which the broadcast media must be put, they argued, was control of the "public mind."

The "War of the Worlds" broadcast, originally intended as a Halloween prank, presents a powerful example. In Michael Denning's brilliant study of this period, *The Cultural Front*, he states:

> "The War of the Worlds" broadcast was at first glance nothing special, though it departed from the usual format by prefacing the long first person narrative of the survivor, Professor Pierson, with the mock news broadcast of the Martian invasion. Its structure resembles the later *Citizen Kane*, but unlike Kane the persuasiveness of the newsreel overwhelmed the pedestrian narrative that followed, triggering a panic. According to sociologist Hadley Cantril's analysis of public opinion polls about the panic, six million people heard part of the broadcast, and over a million of them believed it was a real news broadcast and were frightened by it. The panic came to figure, for writers, politicians, and journalists, the power and dangers of the still relatively new mass culture of broadcasting. For some, Welles was as irresponsible as the right-wing radio demagogues; for others, the program was a salutary warning. For Welles and the Mercury Theater, the panic represented not only national notoriety, but the other side of the people's theater, of the 'popular, democratic machine': the lure and danger of hypnotizing an audience.[4]

It should be remembered that this theatrical performance took place during the period of Fascism's rise to power in Europe and many who heard the broadcast thought it was a news report about a Nazi invasion of the US. Furthermore, the "salutary" lessons of the show were lost on no one when it came to the war effort. In fact, the Columbia Workshop, and Welles in particular, soon became actively involved in the fight against fascism, as radio was put to use mobilizing the American People.

## RADIO AND MUSIC: TROUBLED SYMBIOSIS

Today, it may be more pertinent to pose these questions of all media without special focus on radio, but radio continues to have a unique connection to music that gives it greater importance to music makers than it might have to society at large. For one thing, both radio and music are invisible. They do not require sight, operating only by vibrating the air that, in turn, vibrates the ear drums of the listener. For another, radio has from it infancy, relied heavily on music. Not only do virtually all broadcasts begin and end with some sort of musical accompaniment, but a vast amount of airtime is devoted to music in its own right. Conversely, music has relied on radio for its proliferation. To popularize a work, a composer, or a performer, radio is a crucial instrument. This apparently symbiotic relationship between music and radio has a stormy history, however, that has culminated in the pitting of many musicians against the institutions and corporations that control what is broadcast.

From the 1930's on, radio has played a large and special part in people's lives in spite of encroachment by TV and other technologies. Particularly as it regards music (an analogous situation is radio and sports), listeners were connected to each other through shared enthusiasm for what was heard on a more or less continuous basis. The lines from Bruce Springsteen's "Thunder Road" encapsulates this relationship perfectly:

> The screen door slams
> Mary's dress waves
> Like a vision she dances across the porch
> As the radio plays
> Roy Orbison singing for the lonely
> Hey that's me and I want you only

Prior to the proliferation of 8-track and cassette tape decks, radio was the way music could be transported, literally accompanying a person through daily life. Radio was a constant pulse, always on, reflecting the increasing mobility and tempo of the modern world. Furthermore, as a humorous scene in the film *O Brother, Where Art Thou?* illustrates, radio was instrumental in the proliferation of music at a particular time and place. In the film we see the protagonists, escapees from the penitentiary, going into a rural radio station to try to win a contest the station is holding as a means of attracting musicians to come and perform on the air (which in turn would attract listeners and satisfy advertisers who subsidized the station's operation). Thus the "Soggy Bottom Boys" were born, and through the magic of radio (and a great song!) turned into popular heroes overnight. This comedic tale is truthful and revealing in two important ways.

First, it portrays one way radio actually functioned in its early days in the very large parts of the US that were rural. Prior to World War II, the majority of the population of the US lived in the country, not the city. Radio played religious and secular music mainly indigenous to the regions it was broadcast, relying heavily on performance by local people to attract listeners (and induce them to buy receivers—which was the original profit motive in radio). This was happening at a time when the largest internal migration in US history was taking place from the south to the north, from the countryside to the city.

In another profound insight in *The Cultural Front*, Denning demonstrates that the development of country and western, rhythm and blues and rock and roll were a product of this migration. What has come be known as "American Music" originated in the south, and was literally transported to the rest of the country by the workers flooding into the cities of the east, north and west. In this context two technologies developed simultaneously, the radio and the phonograph (and its extension, the juke box) to carry this music, its sound and sensibilities far beyond the rural communities from which it had originated. This did not entirely displace the previously dominant forms of popular music which were based more on transplanted and modified European song, but it ultimately led to the prevalence of a musical genre that took over the world in the Sixties. The British Invasion of 1964 was young English musicians playing music that originated in the southern United States, the biggest indication up to that time of the ever widening reverberation of this influence.

I recall the day when the Beatles' *Sgt. Pepper's Lonely Hearts Club Band* was released because, just prior to becoming available in stores, KSAN, the hip FM station in San Francisco, devoted an entire day to playing the album. Thousands of young people, myself included, rushed home to catch the broadcast so laden with cultural and historic significance. We sat, ears glued to the speakers, hanging on every note. Then we listened raptly to the comments of the announcer which were, in turn, followed by our own intense discussion of what we'd just experienced. We could be certain that all of our friends and classmates at school had listened too. We knew at the moment we were listening, that this would be the topic of discussion for weeks to come. This event followed years of devoted radio listening on the part of millions. It also signaled changes taking place at that very moment. AM and FM, the role of music in the development of radio and vice versa, the relation between a technology and society, and most significantly, the Sixties with all their radical implications.

AM is short for Amplitude Modulation and FM is short for Frequency Modulation. Marconi's application of the principles of electromagnetic radiation made the first wireless transmissions of information possible in 1895. That air is the carrier of sound has long been known. That it could, over much longer distances, carry electromagnetic waves was a breakthrough, particularly when the apparatus to perform the operation was made practical. Electromagnetic waves travel at the speed of light: 300,000km/hr. Sound waves in the audible range, such as speech and music, have a frequency that is too low for efficient transmission through the air for significant distances. Radio requires a transmitter and a receiver that can convert the sound waves into electromagnetic form and reconvert the transmitted wave back into its sonic form, by which it can be heard through a loudspeaker. Initially this was done by the method of amplitude modulation, which has the benefit of great range and low susceptibility to being blocked by mountains, buildings, etc. However, it has the drawback of being susceptible to interference caused by anything from lightning to electrical devices to other radio stations, and its inherent limitations make for lower quality sound reproduction. For this reason, Edward Armstrong developed another technique, Frequency Modulation, in 1933, which has the advantage of producing higher quality sound and is less susceptible to interference. Its drawback is that its range is limited in comparison to AM. Also, in the early days—1930s and 40s—the receivers were more expensive making them less attractive to the mass market.

Precisely because of these comparative advantages/disadvantages, commercial broadcasting favored the lower quality/greater range of AM. This is the basis on which radio and its special relation to music began and developed. The legendary broadcasts of Wolfman Jack provide a perfect example. From a transmitter in Tijuana, Mexico where regulations were more liberal than in the US, the Wolfman could be heard all the way to the Canadian border. It is important to mention here that there were significant differences in how radio developed in different countries according to the policies of governments, as well as the economic and political factors at work during the early period of broadcasting. World Wars I and

II played a major part in the development of radio and regulations governing its use. Still, it is worth concentrating on the US because its experience, while unique, raises issues that are now being faced globally, notably in the great telecommunications wars and the ongoing siege of publicly owned and operated industries by private corporate entities. We can see this in the specific development of FM radio in the US. There, FM stations were originally launched in the late 1940s and the 1950s to counter the commercial formats of AM stations, which depended heavily upon saturation advertising and repetitive "playlists" of popular songs. FM catered to a more diversified audience and focused on in-depth news analysis and classical or semiclassical music. Now, with the exception of public radio, college radio and pirate radio, no such distinction can be made. Commercial formats and playlists dominate all radio.

For approximately ten years from—1966 to 1976 FM radio—pioneered in San Francisco by people such as Big Daddy Tom Donahue, was the broadcast equivalent of the explosion of creativity being expressed in popular music. It is no accident that it happened in San Francisco at this particular time and in the way that it did. Tom Donahue himself had been a disc jockey on commercially oriented AM stations long before coming to FM and developing the format that became the model for FM radio nationwide. Sly Stone, also an AM radio DJ prior to becoming a major musical force in his own right, was another key participant in this process. While the real action was taking place in the concerts and happenings, the love-ins and freak-outs at the Fillmore Auditorium or in Golden Gate Park where live music was being played, FM radio was an important dimension of the rapidly unfolding cultural revolution. Masses of young people deserted AM radio altogether associating it with bubble gum pop and the crass commercialism of "The Establishment." This cannot be emphasized enough in terms of what actually helped shape music, musician and audience. Nor can it fail to make damning criticism of today's corporate programming of manufactured "stars."

Following the commercialization of FM and the demise of stations formatted in the "Sixties" manner, college radio emerged to partially fill the gap. These stations were non-commercial since they were sponsored by the institutions that housed them, and were used in part for the training of students in communications courses. Their range is usually very limited (they can only be received within a small radius and suffer all the problems of low power and small antennas) and their financial support is inadequate to provide more than the basic tools for broadcasting. However, these limitations enhanced the credibility of these stations, because they were run by young people with a love for radio and music, particularly music that was fresh, innovative and free of the taint of mainstream formula. We'll go farther into what happened to college radio later, but for now, suffice it to say that for music lovers and musicians, the diversity of musical offerings and the lack of commercial constraint made college radio the "network" that replaced what it had descended from: FM radio as it developed in the Sixties.

## RADIO VERSUS MUSIC—FROM FRIEND TO FOE

After tracing, albeit far too briefly, the development of music and radio, it is easier to understand the perplexity with which musicians and music lovers confront the present state of affairs. It has not always been this way. From being a friend and ally, radio has turned into an ominous shadow cast over the lives and work of millions of music makers today. Any recording artist or producer faces a contradiction: needing radio to sell enough records to justify the investment in making them, and not wanting or being able to conform to the dictates of radio programming that insist narrow criteria be met. Musicians and audiences are no longer the creative source in a vital, social linkage. Radio is no longer propagating what arises spontaneously from the populace itself or bringing attention to the finest or most interesting musical expression. Instead, the so-called "free" market is dictating what people should make and hear which is (too much of the time) silly, mind-numbing nonsense. In the study quoted at the beginning of this chapter conducted at Napier University, Edinburgh,

> They found that, with the exception of the early 1990s, the heyday of guitar bands like The Happy Mondays, the proportion of manufactured No 1s has risen year on year—to over two-thirds of this year's 22 No 1 singles.
> At least seven were released by stars created on TV talent shows. Only six have been by real acts, among them Oasis, rock singer Pink and US rapper Eminem. The others, Elvis Presley, George Harrison and Aaliyah, are all dead.
> Last week, Woolworth, WH Smith and Asda even refused to stock the current No 9, "Bunsen Burner", a pastiche of Seventies classic "Disco Inferno", because its singer, 50-year-old John Otway, does not appeal to teenage girls.[5]

Findings such as these (and there are numerous others similar to it), only confirm what many music makers, young and old, feel without really understanding. Many then arrive at the conclusion that if they want to be successful, they must conform. This in itself is a profound shift from the attitudes that propelled rock and roll and soul to the forefront of world popular culture in the Sixties. Aretha Franklin, arguably the greatest singer of the 20th century, could not be signed today. She is not classically beautiful or sexy as codified by MTV. Her roots in the black church and the deep soil of African-American culture are too raw and raucous for neat packaging. Albums such as *What's Going On* by Marvin Gaye or *The World Is A Ghetto* by War—both giant hits—might never be made in today's conformist, artificially constructed climate. They would likely be considered too controversial in the wrong way (read: "Political")—with too limited an appeal.

Manufactured controversy, such as that surrounding sex and violence, is desirable. This is the stuff that stirs the libidinal and transgressive interest of young people and channels it away from the musical or political. The music industry has always attempted to do this. The social forces that were unleashed enabling the "southernization" of American music (in the '30s and '40s), combined with the intense political conflicts that filled music with deep historical significance (in the Sixties) gave musicians a power within the industry that has since withered away. The balance of forces has shifted decisively into the hands of industrial magnates and their insatiable quest for profit at the expense of the music maker and the audience.

Of course, this is a complex problem, involving many contradictory aspects. There is such diversity of musical expression and so many forms of broadcast that it cannot be stated that the situation is categorically "bad" for music. It will be an oft-repeated theme of this book that music and those who make it are endlessly resilient, turning the very limits on expression into vehicles enabling it. This is especially marked in the rise and global influence of hip-hop.

Most importantly, it would be wrong to view the situation as stable. This is not a period of a gradual easing into equilibrium of a well balanced, smooth running machine. The current malaise of popular culture is characterized by the exact opposite. It is profoundly unstable, making the music industry and those employed in it neurotic to the extreme. The pervasive mood of crisis and threat, of a "Golden Age" being over and behind us, indicates that even with unprecedented profits, the music industry is not facing a bright future.

In a recent interview, Robert Plant, lead singer of Led Zeppelin, was asked: "How has the music business changed since you first started in the 60s?"

Plant responded: "The music business? It screams with insecurity. It has been devoured by whiskey companies, online giants and multinational moguls who combine the booty of music, movies and literature to grease the ever bigger palm. The lower minions working down the ladder below the faceless moguls throw money cautiously at whatever artists seem to be the most appropriate to fit the bill. So one slice of mediocrity inspires another."[6]

To grasp the specific role of radio in this, we need to go further back than the Sixties, however. In the early days of rock and roll, Allan Freed, the DJ who claims he coined the term (and actually tried to copyright it!), was indicted for accepting $30,000 from six independent record companies in the "payola" scandal that "shocked" the music industry. The "crime" was the accepting of a bribe from record company promoters to play certain records a certain number of times. First of all, this was and remains standard industry practice, whether the bribe is money, drugs, prostitutes or other "gifts" and second, what was once called "sleaze" is now called "legitimate promotional expense". The crime was never stopped; they just stopped calling it a crime. The need to maintain appearances is based on the struggle that began at the inception of broadcasting between public and private interest, between the informative or educational function and the profit making function. There is a political, as opposed to purely economic, dimension to this arising from the basic question of control of the airwaves. But we must ask: Why is anyone shocked? Similar to the scandals that have recently rocked the financial markets, the only scandal is that people consider it a scandal, since it is at the very heart of capitalist business procedure.

Now, however, new methods are being employed to better obscure how this works. Even in countries where publicly owned radio is still the dominant force in broadcasting (most of Western Europe, for example), questions of impropriety are neatly sidestepped by resorting to carefully manicured surveys of listenership, and by the wholly disingenuous argument that a public service should "give the people what they want." Therefore, if there are more listeners because only "top hits by top artists" are played, we are just doing the public bidding. To be blunt, this is hogwash and completely distorts the actual relationship between all the factors involved in mass communication which are, of course, well known to advertisers and PR professionals since they go to school for the purpose of learning these techniques. That the public be kept blissfully unaware is a precondition of its effectiveness. Deceit, therefore, is the sole purpose of maintaining any pretense of public accountability at all!

In callous disregard of music makers and public alike, major labels dictate what will be played most, thereby marginalizing whatever is not their exclusive property. The Big Five record companies are, themselves, only a part of much larger conglomerates that own media empires including radio and television networks. It is obvious that the shareholders of AOL-TimeWarner want their investment in a particular artist returned, whatever the means. They assume, as a matter of course, that Warner Brothers Records will use all the resources at its disposal to insure maximum airplay in the effort to gain maximum profitability from its stable of "stars." This is so obvious that it begs credulity when we hear the protestations of radio programmers and music directors to the charge that they are mere lackeys of the majors without a shred of independent decision making to their name. In fact, in many cases, they are literally paid employees of these very corporations or others with interlocking boards of directors. But even when they are not, the commonality of interest is revealed in the policies they implement. An example is the case of DRS3, the main, state-run radio station in Switzerland. In 2001 they hired a German programmer to "modernize" their nationally broadcast music shows. His first act was to cut in half the number of songs played. A reduction of 50% means doubling the number of times the remainder are played. As for the criteria for what was kept or not, the results became apparent in weeks. Swiss musicians, except those already "stars," and particularly those on independent labels, were off the air. There was an immediate spike in the percentage of foreign (mainly US and UK) music played, and a significant increase in the percentage of airtime taken by acts signed to major labels.

## BELOW THE AIRWAVES

Yet beneath this sordid manipulation lies a certain logic, a certain necessity, that reveals the depths of the crisis facing us today and particularly the role of radio in it. In a speech delivered to the JP Morgan seminar, Jay Berman, CEO of the International Federation of the Phonograph Industry made this remark: "In 1926, Henry Ford, of motor industry fame, had this to say of music: 'I don't deny the importance of art and music in polite society. But in business it will never be of any value.' Henry Ford would not recognize the international music business today. An industry worth US $34 billion that invests billions of dollars in developing, promoting, marketing and distributing recorded music around the world; an industry that employs hundreds of thousand of people worldwide— 600,000 in Europe alone; and one that, for more than half a century, has adapted to new technologies to meet the changing demands of our consumers."[7] Of course, Berman should have added another statement Henry Ford made in reference to the Model T, "You can choose any color you want so long as it's black." Indeed, the Fordist model of assembly line production remains the model for industrial manufacture—"knowledge economy" psychobabble notwithstanding. When it comes to music and industry, Ford was right on both counts. Music really is "not of any value."

Transforming it into a commodity requires a special effort.

> A singer who sings like a bird is an unproductive worker. When she sells her song, she is a wage earner or merchant. But the same singer, employed by someone else to give concerts and bring in money, is a productive worker because she directly produces capital.[8]

Or, put another way,

> One cannot present the labor of the pianist as indirectly productive, either because it stimulates the material production of pianos, for example, or because it gives the worker who hears the piano recital more spirit and vitality. Only the labor of someone who creates capital is productive, so any other labor, however useful or harmful it may be, is not productive from the point of view of capitalization; it is therefore unproductive. The producer of tobacco is productive, even though the consumption of tobacco is unproductive.[9]

It may not be very popular to quote Marx these days, but what he said is quite accurate and exactly to the point. This operation of making music and musician into commodities, capturing and changing these into "stars" and "hits" is what the music business does. But at the same moment the costs of music production have fallen (and dramatically over the last ten years) the costs of promotion have skyrocketed. These are the key costs in the production of "stars" and "hits" upon which the music business is based. To restate the point, it is not the production of music that makes the music business run. It is the production of "stars" and "hits" that is done by massive, and increasingly costly promotion.

Miles Copeland, head of highly successful IRS records and now an industry consultant, had this to say about music and profitability:

> From my own experience I know investors look at record companies unfavorably BECAUSE THEY DON'T MAKE ATTRACTIVE RETURNS ON INVESTMENT. Basically, it's a high-risk, low-return business, which is why companies are shrinking in quantity and staff. Many of my friends who were gainfully employed five years ago, are out of the business altogether. Many household names, A&M, Geffen, Chrysalis, IRS, etc., have been shuttered. Hardly the product of a highly profitable industry.[10]

Thus, it is without irony that Jay Berman concluded his otherwise upbeat speech with this statement: "Our ongoing strategy is twofold—on the one hand to defend our existing business and on the other build and exploit the new business models of the digital era. As the queen of disco herself,

Gloria Gaynor, pronounced, 'We will survive.'" "Defend?" "Survive??" What do these words suggest is the real state of affairs to which Berman is speaking? Given their propensity for lying, for saying exactly the opposite of what they know to be true in order to achieve their hidden agendas, what are we to deduce from such remarks?

I suggest that what appear to be contradictory claims are both accurate simultaneously. They reveal the sharp contradictions within the economy as a whole—not only the music or telecommunications industries. There are both enormous profits and not enough profits at the same time. Thus, we have on the one hand, industry champions like Berman giving rah-rah speeches to increasingly nervous managers fearing for their prestigious livelihoods, and on the other hand old veterans like Copeland hearkening back to an earlier time when the industry was actually less profitable but was run by people directly involved with music production like himself, Herb Alpert, Chris Blackwell and others who owned and operated their labels themselves. The basic conditions created by promotion usurping music production is what these two are unwilling to put in perspective or draw the necessary conclusions from. Lacking any social conscience or aesthetic principles, they cannot.

## REVOLUTION, THE SIXTIES AND THE CURRENT CRISIS

The two periods that saw the greatest changes in radio were the 1930s and the 1960s. We've already mentioned some of the social upheaval that made the earlier period significant, but in order to understand what happened to music in the latter period we have to look at what was happening in the world at that time. The Sixties, as they have come to be known, were a period of worldwide revolution. A great assault on Power, privilege, government and the injustice and suffering for which they were responsible was underway. From the Tet Offensive in Vietnam, to the anti-war and black liberation movements in the US, to the Paris uprising, to the Cultural Revolution in China, the world was in an uproar, all hell was breaking loose! Naturally, this was given expression in music, and soon after, on radio.

The impact on music was immense, lasting long after the revolution had subsided and "order" was being restored, continuing to this day. First of all, the "southernization" of American culture begun in the earlier period became the form of expression of youth revolt. Rock and roll and soul music completely transformed the musical landscape in the US, the UK and, increasingly, much of the rest of the world. Music that had been brought to the big city by southern blacks and whites in the form of blues, country and western, and gospel was now taken up by the children of those migrants and transformed into a new and explosive admixture that championed the rebellious spirit and visions of a better world brewing among them.

There is a direct, personal connection between the 1934 General Strike in San Francisco, the Free Speech Movement, the Black Panthers and the massive social protests against the Vietnam War that have come to signify both San Francisco and the Sixties, to the world. Direct, because the social life of a left-wing, labor-oriented public was firmly established by the victorious workers of 1934, continuing undeterred by McCarthyism and the Cold War up to the Sixties. Personal, because, many such as myself, who came of age and were swept up by the tumultuous Sixties were the children of those who had been the young soul rebels of the previous generation.

This book is not intended to be a personal account, but my own experience, in this case, is convincing evidence of these living connections. When I first went to a demonstration, it was because my stepfather, who was a longshoreman and had participated in the 1934 General Strike, woke me and my sister at four in the morning to bring us to the University of California campus where the Free Speech activists were occupying a building. To make such connections clearer, my stepfather intervened with the truck drivers who were trying to make deliveries to the University, talking to them as a union brother and convincing them to honor the picket line. They turned away that morning.

I first heard Steve Miller at an anti-war demonstration. I first heard Janis Joplin at my high school dance. I first heard the Grateful Dead and the Jefferson Airplane at the free concerts that took place weekly in the Panhandle of Golden Gate Park. I first saw Bill Graham in the Civic Center of San Francisco yelling at the cops who were trying to stop a performance by the Mime Troupe. When I first attended a rock concert it was at the Longshoreman's Hall, a year before the Fillmore opened to become the shrine of all that was new and liberating in music.

This is what made the "San Francisco sound" what it was. The wonderful talents of the musicians should never be underestimated; but it was into this social situation that they were born and their talents given purpose. It was for these audiences that they performed before and after becoming internationally acclaimed. Why would Creedence Clearwater Revival, the "pop" act par excellence, write songs such as "Fortunate Son" or "Effigy?" Why would Sly Stone write "Stand" or "Tower of Power" or "What is Hip?" The list is long and full of inspired musical moments that not only speak of the time in which they arose, but of another time in which their aspirations could be realized. This was the social mood. Sam

Cooke sang in the very early Sixties, "A Change Is Gonna Come." By 1968 it was happening!

In this milieu, FM radio developed. Musically, a spark had been lit by the Beatles and the British invasion. It had swept away an earlier glut of manufactured teeny stars such as Fabian, Bobby Vinton, Joey Dee and Annette Funicello, who were equivalent to the boy groups and pretty girls of today's vapid pop culture. But shortly after the musical spark had been ignited, social combustion began and blew away the pop pretenses of the British Invasion itself. The Beatles and the Stones had to follow the lead of the Summer of Love and the new world being envisioned in San Francisco. Their music and lyrics underwent major changes due to what was happening there and in the world at large. When one examines the quantity of great music made in this period one has to make the connection with the times in which it was made. It is impossible to evade the implications.

Before returning to the present, two important points need to be made regarding music and radio. First, musically, the revolution of the Sixties never really ended. No sooner had the great musicians of those days ceased to be in the forefront of youth rebellion than punk, reggae and ska broke out, reinvigorating popular culture and trying, as best they could, to rally the new youth to the banner of resistance. The Ramones, Sex Pistols and The Clash, The Specials, The Selecter and The English Beat, Bob Marley and The Wailers, Jimmy Cliff and, from Africa, Fela Kuti—these were among the prominent artists in the '70s and early '80s representing a renewed and renewing challenge to the status quo. In fact, the period of the '80s was the high point of both independent labels and college radio. In a new political climate created by Reagan and Thatcher's counterrevolutionary attack, musicians and radio developed a DIY strategy. Even though many of the artists mentioned above were actually on large independent labels or even majors, they nevertheless spawned an upsurge of indies that were characterized by a close connection to the audiences that bought their records and personal participation in the music scenes that were their business. At the same time, college radio expanded rapidly as a response to rejection by mainstream, corporate-dominated radio (which by this time had taken over KSAN and other pioneers of FM, "alternative" radio programming). Alternative Tentacles, owned and operated by Jello Biafra, lead singer of the Dead Kennedys, is a prime example of this trend.

Second, though much that is referred to above is English language and US or UK-based popular music, the global dimensions should not be overlooked. For one thing, the influence of many of the artists mentioned (and many others like them) extended to Latin America, Africa, eastern Europe and Asia, in turn inspiring musical expressions in the languages and musical forms of those regions. For another, the seeds sown by, and the social ramifications of, the DIY or anti-authoritarian spirit contributed greatly to diverse movements all over the world. The explosion of squatters movements throughout western Europe, the innumerable Centro Sociales in Italy are examples. But the influence was even more widespread when the indirect and intangible are considered. Thus the Zapatistas in Mexico, the Ya Basta group in Italy, the pro-democracy movement in China and many others can be seen in this light.

## WAR OF THE WORLD VIEWS: CLEAR CHANNEL VS. PIRATE RADIO

Closely interwoven as the music and telecommunications industries are, it is not surprising that the consolidation taking place in each is leading inexorably to the combination of all facets of mass communication into one, or a few, even larger and more diversified corporate entities. To increase profitability and purge the nonproductive remnants of the Sixties, companies like Clear Channel have emerged, buying up vast numbers of radio stations, firing staff and imposing programming rules that ensure the greatest exposure to the "stars" and "hits" that produce the greatest profit for their record company counterparts. There is both a practical and ideological component at work in this process. Practically, Clear Channel is eliminating competition and gaining complete dominance of what is broadcast. Ideologically, they are promoting the "free market" vision that hopes to turn everything in the world, but specifically everything in the public sphere, into private property. Thus their target is the entire concept of public ownership of the airwaves, and they lobby (read: "bribe") the necessary politicians to ensure that the FCC makes rulings favorable to their interests.

Opposed to this are two alternatives: public radio and pirate radio. In virtually every country in the world, including the US, some frequencies are reserved for public radio. Indeed, in some countries there is only public radio, which usually means that it is run by the State, not a private enterprise. While in itself a contentious battleground, public radio nevertheless represents the principle that there is a public sphere, which includes libraries, schools, museums, parks and lands, and a wide variety of scientific and artistic endeavors. This poses a direct and serious threat to Clear Channel and everything it represents.

Here are two antagonistic world views. Both mobilize music and musician to persuade the listener that "this is what's important to YOU!" It is abundantly clear that Clear Channel will use the power of money and the power of deceit—the proper name for Public Relations—to defeat its rival and gain control of the airwaves. While this battle rages and public radio and the public sphere fight for survival another kind of challenger has entered the field: pirate radio.

Pirate Radio is based on two simple facts: 1) radio broadcasting is cheap and easy and, 2) people love to do it and don't need to be paid to do it. A "pirate" radio station is an unlicensed, illegal station broadcasting in violation of the laws of the country it is located in. The name refers to the ships that floated powerful transmitters off the English Coast in the mid-sixties. And it didn't end there, as Alex Petridis, writing for *The Guardian*, discovered. "Ever since Simon Dee's first broadcast from the MV Caroline in 1964, pirate radio has played a crucial role in forming Britain's musical taste. Now the phenomenon is bigger than ever, the airwaves in the cities so crowded that the pirates are being pushed into the suburbs and the countryside." Petridis goes on to describe the process: "Stations rise and fall with dizzying frequency—the victims of internal feuding, a lack of suitable studio locations and raids by the DTI's Radiocommunications Agency—but there is always someone to replace them. So far this year, the RA has raided 179 pirate stations in London. Most went straight back on the air. As the RA dolefully admits: 'There's no easy victory or cure for pirate radio. You take them down, they put them up again. You can't be sure people won't re-offend. You're just dealing with a specific complaint at a specific time.'"[11]

This phenomenon is extremely widespread. Certainly, the potential exists for it anywhere in the world. There are several significant aspects to this. First, music plays an even greater role on much, if not all, pirate radio than any other format we've discussed, including commercial, public or college. Love of music is often the main motive for those undertaking the risk. Second, the commonality of interest between the pirates and the great majority of musicians who will never be "stars" or write "hits" is obvious; what greater symbiosis could there be between makers of music and broadcasters of music? Third, the challenge to capital is similar to the one posed by the internet and the free downloading of music, but with a twist: you don't even need "new" technology to do this. No land lines. No crashing software. No Microsoft or AT&T. Fourth, the basic community-forming functions that both music and radio can perform are localized and immediate. They represent the potential for actual, daily involvement in processes that are imaginative and expressive, by almost anyone with the desire to acquire the needed skills. The "stars" can have their "hits," but we have each other, and that's far more meaningful and fun than passively awaiting the next bombardment of bullshit from Big Media.

It should be mentioned that what happened to FM following its heyday happened to a lesser, but still significant extent, to college radio. DJs were courted by major labels, bribed with dinners, drugs, offers of jobs and other enticements. The "network" was systematized by CMJ and other journals and organizations connected to the music industry, making it one more channel for the promotional budgets spent creating "stars" and "hits." This does not mean that college radio is "dead" in the sense that FM certainly is. It remains non-commercial and continues to be an avenue for underground and non-mainstream artists to be heard. But by virtue of its control by educational institutions that have no inherent interest in either radio or music, it is subject to the twin influences of the corporate control of music and the corporate control of education, specifically the research departments at many universities now directly tied into large pharmaceutical companies or the Defense Department, to name only two examples. This does not mean it will disappear without a fight, however, and it will be very important how the War of the World Views unfolds in this specific area of mass communication.

In any case, the Clear Channels of the world do not have a "clear channel" in regards to the public, music makers and music lovers in particular. There has long been, and will continue to be, widespread opposition to their rapacious plunder of what "clearly" cannot belong to anyone. Furthermore, while they and the Big Five record companies conspire to produce "stars" and "hits" the vast majority of music makers pursue their craft, known only to those who share and enjoy the result. But this is a very large number of people. It may not constitute a market in the capitalist sense. But it is adequate to provide sustenance to those engaged in it. In fact, it always has, and nothing about the "New Economy" can change that.

If the moaning of industry representatives about the sorry state of their multi-billion dollar game has any basis in reality and is not merely a ploy to deceive, why are they still in it? If they are not lying about the threat to a business that has been so lucrative, they should be motivated to ask basic questions about why they are killing the goose that laid the golden egg. In other words, the constant repetition of the same relatively small number of songs by manufactured artists that require an enormous investment to market begins to bore, particularly since you frequently hear the same songs played all the time in supermarkets, shopping malls, football games, etc., as well as on the radio. A limit is being approached, where it is conceivable that the average person might think, "I hear this damn song all the time, why should I pay to hear it again!?" This is a conundrum analogous to an industry set up to market the color green. The color green is everywhere. How can you convince people to buy something they see all the time, wherever they look? When goods or services can be made so cheaply and in such abundance, yet require massive infusions of capital in order to sell, the irrationality, even from a business perspective, presents itself full force. Advertising, promotion, hype, is effective. Precisely because it is effective it is necessary, and more and more so. Demand increases for the product that advertising itself has become. The escalation of promotional costs creates an absurd situation in which the product, music, is worth far less than the value of its promotion. Although enormous profits still fill the coffers of the major labels, the system they are running is unsustainable. It must crash.

## TURN OFF, TUNE OUT, DROP IN

Short of another social revolution like the Sixties, a radical transformation of telecommunications is unlikely. The internet is not going to bring this about any more than television or radio did. Though there are wonderful benefits the internet offers, like all technology, it is only capable of doing what people, collectively, do with it. I have chosen not to address the internet in this context, because for music it is essentially redundant. In spite of the claims of its gaga-eyed gurus, it has had no impact on music making and is unlikely to any time soon. It is a vital tool in the hands of political organizers, and for private and professional communication. It can be a very useful means of doing research. But a TV combined with a telephone combined with a typewriter do not a revolution make. Commitment, sacrifice, struggle and wisdom under specific historical conditions might, but not technology.

And, kids, download to your hearts' content. If you dig the music, though, please show some love and respect for the artists who made it. Find a way to support them. Make a donation, go to a show, buy a CD, write an email. Do something. But, otherwise, have a great time! Music will always be there for you, if you're there for music.

As far as radio goes, turn off the mainstream stations, tune out the mindless drivel, drop in to a friend's house or a local concert or a music store selling vinyl. Start finding music you really love, and stop listening to music you don't have to feel. If it doesn't move you, if it doesn't stir your emotions or your thoughts, don't listen to it. There is still much to be enjoyed about radio itself. There is much to be discovered in the turbulent eddies of the air. But as with music, you have to invest some time and energy in finding what is truly meaningful and most importantly, can be shared with your own community of family, friends and fellow workers.

# FOOTNOTES

1    Three thinkers exemplify this: Ludwig Wittgenstein, Martin Heidegger and Marshall Mcluhan. Each in his own way expressed dismay at the failure of Reason to fulfill the Enlightenment's promise of delivering humanity from war, pestilence, famine and ignorance. Philosophy was no match for religion or irrational prejudice and the natural sciences were, in the end, only capable of making technology. Faced with World Wars, the atomic bomb and Nazi death camps, on the one hand, and radio, television, advertising and propaganda on the other they developed an almost mystical fixation on the machine as maker of man. Or, put another way, we are dominated by the very tools we developed to give us dominance over nature. Combined with the use of the social sciences for devising means of molding popular consciousness, we have the recipe for disaster from which there may be no escape.

More specifically, Wittgenstein, who concluded his famous *Tractatus Logico-Philosophicus* with the words: "What we cannot speak about we must pass over in silence," denied the possibility of truth as a category of thought. Accordingly, the only course open to philosophical inquiry is language. Talking about talk. His enduring influence is in Logical Positivism such as that expressed by Stephen Hawking (*A Brief History of Time, The Universe in a Nutshell*) Hawking, in turn, is a veritable cavalier in the crusade against truth as a category of thought. All we can possess is information or knowledge. Wisdom is doubtful as a proposition worthy of pursuit by science. Moralists or the religious can offer opinion inviting our faith but can make no claims to verifiable truth.

Heidegger's ontology—the study of being—was represented in his book *Being and Time* (Sein und Zeit, 1927). This had enormous influence on existentialism as a movement and many subsequent philosophers, including Jean-Paul Sartre and Hannah Arendt. He was awed by technology and focused on the compression of time and distance brought about by telecommunications and high speed travel. He looked to the poet with nostalgic longing. Perhaps, he ventured, it is through the poetic that we can return to authentic being. This tension between the technologic and the artistic took on a spectral aura that continues to haunt academia and much popular discourse.

Marshall Mcluhan coined the phrase, "the medium is the message." He argued that it was not the content or ideas expressed in a radio or television program, but the mechanisms of transmission that mattered most. Just as our use of language was shaped by its written form and our minds limited by the book as medium, we were being molded by the new electronic media of radio and television. There were grave threats and bold promises here. If we understood these hidden effects we might really change the world. We could only superficially alter it, however, if we remained bound by forces of which we were unaware. Published shortly before the Sixties really exploded, these ideas gained mass popularity while riding the crest of a great unshackling going on throughout society. *The Age of Aquarius, The Electric Kool-aid Acid Test*, consciousness expanding intergalactic psychic transmission—all were of a piece during a time of literally world-wide revolt against everything that was old and in the way. While much of this may seem corny and dated today, "the medium is the message" and Mcluhan's near-divinity as a prophet of a new world, deserve closer examination, since they continue to influence important issues facing music and radio—both as mediums themselves, and the uses to which they are put.

Today, such thinking is pervasive even as many people are unaware of its sources. Indeed, most of the last half of the 20th century was marked by a morbid fascination with endings—death of God, death of philosophy, death of Man, etc. All anyone wants to talk about, it seems, is the finite, the limited and the dead. This, in opposition to the infinite, the universal and the unpredictable.

What utterly demolished this dismal view was People's War, exemplified by the Vietnamese and the famous Black Panther slogan supporting that struggle: "The spirit of the people is greater than the man's technology."

2    "There is no such thing as society. There are individual men and women, and there are families."—Margaret Thatcher to *Woman's Own* magazine, published on October 31, 1987.

3    It is significant that the career of Edward Bernays, the "Father of Public Relations," coincides with the rise of broadcasting. It was Bernays, after all, who in his book *Propaganda* espoused the techniques for the manipulation of the popular will. These techniques require the deception of the public. In other words, Public Relations cannot be effective if the public is aware of what is happening. Bernays' career is worth a closer look.  Stuart Ewen, a professor of media studies at Hunter College in New York and author of a number of books on the media and public relations, most notably *PR: A Social History of Spin,* had this to say: "Bernays was this guy who introduced mass psychology to the standard practice of PR. Bernays takes Lippman's theory of public opinion and puts it into practice to sell soap, bacon, cigarettes, all kinds of things. He was the double nephew of Freud. His mother was Freud's sister. His father was Freud's wife's brother. So this is a guy who was born in Vienna, who came to the U.S. early on in this century. Literally the unconscious is like dinner conversation at the Bernays's household. One of the most famous of his promotions is when he went to work for the American Tobacco Company. One of the problems at the time was that women were not smoking enough in public. Why? You have to realize that this is a period of time when the health problems surrounding tobacco were considered relatively minuscule and where even doctors are giving testimonials in cigarette advertisements and women are being encouraged to reach for a Lucky Strike instead of a sweet, that this is a good diet aid. But still, there is this idea that a cigarette, this kind of miniature phallic symbol, is a symbol of masculine rights, precisely because men can smoke in public and women can't. So he goes to a group of feminists—his wife, Doris Fleishman, was a feminist and very actively involved in these issues and pushed him in many of his campaigns. He goes to this group of former suffragettes and convinces them that they should have a march down Fifth Avenue carrying cigarettes in the air as torches of freedom. So he takes the symbol of masculine power, puts it in the hands of women, has them march, and all of a sudden the cigarette is not about tobacco, not about taste, not about smoke, it's about freedom."
Interview with David Barsamian in *Z Magazine.*

It is also worthy of note that *Propaganda* was addressed to the captains of industry who, according to Bernays, are the real Power in a democratic society. It should be no surprise that the Nazis came to power by, among other means, applying the techniques Bernays proposed concentrating specifically on radio transmission.

4    Denning, Michael. *The Cultural Front.* Verso Books, 1997, p. 382.

5    Morrison, James. "Pop charts dominated by 'junk', study says." *The Independent.* October 13, 2002.

6    If you have internet access, you can visit the IFPI website for all the material quoted in this book. The IFPI is a bit more sophisticated than the RIAA in the presentation of its arguments. Also, it provides an international perspective whereas the RIAA is almost totally focused on the USA. http://www.ifpi.org/
http://serious.manicnirvana.com/articles/2002/0002misc/060602guardonline.html

7    Copeland, Miles. "Are Record Labels Greedy?" http://www.riaa.com/news/guest-columns/milescopeland.asp

8     Marx, Karl. "Travail productif et travail unproductif." *Materiaux pour l'economie.* Gallimard, p. 393.

9     Marx, Karl. *Theories of Surplus Value.* Foreign Languages Publishing House, 1963, p. 394–395.

10   Copeland, Miles. "Are Record Labels Greedy?" http://www.musicconnection.com

11   Petridis, Alexis. "Hold tight the massive." *The Guardian.* November 22, 2002.

# THE MIDDLE
## OF THE BODY

MUSIC, DANCE
AND FESTIVAL

Music originates in the body. The beating of the heart, the tempo of breathing, the rhythm of a steady gait extend outward on reverberating waves of sound, generated, first and foremost by the voice, the hands and the feet. Singing, clapping, stamping. This intimate physicality connects music directly to dance and these two are forever woven together in an undulating, pulsing thread running through all that each does separately. It is an interdependence of possibility as dance and music continually refer to each other for motive force and actual realization. This is not, in the first instance, a matter of performance, the separation of the social body into two parts performer and audience. It is instead in the festival where all participate in singing and dancing that music and dance first manifest their rejuvenating potency. In considering all the dimensions of the question of music and society, one is constantly drawn back to this ground, this earth, upon which all else is constructed. What music proclaims and calls forth is the potential for another, better world. Its effect is to transport from this place to another place without physically leaving this place, and it achieves this first and foremost by uniting and inspiring the dancing multitude, transforming it into a collective body.

This takes place at the Feast. It is full of laughter and the particular, grotesque humor that characterizes the popular. It is the uncrowning of kings and the crowning of fools. It is the elevation of the lower body above the upper. The mockery of propriety and seriousness by public display of the actual site of birth and death, of fornication and defecation: the genitals and the bowels. Fucking and shitting. The judgment of the laughing people is to bring down the high and mighty and replace them with the grotesquely exaggerated prick, twat and asshole! Pomp and pageantry express the solemnity of Power and privilege. Licentious song, bawdy dance and ribald laughter explode such pretensions and expose them to the body that is the origin of all humanity and to which all must return.

This is the meaning of carnival. It was eloquently celebrated in the work of Francoise Rabelais, later discovered and analyzed by Mikhail Bakhtin. Bakhtin showed that the roots of Rabelais' work lay in the popular culture and grotesque humor of his time and place: France of the late 15th and early 16th centuries. The significance of this for an understanding of music and dance, not to mention society as a whole, cannot be over-stated. That Bakhtin's book was written in Russia in 1930 but not published there until 1965, says a great deal about the controversial nature of its contents, its latent threat to any authority. That it remains largely unknown except in certain academic circles is a problem I hope to contribute to remedying. Our focus here continues to be music. But while music creates a context by its performance, it nonetheless takes place within a larger, social one and invariably plays its role by way of interaction with all the forces contending for dominance within society. In this regard, Bakhtin's exposition of Rabelais sheds a great deal of light on a situation, the world of carnival, wherein music plays its vital role to the fullest, charging and being recharged by the dancing body. Energizing and galvanizing the wild abandon that is both cause and effect of the body being freed, through rhythmic movement, to join other bodies in a public display of the social body.

What is important to keep in mind are the essential components of carnival as identified by Bakhtin. The Feast. Laughter. The Body—particularly the genitals and bowels. These are not static categories but exist in continuous, vigorous movement of lower to higher and vice versa. There is an overturning taking place. Bakhtin puts it this way: "This travesty of one of the basic teachings of Christianity is, however, far removed from cynical nihilism. The material bodily lower stratum is productive. It gives birth, thus assuring mankind's immortality. All obsolete and vain illusions die in it, and the real future comes to life."[1] We will return to this point throughout the remainder of this chapter.

For music makers today, these issues present enormous challenges while offering imaginative possibilities too long ignored or pushed to the margins where they can be rendered curiosities having little social effect. Why is this so? Everywhere we turn we are invited to "Party," to "Have A Good Time." There are raves and techno parties virtually every night in every city in the world. There are '70s, '80s, and now '90s, revival nights where the disco, soul, r+b, funk, dancehall, reggae, African, calypso or other genres of music are played. There are cover bands on all continents playing the great dance hits of whatever generation or genre one might wish. There are huge festivals and Love Parades that happen with seasonal regularity attracting enormous crowds of revelers. In fact, in Basel and other Swiss cities, in New Orleans, in Brazil and Trinidad, carnival itself, continues as a tradition, thriving unabated down the centuries. (This, incidentally being the one carnival, there were many in the middle ages, that as Bakhtin explains, "did not coincide with any commemoration of sacred history or of a saint but marked the last days before Lent, and for this reason was called Mardi Gras or Carême-Prenant in France and Fastnacht in Germany" and Switzerland).[2] It might appear that Rabelais' vision has finally triumphed in the flowering of democracy and the vast expansion, even the privileging of celebration and festival.

Yet, it is my contention that there is, amidst this nearly continuous partying, a multiple displacement going on that removes the Feast, the laughing people, the body and the fundamental role of music to a shadowy underworld, visited occasionally by anthropologists and tourists, but imprisoned and rendered impotent in isolation. It is my further contention that this has been going on for centuries and continues to this day. It is part of an endless effort to control the popular will that always immanently threatens Power. It has met much resistance, each successive effort to channel the carnival spirit into "safe" expression being faced with popular opposition, culminating in the most recent example of the return of the "world of carnival" in the Sixties. Subsequently, the removal was begun again with a vengeance.

## THE CARNIVALESQUE IN CONTEMPORARY CULTURE

Exemplary of the carnivalesque in contemporary popular culture is the work of George Clinton and the bands he led—Parliament and Funkadelic. In an album released in 1977, *Funkentelechy vs. the Placebo Syndrome*, all of the elements of Rabelaisian carnival are on display. An entire cast of characters, masked and grotesque, is created to play their roles in a festive mocking of both the "unfunky enemy" (Sir Nose D'Voidoffunk) and the fake or inauthentic (The Placebo Syndrome). Jocular reference to bodily functions and the use of goofy parodical sounds in the music itself evoke great hilarity. The entire operation is driven by a propulsive rhythm that is deceptively complex and sophisticated on one level while being simply irresistible on another. Dense with counterpoint and lyrical asides, the music creates a great, roiling, harmonious cacophony that is determined in its irreverence, cosmic in its silliness and profound in its playful exuberance. There is everything and nothing political about it. It certainly does not take itself seriously.

This album was released at the high point of the popularity of funk. It followed several earlier albums by Clinton and his large ensemble of musicians (sometimes numbering as many as fifty). These were, in turn, directly descended from the lineage of James Brown, Sly Stone, The Meters and War—all artists that shared elements of the carnivalesque approach. Clinton's work, which continues to this day, was always the most consciously and fully realized in this regard. It expresses more explicitly than most the mockery of the high and mighty—the crowning of the fool and the uncrowning of the king—that is at carnival's heart. The name Parliament stands as the perfect high/low reversal. When this motley assemblage of mutants and weirdos (and black ones at that) gets to be the actual, governing parliament, the world will truly be turned upside down!

The characteristics described above are shared in different ways by all kinds of popular music that might be broadly named rock and roll. In fact, the spirit of wild abandon called forth by the music and assembled in mass gatherings of hippies, freaks, political radicals, poets, artists, jugglers and magicians are emblematic of the entire period from the mid-Sixties until the mid-Eighties of the last century. Even as its social base shrunk and its breadth of influence was circumscribed, the spirit was carried on by artists such as Clinton, The Grateful Dead, Frank Zappa and others. Certainly, it is alive and well in many quarters to this day. The point here is not to say that what is authentically carnival is dead. Far from it. The point is, rather, to identify and defend the timeless qualities that have been represented in specific ways in our own time and put them to use in combating the Placebo Syndrome and its agent, Sir Nose D'Voidoffunk.

Compare the music described above with all the deeply serious "partying" going on today and one begins to see core differences. But before we examine these differences, we need to clarify Bakhtin's use of the word "ambivalence," since it is central to his analysis. "All these ambivalent images are dual-bodied, dual-faced, pregnant. They combine in various proportions negation and affirmation, the top and the bottom, abuse and praise." To illustrate this he quotes a scene from Rabelais' *Gargantua and Pantagruel*, in which Gargantua's wife dies as their son is born. "In this situation," Bakhtin writes,

> Gargantua suffers great embarrassment: "A terrible doubt racked his brain: should he weep over the death of his wife or rejoice over the birth of his son?" And so he cries "like a cow," but then, thinking of Pantagruel, exclaims: "Ho, ho ho ho, how happy I am! Let us drink, ho! and put away our melancholy! Bring out the best wine, rinse the glasses, lay the table, drive out those dogs, poke up the fire, light the candles, close that door there, cut the bread in sippets for our pottage, send away these beggar folk but give them anything they ask for! You, there, hold my gown! I shall strip to my doublet to entertain the gossips better."
>
> As he said this, he heard the priests chanting litanies and mementos as they bore his wife off to burial.[3]

This ambivalence is also expressed in the mask. Bakhtin says, the theme of the mask [is] the most complex theme of folk culture. The mask is connected with the joy of change and reincarnation, with gay relativity and with the merry negation of uniformity and similarity; it rejects conformity to oneself. The mask is related to transition, metamorphoses, the violation of natural boundaries, to mockery and familiar nicknames. It contains the playful element of life; it is based on a peculiar interrelation of reality and image, characteristic of the most ancient rituals and spectacles. Of course it would be impossible to exhaust the intricate multiform symbolism of the mask. Let us point out that such manifestations as parodies, caricatures, grimaces, eccentric postures, and comic gestures are per se derived from the mask. It reveals the essence of the grotesque.[4]

In broader social terms, the ambivalent mask can't be "captured" for political use by left or right. An example: the album cover for Funkadelic's *Uncle Jam Wants You* shows a photograph of George Clinton sitting in an oversized rattan chair exactly like the one Huey Newton sat in for a world famous photo a few years earlier. The original Huey Newton photo was serious revolutionary imagery designed to visually recall the lofty goals of the Black Panther Party. Was Clinton parodying Newton? Was he making fun of an icon of the Black Liberation struggle? This is ambivalence thrusting in several directions at once.

The response of Stalin to Bakhtin's work was to quash it with as little fanfare as possible. Bakhtin was arrested, sent to teach in a small town in Kazakstan and his writings were ignored. Since his work concerned popular culture and was not overtly anti-Party, it was best to just sweep it under the rug. Where the Nazis and other Inquisitors would smash and ban, liberals and leftists have tended to form "alliances" with the "world of carnival," feeling an uneasiness with the laughter that might just be directed at them, but not being able to oppose it since it is quintessentially popular.[5]

The Funkadelic album was subtitled "Rescue Dance Music From the Blahs," recognizing, even in 1979, the displacement already under way. The whole album was an hilarious parody of disco. The album title's play on official US recruiting posters perfectly represents Bakhtin's meaning of ambivalence.

We must turn now to an examination of the constituent parts of Bakhtin's analysis so we can better grasp what are the key ways the "world of carnival" is being displaced and how to use it anew.

## THE FEAST

Today the Feast has been displaced by the spectacle. Usually held outside the city center in sports stadiums, open fields, or large halls suitable for their staging, such events have nothing whatsoever to do with the Feast. The true Feast took place within the town or city, in its marketplace or social center, displacing normal everyday life and overwhelming the routine, mundane functioning of society. This still happens in those places where the carnival tradition remains strong. But rock or other music festivals bear no resemblance to them, nor even to the great disorderly festivals of the Sixties that are their progenitors. The rave movement attempts to resurrect key elements of the Feast, occasionally succeeding, but is ultimately incapable of doing so, in part because of the temporary and transitory nature of such events themselves. In contrast, the Feast requires a connection to a historic marker, a time from which the timeless erupts. All great medieval Feasts corresponded either to astronomically measured, seasonal events or those designated by the Church or local custom. To quote Bakhtin:

> Besides carnivals proper, with their long and complex pageants and processions, there was the "Feast of Fools" and the "Feast of the Ass"; there was a special free "Easter laughter" (risus paschalis), consecrated by tradition. Moreover, nearly every Church feast had its comic folk aspect, which was also traditionally recognized. Such, for instance, were the parish feasts, usually marked by fairs and varied open-air amusements, with the participation of giants, dwarfs, monsters, and trained animals. A carnival atmosphere reigned on days when mysteries and soties (foolish plays) were produced. This atmosphere also pervaded such agricultural feasts as the harvesting of grapes (vendange) which was celebrated also in the city. Minor occasions were also marked by comic protocol, as for instance the election of a king and queen to preside at a banquet "for laughter's sake."[6]

The modern festival is disconnected from history, astronomy, the bounties of the earth or the celebration of tradition. It is a baldly commercial affair which might, at times, present great music and even be a lot of fun, but it cannot be a Feast.

Special mention needs to be made of the role of dance in all such Feasts. In stark contrast to the formless dancing of the present music festival or party where every individual moves in their own untrained way, the Feast, and the music performed there, was powerfully marked by dances. There were actual learned movements that, while very simple, were shared and performed collectively. Vestiges of this practice exist in numerous cultures the world over. But in mass, popular culture they have largely disappeared. Such movement is confined to the music video or the concert stage where trained professionals exhibit gymnastic, coordinated movements to awe and render motionless the onlooker. This has displaced the collective, shared activity and removed it to the dancing school or ethnic preserve, where it can be a tourist attraction and no more.

Last but not least is the importance of play. Among the most stark reminders of how things have changed is the absence of play in today's giant music festivals, rock concerts or dance parties. Games of chance with their prophetic and prognostic attributes, dice and cards being the prime examples, have traditionally played a large part in feasting. They are closely related to the role-play and transfiguration of the mask, visible manifestations of the Feast's general atmosphere of playfulness. One might say that today's great spectacles seriously lack an essential lack of seriousness!

"Carnival," says Bakhtin,

> is not a spectacle seen by the people; they live in it, and everyone participates because its very idea embraces all the people. While carnival lasts, there is no other life outside it. During carnival time life is subject only to its laws, that is, the laws of its own freedom. It has a universal spirit; it is a special condition of the entire world, of the world's revival and renewal, in which all take part.[7]

## LAUGHTER

There is a specific form of festive laughter within the general category of Laughter. Laughter is ancient and universal. Not only do all people laugh, but the causes and effects of laughter have been the subject of great controversy and deep study for thousands of years. It has been forbidden and punished by priests and potentates while simultaneously celebrated by their opponents among philosophers, scientists and artists. It has been forced, rhetorically and practically, into the lowest realms of the hierarchy of human activity, and it has been elevated to the loftiest heights in the pantheon of human aspiration. "Early Christianity," writes Bakhtin, "had already condemned laughter. Tertullian, Cyprian, and John Chrysostom preached against ancient spectacles, especially against the mime and mime's jests and laughter. John Chrysostom declared that jests and laughter are not from God, but from the devil. Only permanent seriousness, remorse, and sorrow for his sins befit the Christian."[8] Conversely, certainly in part due to the impossibility of stamping it out, the Church permitted laughter in its proper place.

> During the Easter season laughter and jokes were permitted even in church. The priest could tell amusing stories and jokes from the pulpit. Following the days of Lenten sadness he could incite his congregation's gay laughter as a joyous regeneration. This is why it was called "Easter laughter." The jokes and stories concerned especially material bodily life, and were of a carnival

type. Permission to laugh was granted simultaneously with the permission to eat meat and to resume sexual intercourse (forbidden during Lent).[9]

By the time Rabelais began writing, during the Renaissance, the popular humor of preceding centuries was bursting out of the official bounds set upon it and being recognized by scholars and writers for the vital and subversive force it surely is. This got Rabelais himself into difficulties. The Sorbonne declared his works obscene. Clearly, his immediate and widespread popularity demonstrated not only his genius but the chord he'd struck among the people. What Rabelais grasped was the power of laughter in general and in a particular form arising from folk culture of great antiquity. This Bakhtin describes as grotesque realism. It is always festive and all Feasts, in order to be Feasts, must give free reign to its expression.

Everyone tells dirty jokes that are "dirty" precisely because of their reference to fornication and defecation, the genitals and the bowels. If we are embarrassed by them, we become their object. If, rather, we recognize in them their wisdom and universality then we join the festivity. Indeed, folk humor the world over is characterized by such reference to the material bodily functions. Being "earthy" or "down to earth" not only describes a quality of a person, but a process of making earthy or bringing down to earth, which is accomplished by situating life in these zones of the body and with devastating effect, by mockery and ridicule of the sanctimonious. The grotesque aspect is important in its exaggeration of size, potency and cosmic significance. "This exaggeration," says Bakhtin, "has a positive, assertive character. The leading themes of these images of bodily life are fertility, growth and a brimming-over abundance. Manifestations of this life refer not to the isolated biological individual, not to the private, egotistic 'economic man,' but to the collective ancestral body of all the people."[10] Examples of this abound in the works of Rabelais and Clinton. Indeed, it is what defines them and sets them apart from many of their contemporaries, yet connects them to a deep reservoir of understanding among the mass of humanity.

This can be contrasted to other kinds of humor that are either of a purely negative character or do not contain the grotesque. Such are irony and sarcasm, often used in rhetorical fashion to demolish a political opponent or reduce an enemy to powerlessness. In many cases this type of humor displays the wit or erudition of the individual telling the joke, making the rejoinder, or arguing the case, but does not include the audience except as spectators. Unlike festive laughter, such "putting down" is not ambivalent. It intends to keep down what it has put there. It is not regenerative. It can be directed at an ethnic or religious group, women, homosexuals, indeed any other who is thus not included in the immortal Body (the human community celebrated by the Feast). The result may be funny, at least to some, but missing are the elements essential to grotesque realism and festive laughter.

Actual meanness or humiliation, which is a form of exclusion, does not exist in festive laughter. It can appear, but it will always be a mask in a complex relationship between appearances and reality within the context of play. Even the most debasing, abusive statements made in the carnival style are meant to include the butt of the joke, to draw into the community, by leveling all. In contrast, cruel jokes, made to single out an individual or group and make them ashamed or to lower them beneath the one making the joke are not found in the laughter of the Feast.

Outright, side-splitting hilarity is rarely the product of the ironic or sarcastic. This is, on the other hand, an essential effect that must be produced by grotesque realism or it simply isn't funny at all. This contrasts heavily with the snicker or the chuckle—the response elicited by other kinds of humor. The nudge-nudge, wink-wink, unless grossly exaggerated and parodied, is always an "inside" joke.

There is a strong tragic character in much humor, as opposed to the entirely comic character of the grotesquely realistic. A good deal of what is shown on TV, on situation comedy and game shows, is of this type. People laugh at their own frailties and shortcomings, or at their blunders and *faux pas*, but nowhere is there a sense of being rejuvenated and revitalized by the truths revealed in laughter. Rather, there is a resignation in the face of the fundamentally selfish, egocentric, acquisitive and ultimately destructive character of human beings (which implicitly justifies the police). This is the opposite of what the humor of the Feast is all about. The entire purpose of its wild destructiveness and abusive gaiety is to degrade in order to rejuvenate. It brings the great head down to the level of the lowly genitals and bowels precisely to remind that it is from the genitals that life springs eternally, and from the bowels death is expunged to return to earth, further rejuvenating life.

It is the uncrowning of kings and the crowning of fools, the overturning of the entire social hierarchy that is crucial to festive laughter. That it originates in a rigidly hierarchical society is obvious. That it continues to resonate to this day reflects the fact that, even in our supposedly classless, democratic present such hierarchies remain. It is not accidental that in modern, liberal societies, the Feast, laughter and the body, in their grotesque realistic expression, are most vitally manifest in the cultures of the descendants of African slaves. In their struggle against the rigid stratification slavery imposed, they adopted and modified carnival itself. The festive laughter of grotesque realism speaks volumes about their common ancestry, history and struggle for liberation. This is the vital link between Francois Rabelais and George Clinton. It is the reason that "nigger music" was violently suppressed and kept away from white people in the United States. It is also the reason that, when it could be contained no longer, it had the enormous, unleashing effect that we name rock and roll and all that followed. Keith Richards of the Rolling Stones once commented that the fall of the Berlin Wall and the collapse of the Soviet Union was as much a result of the influence of rock and roll as it was of any overtly political act. While this may appear to be an oversimplification, it points out an important absence in much "serious" discussion of society and history. It identifies the threat to authority that is posed by the Feast of the Laughing People and the celebration of the material body. This laughter topples tyrants.

It must be noted that outside of comedy or children's shows there is little laughter in music today. It's difficult to imagine a song like Big Joe Turner's "Shake, Rattle and Roll" being popular now. Its famous line, "I'm like a one eyed cat peeping in a seafood store," with its humorously veiled sexual reference, was characteristic of an entire genre of music. The same is true of Fats Waller's, "I Want Some Seafood, Mama." Waller's humor, in fact, was particularly carnivalesque in its employment of the grotesque or exaggerated. "Your Feet's Too Big," containing the line, "Your pedal extremities are colossal," could have been lifted directly out of a novel by Rabelais.

In fact, the vast reservoir of popular humor found in much blues, jazz, and the forms they spawned has largely disappeared, to be replaced by sadness, anger, threatening postures or sentimentality. The closest most current popular music gets to anything remotely humorous is the carefree or "I just wanna have fun" attitude. But this is not funny at all. Indeed, it is inadvertently sad since it begs the question, "Why don't you, then?" George Clinton released an album not long ago called, *Hey Man, Smell My Finger* which, in the title alone, hearkens back to the kind of bawdy reference he's famous for and that was once common. There are numerous others in various styles of popular culture that include the festive and comedic in their work. Most of this is still located within the African-American musical tradition and even there, it has been displaced by the angry, the unambivalently abusive, self-loathing and destructive. Bakhtin's summary comments are worth quoting at length, both for what they say and for how, in contrast, things sit today.

Besides universalism and freedom, the third important trait of laughter was its relation to the people's unofficial truth. The serious aspects of class culture are official and authoritarian: they are combined with violence, prohibitions, limitations and always contain an element of fear and of intimidation. These elements prevailed in the Middle Ages. Laughter, on the contrary, overcomes fear, for it knows no inhibitions, no limitations. Its idiom is never used by violence and authority.[11]

## THE BODY

The material bodily function we have been discussing includes, but is not limited to, sex and sexuality. Furthermore, in its comic aspect, sex is sweaty, stinky, energetic and noisy. In a word, it's funky. The bodies involved are never the forms idealized by romantic or idyllic imagination. Corpulence is symbolic of abundance and is displayed abundantly in carnivalesque representations of the body. Gargantuan buttocks and pendulous breasts are fecundity itself. Genitalia are extended and engorged, representative of the bursting forth of life. This starkly contrasts with virtually all images of the body on display anywhere in the world today. Certainly, the ideal is completely different. And it is completely devoid of the comic aspect. The sex is pristine, romantic, lovely, hot (but not sweaty), never a hair out of place, smooth and graceful and above all, totally infertile.

Sex and the body are now separated from both defecation and rebirth. The pregnant body of a woman is never sexualized. The female sexual body, conversely, is firm and hard, lithe and smooth, protuberance of breasts and buttocks geometrically symmetrical to the head, waist and legs. It produces nothing either of life or of death. It is a great fornication machine.

It needs to be said here that what may appear to be gross generalizations are nothing of the sort. What we are calling attention to are qualities and characteristics of polarized and conflicting expressions broadly deployed in the world. Good and bad do not apply in a moralistic sense. Further, it must be kept in mind that at no time in history was the "world of carnival" dominant in the world at large. Always it has been an eruption—some would call it a festering boil!—in the larger, officially sanctioned world. But it is precisely in examining the body that we see the sharply contrasting views of what is real. In the idealized image of the beautiful sexually-arousing body omnipresent today, we see something totally unreal even when it is a photograph of an actual person (called, interestingly enough, a "model"). Conversely, the grandiose, exaggerated, frequently masked and fantastically costumed body of carnival is actually reality presented through its comic aspect. It is in this sense productive of truths about social life, whereas its "official," sanctioned opposite is a producer of lies.

Leaving aside all the broader social implications, this manipulation of images has negative consequences for music, and specifically for the festive component we are discussing here. Obviously music and musician suffer directly when a requirement for recognition is a pretty face or athletic build. Many of the best composers and performers the world has known were not handsome or beautiful. By today's twisted logic, they wouldn't look good on TV, so forget them. Even more significant is the fact that mass confusion over sex and sexuality has led to the vast proliferation of songs about loveless sex or sexless love. The splitting apart of the material body into discreet compartments that can be itemized and correlated with specific musical genres, age-groups and product lines impoverishes music by making it serve banality, perpetuating a phobia of real life. Music is being forced into the role of sex stimulant, a sort of sonic Viagra, its beat constant and relentless, its volume loud and overwhelming, its emotional content nonexistent and its particularity indistinguishable. It is elevator music for mating rituals conducted in the public/private anonymity of the modern disco or dance club, all following rigid schedules predetermined by the working week and the quantity of drugs available. There is no joy here. There is no comedy. The musicians involved are literally industrial workers producing endless copies of the same thing. There are aficionados who will say otherwise, pointing to all the styles and subgenres that proliferate like fungi in a sport shoe. But after a generation has passed, a lot less people are being fooled by it. The polarizations are intensifying and rebellion is, again, stirring amongst the rabble.

This is where the material bodily function of a fart can actually clear the air! The utter seriousness of this contrived, narcissistic beauty contest begs for comic relief. At its core is vanity, and vanity was always one of the principal targets of the Laughter of the Festive Body. Everyone knows that real sex is a somewhat messy affair of bodily fluids and peculiar odors, that people shit, piss and fart from the same regions that they lick and suck. This knowledge is hidden by the world of vanity, and celebrated by the world of carnival. The ambivalence of festive laughter decisively separates it from locker room or frat-boy humor in a profound way: the frat-boy sneers and degrades in a transference of sex and conquest, intimacy and control and only in a cowardly way, surrounded by like minded "buddies." Carnival celebrates openly and inclusively, defiantly puncturing pretensions of solemnity in a public way, and everyone is included. It denigrates and mocks, not the bodily functions by which it is never embarrassed, but the official hiding of them behind a veil of sham innocence and moral purity.

This has long been a powerful feature of black secular music and was savagely repressed by the white man. It was always confused in the warped mind of the racist with the wanton sexuality they attributed to the nigger/half-man, who was the invention of their own, slavemaster imaginations. This has never only been about economics, the music industry, corporate media or, even, the white man in the White House. What always tormented the tormentor was the celebration of the life-giving processes of the human body itself in its contradictory multiplicity, as a sexual dyad of man and woman, or copulating pair. The political explosions of the Sixties would never have been possible without this carnivalesque component that in a very real sense prepared the ground. In fact, the George Wallaces, the Strom Thurmonds and all their hooded pals were right. "If white kids are exposed to nigger music, we're lost!" This is again what connects Rabelais to George Clinton. Rabelais was an erudite intellectual who knew exactly what he was doing in a tumultuous time. Clinton is similar in that he profoundly understands what is happening in his historic time, and his talents, like those of Rabelais, have been deployed in a most subversive enterprise. The two are connected in a timeless celebration of the Feast, Laughter and the Body.

The Village People provide another example. At the same time that Clinton's *Funkentelchy* was released, and on the same label, Casablanca, this group was assembled to take advantage of (read: Exploit) the burgeoning gay music market. It was a calculated move that one might expect to be totally devoid of genuine musical or social attributes (D'Voidoffunk, as George Clinton would say). Due to fortuitous circumstances, something emerged that quintessentially captured both the carnivalesque spirit and the imaginations of millions world wide. A racially mixed group costumed to play stereotypical roles in gay fantasy of sexual attractiveness (cop, construction worker, biker, cowboy stud, etc.), the Village People had three big hits, "Macho Man," "YMCA" and "In the Navy." These were parodic in the extreme. Getting the US navy to allow them to film a video aboard an actual warship was the ultimate coup. This was masking, mocking and partying all in one! Every lyric contains double entendre. It can be read as perfectly innocent, inoffensive pabulum but interpreted through the lens of gay experience, it is all about celebrating the sexual, desire and the material body.

## THE PLACEBO SYNDROME VS. FUNKENTELECHY

It is evident that, today, The Placebo Syndrome has temporarily gained the upper hand over the Funkentelechy. Not only has the fake, inauthentic, unfunky, been substituted for the genuine, but a brutal reassertion of fear-based propriety has invaded the "world of carnival" and placed security guards at the entry points. Two processes, closely linked but distinct in their appearance have been initiated and with great effect. We'll examine them separately and then show their mutual dependence.

Fear has long been the basis of political Power. It is indispensable for the small number of the privileged to dominate the large number of the unprivileged. Its most resolute and invincible enemy is the laughter of the people. To subdue this enemy, fear must be given specificity and linked directly to the social sites where laughter is most likely to break out. Thus we have the fear of sex, its connection with death and plague, and its safe site of practice designated as wedlock. We have the fear of inebriation and its connection with death via madness, violence or disease and its safe site designated as permanent sobriety. We have the fear of the child and its connection with death via sex, drugs, violence and music and its safe site designated as the fortress of the two-parent family. We have the fear of music itself as a sinister purveyor of sin and vice and its safe site designated as nowhere out of earshot of the priest, teacher, policeman or parent.

These fears need to be carefully and constantly maintained, or they lose their potency in the natural course of time, since 1) they are largely unfounded, and 2) they lead to a miserable existence. This by and large is the function of the news media, but in order to be effective it requires the mobilization of religious fundamentalists who can spread fear house to house and ostracize or punish those who do not succumb.

The entire edifice of the Sixties and all the pro-democracy movements that broke out in Eastern Europe and China in the late '80s successfully destroyed these fears in large part by deploying the "funkentelechy" particular to their cultural milieu. Now, "entelechy" means the realization of form giving cause as opposed to potential existence. The "funk" prefix makes such realization carnivalesque. Any successful struggle against the forces of fear in the political arena must be accompanied by a vigorous effort to unleash the Funkentelechy among the populace at large. Manifestations of this include the new ways the global justice movement holds its demonstrations using outright carnival imagery, wildly costumed drum corps, giant puppets and so forth. This is an important development since one specific target of the fear campaign of today is the world of carnival itself.

The other side of fear is the co-optation and marketing of transgression. At precisely the historic moment when the inevitable triumph of democracy and the free expression of the popular will was being proclaimed, all that was spontaneously celebratory or personally liberating was being transformed into efficient, rational markets. Thus, masturbation was commodified in the giant porn industry. Participants in every form of sexual expression from prostitution to bondage and S&M were designated "communities" and had representatives to speak to the broader public about their unique needs and problems. Meanwhile they were becoming specific market niches for the goods and services of firms suddenly made "respectable" through the wide public acceptance of what had previously been considered perverse.

The same, in a different way, took place with drugs. The problem in the case of drugs is that without formal illegality, there is no market value. None of the drugs most often used to alter conscious states cost much to produce or distribute; wine is far more expensive to grow and process than cocaine or heroin. On the basis of this prohibition, however, drugs of all kinds proliferated becoming the basis for the economies for several countries (Colombia and Afghanistan, for example) and the basis for most partying throughout the world.

Lastly, and closest to our main subject, the music of which George Clinton is the finest exponent was cleverly replaced by a replica that bore some resemblance to the original but, like any placebo, cannot have the same effect. This was a complex move and, in all its dimensions, is the subject of this book. Mindless fun along with evolutionary changes in popular music displaced the Funkentelechy. George Clinton from the beginning has said, "Free Your Mind and Your Ass Will Follow!" But the party (rave, rock concert, music festival) became the market place for specific sexual practices and specific drugs. Each genre was known to its "community" to offer its own particular array. Instead of music being the gathering point, the center of activity and principle reason for attendance, it became the brand or trademark for identifying which transgression was therein permitted and sheltered. Furthermore, music became the Muzak for a supermarket of sex and drugs. If you want S&M and poppers, here's the sound you dance to. If you want orgies and ecstasy, here's the sound for you. If you want old fashioned whores and cocaine, here's the sound for you. And so forth. The whole explosion of techno and dance in the '80s and '90s was fueled by cocaine and casual sex. Entire islands were devoted to it (Ibiza in the Mediterranean, for example). Huge enterprises such as the Ministry of Sound, were built on it. The Placebo Syndrome came roaring back on a wave of pounding beats, energizing drugs and free sex. There is no transgression under the flag of the Free Market.

It is the combination of fear and marketed transgression that are deployed by the "Masters of the Universe" today. Sir Nose D'Voidoffunk and his mercenary minions have found a formula by which to upgrade their software, as it were, tweaking the program to more successfully delude and confuse. But this is precisely why it is so vital to understand the ancient codes and modern expression of the festival of the laughing people, Funkentelechy.

## FOOTNOTES

1     Bakhtin, Mikhail. *Rabelaise and His World.* Indiana University Press, 1984, p. 378.
2     Ibid. p. 8.
3     Ibid. p. 407.
4     Ibid. p. 39.
5     "Mikhail Mikhailovich Bakhtin b. Nov. 16, 1895, d. Mar. 7, 1975, was a Russian philosopher, linguist, and literary theorist whose ideas have had a substantial impact on literary criticism, both in Russia and, since the 1960s, in the west as well. Bakhtin was, for many years, a teacher at provincial universities within the Soviet Union. (Arrested in 1929, he was exiled for six years to a collective farm in Kazakhstan.) He managed to take up residence in Moscow only in 1969."— "The Bakhtin Circle." *Grollier Encyclopedia,* 1997.

    "Bakhtin...was arrested, presumably because of his connection with the St. Petersburg Religious-Philosophical society, and was sentenced to ten years on the Solovetskii Islands. After vigorous intercession by Bakhtin's friends, a favourable review of his Dostoevskii book by Commissar of Enlightenment Lunacharskii and a personal appeal by Maksim Gor´kii, this was commuted to six years exile in Kazakhstan."—*Internet Encyclopedia of Philosophy.* http://www.iep.utm.edu/b/bakhtin.htm
6     Bakhtin. p .5.
7     Ibid. p. 7.
8     Ibid. p. 73.
9     Ibid. p. 78.
10    Ibid. p. 19.
11    Ibid. p. 90.

# OUT OF CONTROL

## MUSIC OF LIBERATION
## AND THE LIBERATION
## OF MUSIC

All I ever had, is songs of freedom.

BOB MARLEY, "REDEMPTION SONG"

S ince the three revolutions at the end of the 18th century—the American, the French and the Haitian—the possibility called Freedom has seized the world. Yet it was torn apart at birth: African slavery and the Rights of Man. Genocide and the Declaration of Independence. Capitalism and Liberty and Justice for All! Enlightenment ideals arising within a Europe convulsed by popular revolt and bent on the colonial conquest of Africa and the Western Hemisphere.

Clashing dreams give birth to clashing sounds. One man's dream is another man's nightmare. And one man's music is another man's noise. Thus it is that the drumming of the African slave struck such terror in the heart of the master. For thousands of years, music has borne in its heart the rhythms and the melodies of human bondage. Since revolution ripped the fabric of time, slavery and liberty, music and politics, have been indissolubly locked in a danse macabre. Of death and of jubilation.

Rulers have always sought to control music. At the same time, the oppressed have sought to unleash it. In religious ceremony, waging of war and the refinement of the elites, music was given its proper function. In mourning misery, inspiring resistance and in festive celebration, music was given its improper function. But once the struggle for Freedom began in earnest and particularly in the 20th century, music and politics were bound together in a peculiar way. When Frank Zappa said, "The right would like to put you out of business and the left would like to hire you, and I'm not for hire."[1] he was pointing to the dilemmas this posed.

Politics is the struggle for power. But there are two kinds of power. Most European languages have two words for these two different kinds of power—potestas and potentia, pouvoir and puissance, Macht and Vermögen. English requires qualifiers such as power over vs. power to or coercive force vs. motive force. This linguistic ambiguity has concealed great confusion, and I will use the capitalized Power to designate coercive force, domination or rule, and the uncapitalized power to mean potency, vitality, possibility, or creative drive. There is in each kind—Power over or power to—a threat to negate the other, to humiliate and ridicule its hollowness. Might makes Right, vs. Right makes Might. There is also the continuous effort of each to evoke the other, to wear its cloak. All hierarchical societies are saturated by this tension. There is a slippage into and out of the different and opposed kinds of power—constantly, and in every situation.

Since the American, French and Haitian revolutions, Freedom has been made to mean the Power that will release power. Power for the good of all so that all might share the power—the full potential of human life. Power that in principle and practice limits itself, that power might be free. Thus, when called upon, power has served Power as furthering its own interests. The problem is that Power lies. The resulting confusion makes it necessary to distinguish between two contradictory kinds of politics: those of the oppressor and those of the oppressed. The first seeks the permanence of Power, the second its ultimate elimination altogether and with it the elimination of politics. The politics of domination vs. the politics of liberation. But while there is an obvious sympathy between music and the politics of liberation, there remains a striking difference between music and any kind of politics.

Politics organizes violence. Music disorganizes politics. Politics insists with the word and the weapon that it determine what music should do. Music insists that neither word nor weapon are adequate to the task. Politics claims it gives music purpose and meaning. Music claims it can exist without politics. The Power of the one is opposed to the power of the other.

As a result, two contradictory responses have developed, neither of which solves anything. On the one hand, many have turned to music itself as liberation. Many view musicians as the oracles of Truth. Many see in music a path to salvation and a resolution of the conflicts politics is responsible for creating but cannot solve. On the other hand, people dedicated to struggles for liberation have continued the age-old attempts to control music, to force it to serve the struggle or be banished.

## THE POWER OF MUSIC VS. THE POWER OF POLITICS

Music and politics directly correspond at one point: belonging. This is yet another word that in English has two completely contradictory meanings. This belongs to me. Or we belong, together. Ownership versus membership. Exclusion versus inclusion. Property versus the Commons. Music and politics are both fundamentally concerned with belonging in the sense of membership, the Commons. The making of belonging. For music making, the Commons is the purpose for which it exists. For the politics of Power, it is for rule over the Commons. For emancipatory politics, the politics of the power to, it has always and can only mean: how will the Commons decide for itself?

Capitalism makes belonging (in the sense of property) its only principle, to the exclusion of all others. Its purpose will always be the same: to transform music (and everything else) into possessions of which the rich will always have the most and everyone else will have the least. The development of liberal democratic forms serve it politically as the best way to manipulate the Commons into "voluntary" servitude to capital. The problem music presents is that it requires nothing but human bodies to make it and it produces immediate effect. Particularly when impoverished humans make it, it produces the Commons that it needs to exist as itself, as music.

Since revolution ruptured time and posed the radical conception of all Humanity as a Commons (liberty and justice for ALL!), music has shared this purpose and effect with emancipatory politics. In this sense music is communist. Not in the usage of that term as relates to Parties or States, but as it relates to the Commons. Emancipatory politics can aim at nothing less than the ending of Power, since Power is always the reduction of the Commons to a state of literal or virtual servitude via the State—whether that State be liberal democratic, fascist, communist or otherwise. How the Commons will decide what forms of social organization will free the People from coercive Power remains the great challenge of the unfinished revolutions of the past two hundred years. For music, the question has long been settled.

Music has the power of producing this effect in its makers and their audiences. It does so frequently. In fact, it is what most people seek when they go to a concert or have a close relationship with the music of a particular performer or group. It is precisely this sense of belonging evoked by music that makes it the envy of politics. It is why, when politics has degenerated into policing the masses and mediating disputes between the rulers, people would much rather listen to a good band than hear a speech. No one expects anything but lies or platitudes from speeches. Everyone seeks real belonging from music.

Recognizing this, ruling elites have employed a strategy in which replacement is more important than suppression or cooptation. Their goal is to replace real music with Anti-music precisely in order to encourage a sense of belonging to them: sharing their ideology, their Church of the Free Market as well as, literally, belonging to them in the sense of loyal, obedient slaves. A herd and not a Commons. This is why music has no choice but to serve the struggle for liberation. Because it is the Commons, generated by music, which music needs to exist. It is the task of emancipatory politics to define the Commons in the terms that originated in the events of the revolutions of the last decades of the 18th century. It is the task of emancipatory politics to enunciate and demand the end of Power, as the goal towards which thought and deed must be directed today. Music must serve this cause, because that is what music does and why it does it. Without a Commons there would be no music, only sound.

## NO FUTURE

It's London, 1977. From a boat on the river Thames into the "jugular vein of Empire," the Monarch's Silver Jubilee, the Sex Pistols launch their sonic assault "God Save the Queen." It's a decade after the revolutionary Sixties and, as we now know, a decade before the fall of the Berlin Wall. Rock and roll was a coopted, complacent shadow of its former rebellious youth. Not only did punk emerge as a general outburst against the living death of a decaying Britain, it was a specific attack on the aristocracy of rock. "Because," as musician/filmmaker Don Letts recently noted, "of course, all the white guys were totally fed up with all those terrible rock bands that were around at the time, playing dreadful, arrogant stadium rock. They wanted to deal a death blow to all those bands, and they went on to do that: for a while at least, they savaged those bands, totally deposed them."[2] They exposed the fraudulence of rock's liberatory pretensions- "The Great Rock and Roll Swindle"—while, at the same time, seizing rock's instruments to make anger and passion matter again. What was, in fact, a very small number of people, made an enormous global impact by aiming directly at supposedly axiomatic views of music and politics, at once ridiculing the betrayals by "leaders" of both. The good news was that there wasn't any—unless you wrote it yourself. The Sixties were finished. "No future," sang Johnny Rotten.

At the same time other vital elements were bursting forth from multiple subterranean sites of music and resistance. In the London of '77 and directly linked with punk it was music from Jamaica. In New York and also linked with punk it was the first tremors of hip-hop. Moreover, the rapid acceleration of transcontinental, international musical exchange had reached critical mass. Exiles, refugees, laborers, escapees from war, famine, persecution and poverty were moving in unprecedented numbers all over the world. Music was beginning to sound as if it were coming from everywhere and nowhere at the same time. Influences, inspirations, from a long way away were now here in the heart of the young soul rebel. What was later to be known as World Beat, was being anticipated, inaugurated, by, among others, Fela Kuti in Nigeria, whose influences included James Brown and the Black Panther Party.[3]

Descending directly from the storms of '68, these sounds blew away a popular culture weighed down by riches and fame, glamour and glitz, betrayal and disillusionment; the bitter fruits of cooptation. Anyone could see that this cooptation of rock and roll was part and parcel of the Thatcher/Reagan strategy for reasserting control over rebellious youth while pursuing a counterrevolutionary agenda. But it didn't end there. That klaxon we heard was the death knell for the ideology of the Soviet-dominated Left, particularly as it concerned music. All the old positions, already seriously disoriented by blows dealt during the Sixties, were blasted out of the water. The links connecting the Soviet Union and the USA were suddenly exposed. After World War II both antagonists in the Cold War had erected and maintained a world system to channel radical energies and contain all threats to order. Opposed to this, a spirit of subversion filled the air. A barbed wire solidarity of a new Us against all of Them was proclaimed. "Who are the real revolutionaries?" sang Bob Marley.

A basic assumption was: music is for participation, not passive reception. With little technical skill but lots of passion, young musicians picked up instruments including the turntable, which was, at this time, transformed into a musical instrument, and went about making music. From block parties in the Bronx to "Rock Against Racism" concerts in London, people rallied to act, to take part, to Do It Yourself. This struck directly at the heart of the arguments that had burdened music theory and music makers for two centuries. Most previous discussion was based on a divide between performer and audience. Moreover, the perspective of the music maker is virtually absent in the millions of words about aesthetics, politics or the popular versus the fine arts. Here was an outburst of creative force that struck down such distinctions by declaring that anyone could play, and everyone should! It forced a reevaluation of supposedly settled questions about what was good or beautiful about music. It urgently asked which qualities best express the feelings and aspirations of people determined to free themselves from the clutches of authoritarian regimes.

In a peculiar way, this was a desperate, valiant effort to bring back to life ancient communal purposes and practices of music. This did not mean "folk music" as it had been contrived in the 30s and revived in the 60s. New technologies of music making were embraced. But, in the frontal assault on the institution popular music had become, it was necessary for the excluded to turn away from precisely those features that had come to define popular music. The music that was ostensibly "theirs." Too many of the bands and artists of an earlier time had distanced themselves from the very sources of their music and popularity. Their technical virtuosity and more and more polished recordings reasserted barriers they had originally set out to break down themselves.

In any event, the angry defiance of '77 encountered music's historical repository, the source from which music springs. In turn, music was replenished, in lasting ways, by specific transformations of noises, technologies, ugliness and deconstruction. Countries, nation states, could no longer contain what music was becoming and, in fact, had been far longer than the nationstate itself. While this had in isolated, marginal efforts been a part of music making for most of the 20th century, punk rock and hip-hop thrust these sounds into the middle of the battle, forcing every musician to take stock of what they were doing and whether it had any relevance any more.

And one more thing: women started to play instruments! The days of the "chick singer," when females were only allowed to participate as vocalists, were shunned as young women took up guitars, basses and drums and began to join in the proceedings. This has made a lasting impact and is one special way to note the differences between music and Anti-music. It is characteristic of the period between '77 and the present that a steadily growing number of popular music groups from many countries, include, or are made up entirely, of female musicians. If anything characterizes Anti-music, it is the re-institutionalizing of the female in the traditional role of sex-pot, dancer, singer.

Punk rock, hip-hop, reggae/dub and world music burst forth simultaneously and marked the receding waves of world wide revolt that, in 1968, appeared on the verge of "changing the world." They were an enunciation of failure and a denunciation of surrender. As we shall see, they spawned and continue to inspire, another larger generation of musicians and rebel youth. They carried forward a militance and internationalist spirit into the next phase of musical and political contestation, while exposing jagged rifts left by unsuccessful struggle. Ultimately, they revealed a truth hidden in the tumult of nearly two centuries of revolution: Music is not politics.

## NO PAST

"Turn on your TV and you'll hear the Clash's 'Should I Stay or Should I Go' and 'London Calling' selling beer and cars.

"Does this mean we lost the war? Is music now so hopelessly compromised it can't hold credible meaning?"—Dave Marsh, *Corporate Sponsorship of Music*

An article appeared in *Time Magazine* titled, "Can Bono Save the World?"[4] It told of this musician's campaign to end Third World debt. In the article, Bono says, "U2 is about the impossible. Politics is the art of the possible. They're very different, and I'm resigned to that now." This statement displays the utter confusion of music and politics that has dominated discussion about both over the last century. There are three important arguments to be made:

1. Music (including that of U2) is precisely what is possible.

2. Politics is not an art and it is, for the oppressed, always about the impossible.

3. Being a good musician does not make one a good political leader.

A sidebar called "Political Rock Evolution" lists Bob Dylan, Marvin Gaye, Bob Marley, The Clash, Bruce Springsteen, and Public Enemy. This is one jaw of a steel trap. The other is another statement Bono makes, "let's only have goals we can go after." According to Bono, we have music that is "the impossible" opposed to goals we can achieve. Does this mean the musicians listed above were liars? That "Political Rock" is deluded? Is the enormous influence of such artists a product of drug induced dementia? On the other hand, does the "realistic" campaign Bono is waging against Third World debt mean he thinks these debts are legitimate business obligations? Does "realism" mean accepting the imperialist plunder of the world? This is both a betrayal of music and profoundly wrong, historically.

Of course, it fits nicely into the view being promoted that liberal democracy is the only game in town. The best the suffering multitudes can hope for is better manners from policemen and cleaner toilets at the salt mines. Music is useful as a "safety valve" for people's frustrated hopes or, better, as an instructor of obedience; the passive acceptance of the "possible" as defined by the Powers That Be. Musicians who really want to "make a difference" should follow Bono's lead and sing of a politics of submission. Booker T. Washington for the 21st century. Yet, even with its twisted argument this article poses a question vital to us all.

What has come to be expected of music is both too little and too much. Music cannot make revolution. Music cannot bring about political change. As Malcolm X once said, "You can't just be singing up on Freedom, you got to be swinging up on Freedom." Music does something else, though. It inspires the collective imagination of an end to Power, right now.

What has come to be expected of politics is simply too little. Politics, for the powerful, is to maintain and expand their Power. Politics for the powerless is the shattering of all the limits placed on them, the realization of those very dreams and aspirations that the powerful say are "out of the question." This is how every advancement in the conditions of life for the great majority of people has been accomplished. It takes collective action and the enunciation of what is called impossible by the ruling elites to bring about liberation.

When politics is thought of as the art of the possible music is forced to take on an impossible role. Oppressed people turn to music to soothe their battered souls, to give them strength to carry on and to celebrate whatever hopes they may have of a better life. People seek in song lyrics the wisdom and insight lacking in political leaders. They turn to musicians because there is a lack elsewhere. In fact, it is the absence of political vision that is attested to in the shock and dismay so often expressed at the lyrics of hip-hop, or the anti-social stance taken by certain rock groups. The limits some would place on artistic expression betray the lack of political imagination for a society transformed.

It is only when politics begins to wage the struggle for liberation from suffering and injustice that music of the oppressed joins with it, consciously, in the work of musicians as members of society who have particular skills. It is only when liberation itself is articulated and made the goal of popular action that it can share music's most important functions: liberating the spirit, defying the so-called "realistic" and proposing the unity of humanity.

## THE MUSICIAN AS SLAVE
## AND THE SLAVE AS MUSICIAN

Of course, Bono was not speaking as a musician. He was speaking as a star, a celebrity. He has been elevated from the mass of struggling musicians to the lofty heights of fame in the manner perfected since music became a commodity.

For many centuries and in many societies, musicians were slaves or servants to the aristocracy. Recognizing the power of music and needing to capture it, the rich and powerful have long enslaved or employed musicians. In fact, as musician Gordon Rumson says,

> musicians, as a class, have been rather low on the social totem pole for a long time. Indeed, in many cultures to be a musician is just a few steps above a beggar. My teacher of Arabic music, the late Dr Jafran Jones, informed me that in Tunisia under its old penal codes, legal testimony could not be accepted from children, women, alcoholics and musicians. In some of the legal schools of Islamic law musical instruments are the invention of the Devil. If they are stolen there is no punishment of theft.[5]

Further, many of the most beloved and exalted composers such as Bach, Haydn and Mozart were indentured servants with signed contracts obligating them to absolute obedience to their lords and masters. In *Noise*,

Jacques Attali traces an evolution from "the Musician-Valet to Musician-Entrepreneur."[6] Attali describes the progression from actual slave, to indentured servant, to seller of musical wares. The bourgeois client replaces the monarch, aristocrat or church as controlling interest in the production and consumption of music. There is a direct line between the musician as slave/valet of the ruling elites and the modern day composer.

On the other side, there is the music of the slaves, the music made by the laboring people for themselves. Music was always completely different here. It was an integral part of social life. It was not isolated in performance, it was not a statement by one separated group (musicians) to another (the audience). It was the statement of all to all within the laboring, the ceremony or the festival. There is a direct line between this music and the popular music of today.

As we shall see, most music theory, past and present, has concerned itself with the former and not the latter. The music of the musician as slave/composer and not that of the slave/laborer as musician. Further, almost all that has been written about music concerns listening. What we will concern ourselves with here is making.

Attali, who begins his book by speaking of the need to listen to the world as opposed to looking at it, ends by speaking of composition (meaning the making of music) as vitally important precisely as a means of extricating music and musician from the "cash nexus", the commodification of everything. "Composition," he says, "liberates time so it can be lived, not stockpiled. It is thus measured by the magnitude of the time lived by men, which takes the place of time stockpiled in commodities." I would amend this by saying making music does not, simply, "take the place of time stockpiled in commodities,"[7] but it is what was stolen to make the commodities in the first place—a point we shall explore further.

This distinction is particularly important now when we are being asked to believe that such questions are no longer controversial. The popular is socially dominant. Musicians are revered. What's the problem? The problem is that society is still riven by violent antagonism between the rulers and the ruled. There is still, albeit in modified form, a tiny group of masters lording it over an enormous population of slaves. The rich vs. the poor. This produces suffering and injustice and the struggle against them. In this conflict music and politics are consciously linked or de-linked by opposing forces, depending on their political agenda. In the case of the master, music is kept to its "proper" functions as noted above. In the case of the slave it is the opposite, "improper" functions that continually reemerge.

# NOISE AND SILENCE—THE LISTENER

It has been frequently stated that music arises between noise and silence. This certainly fits prevailing notions of social order. But it is not true and it must be exposed if we are to unravel the perplexities surrounding music and politics.

Music was made before noise existed. In fact, in the 16th century, the word "noise" was used to describe a group of musicians! (This usage is obsolete but is noted in *The Oxford English Dictionary*.) What actually precedes and follows music is sound. But music and noise can only be produced by people. What is noise if not certain sounds produced by people, their social activity, their machines, their weapons, their own sonic expressions (yelling, applauding, fighting, etc.)? By failing to identify music as the origin of noise, we inadvertently support the logic of elites who tell us that all human production must be organized by Power to create social order from chaos. (or noise). This is exactly what music itself opposes. When a group of slaves gathered in the hills above Port-au-Prince to play their drums and invoke the spirits of their ancestors, they were not trying to maintain the prevailing social order. On the contrary, they were using music as one means to destroy this social order because it was oppressing them.

Music is first and foremost a collective activity that produces active collectivities. As such, music for the slave is noise to the slave master. As it anticipates a social order without Power, music is noise for those who seek to maintain that Power. Noise, in this relationship to music, is not simply "in the ear of the beholder." It is the word used to identify the threat posed by disorder. This is both figuratively and historically true. Figuratively because it addresses the linguistic opposition of noise and music. Historically, because work precedes slavery and music came into the world before there was anything to call noise.

Music is not situated between noise and silence because silence does not exist on Earth. As John Cage noted, "In the late forties I found out by experiment (I went into the anechoic chamber at Harvard University) that silence is not acoustic. It is a change of mind, a turning around."[8] Wherever humans live there is sound, even if only the pumping of the blood. Silence is possible where there are no humans and there is no air (outer space and death). We'll get into Cage's insights in a moment. What is important to recognize is that there is sound and there is music. Noise came into the world as a consequence of politics. It is used by Power attempting to control music. Silence, on the other hand, is simply a concept, a thought about infinity or about non-being (death, for example).

Thus it has dynamic implications and great value to the music maker, but it does not exist as a dialectical opposite of music. In fact, noise and silence are embraced by and incorporated into music all the time (Mozart quipped that the most important components of his music were the rests). It is only when politics/Power tries to capture music that noise and silence are pitted against it. The music of the slave is called noise and it is silenced.

Why does this matter? Because in attempting to understand what music does, in order to defend it, most theorists have made three crucial errors:

1. Identified all music with that of the musician as slave/composer, failing to take into account music produced by the slave/laborer as musician (often speaking of the latter as existing only in a time before modernity when, in fact, it never stopped being made.)

2. Creating an inversion based on the prevailing view of politics/Power of the actual sequence of music and noise. This is an acceptance, a submission to the order that makes Power dominant over power, of kings over composers, of the music industry over music. Sound preexists humanity. Music and humans arise together. Noise follows. In fact, noise and (relative) silence are incorporated by music because music is a productive activity that can make use of all sound.

3. Thinking only as listeners, never as makers. But music is made and its makers have a specific and different relationship to it than do listeners. (even if they are also listeners).

Theodoro Adorno is one important theoretician of music who makes these errors. His efforts were sincere and committed to the defense of music against capital and politics/Power. But Adorno virtually eliminates all music except that of the musician as slave/composer. His is a defense of the composer, per se. His model was Beethoven who, in the words of *The Oxford Companion to Music* was, "Acknowledged in his lifetime as a musical Titan, a hero who rose from humble origins and conquered extreme adversity with his genius, he lifted music from its role as sheer entertainment and made it the object of hushed reverence—music written for its own sake as an elevating power. Great composers today are appreciated as worthy of enormous respect, and this is due in no small part to the changed perceptions of music's function that Beethoven brought about." That Beethoven openly celebrated the French revolution and championed the cause of humanity's liberation reinforced the esteem in which he was held by revolutionaries and revolutionary theorists.

Faced with the rise of the Nazis and the literal ending of the German musical tradition from Bach to Schoenberg, Adorno can hardly be blamed for his passionate and one-sided views. But his renewed popularity in the fields of cultural studies and critical musicology renew the need to criticize his work. While he brilliantly exposed the Culture Industry and presciently identified its current effects, Adorno's view leads to capitulating to the Culture Industry he denounces. Partly this is a result of his virtual negation of the popular and the near total identification of music with the composer. Partly, it is a result of the inability to extricate music from politics. In any case, many who have followed his line of thinking seriously downplay the productive force of music and, specifically that of the slave/laborer as musician, because they can only see the triumph of capital and the commodification of everything. Simon Frith postulated that rock and roll is not "a folk or community music of teenagers and youths, but a popular leisure activity provided for them." This may contain an element of truth. It may be correct in suggesting that capitalism can only be overthrown through political struggle and not by singing songs. But it nonetheless conflates music with noise, and Power with power. It fails to grasp why people continue to make music, not only consume it.

This, in turn, is a result of the third problem: that of speaking only from the point of view of the Listener.

John Cage went so far as to propose the composer be Listener. "My work became an exploration of non-intention," he wrote.[8] His aleatory (or chance) music was, in effect, making a listener out of the composer or music maker. This is provocative on a number of levels. First, opposed to the egomania surrounding the star system it is a revelatory intervention. Mocking the pomposity and pretensions of "high art" and its elite supporters, it exposes the dead end at which they have arrived. Second, when emphasis is placed on discovery as opposed to invention, when chance is welcomed as productive of possibility, there is a rejuvenation of the vibrant connection between music, musician and sound. It signals a fundamental breakdown of the bourgeois factory model of the conductor and orchestra following the score. Third, if anyone wants to play music they have to listen first!

Cage wrote in his book, *Silence*, that the composer should, "give up the desire to control sound, clear his mind of music and set about discovering means to let sounds be themselves rather than vehicles for man-made theories or expressions of human sentiments."[9] In a sense, he represents the limit of the musician as slave/composer. Not that composers don't continue to compose and make wonderful music. As Edgar Varese said, and Frank Zappa frequently quoted: "The modern day composer refuses to die." But Cage spent his entire life overthrowing the very definitions by which the musician as slave/composer had been molded. With the composer as listener he sought to free the composer from the relationship to Power that had been his plight for thousands of years. Adorno and others mention this in passing in their work, but fail to grasp its significance since they are totally immersed in the political critique and cannot imagine as Cage did anything beyond the prevailing social order that attempts to capture music as a tool to perpetuate itself. What Cage actually represents is the ultimate critique of this position from within the domain of music. His was an insistence on the independence of music from any control—even that of the composer!

All this, however, operated in a world apart from the slave as musician—from the laborers, the populace, the multitudes who have always, everywhere, made music for themselves.

## MUSIC OF THE SLAVE—THE MAKER

WEB DuBois wrote *The Souls of Black Folk* in 1903. He wrote eloquently of the "haunting echo of these weird old songs in which the soul of the black slave spoke to men." In doing so, DuBois more accurately expressed the vital role that music of the slaves played than most writers about music, precisely because he viewed it from the point of view of the maker—not the listener. Because of this, his work is a stunning critique of the way music is most often written about, exposing, as it does, the failure to grasp this fundamental concept that the source of all music is, ultimately, the makers of the world, the slave/laborers. Furthermore, DuBois poses this in stark contrast to the presumed superiority of the music of the ruling elites.

> Little of beauty has America given the world save the rude grandeur God himself stamped on her bosom; the human spirit in this new world has expressed itself in vigor and ingenuity rather than in beauty. And so by fateful chance, the Negro folk-song—the rhythmic cry of the slave-stands today not simply as the sole American music, but as the most beautiful expression of human experience born this side of the seas.

Not only does this correspond with the facts, it is closely aligned with the argument advanced by Tolstoy regarding true art. DuBois continued,

> Ever since I was a child these songs have stirred me strangely. They came out of the South unknown to me, one by one, and yet at once I knew them as of me and of mine. Then in after years when I came to Nashville I saw the great temple builded of these songs towering over the pale city. To me Jubilee Hall seemed ever made of the songs themselves, and its bricks were red with the blood and dust of toil. Out of them rose for me morning, noon, and night,

bursts of wonderful melody, full of the voices of my brothers and sisters, full of the voices of the past.[10]

It must be emphasized that DuBois was not describing "tradition," "primitive," "folk" or some other "prior to" or "outside" category. The music of oppressed people may trace its roots back hundreds or even thousands of years. But it is not, generally, adherence to specific rules or fixed practices that make it a category. The music of the oppressed is "right now" music. It is always intimately linked to generations of suffering and struggle within particular contexts, but it derives its vitality from being made right now and because of what it does right now for the sufferers. It is immediate, urgent, alive, and at the same time it is eternal, ancient, timeless. This becomes even more clear when one considers what Tolstoy predicted would be the music of the future. "The content of the art of the future will be only those feelings that draw people towards union or already unite them; as for the form of this art, it will be accessible to everyone. And, therefore the ideal of perfection in the future will be, not the exclusiveness of a feeling accessible only to some, but on the contrary, its universality."[11]

This great divide between music made by the musician as slave to the wealthy, and that made by the slave as musician is not limited to one geographical zone or time period. And it goes further than simple definitions of high and low culture or categories of political economy. It is at the root of an understanding of music made in many parts of the world for at least 3000 years and it is of utmost importance now, within the specific conditions created by the slave trade, the African diaspora and subsequent revolutions. While this music is only one among many glorious forms its influence is global and intense. It is, therefore, representative of many other musics whose origins are slavery or involuntary servitude. This includes the musics of the Greek, Roman, Byzantine and Islamic empires, virtually all of Europe up to and including feudal Russia, as well as India and China. The evidence that music of the slave was of social significance is attested to by the writings of contemporaries in various societies.

In Plato's two works that addressed education of the young, *The Republic* and *Laws*, he dwells at length on music. He specifically defines its characteristics as an opposition between that which is fit for members of society and that which is fit for slaves. This is noteworthy precisely because it was written at a time when there was no need to justify slavery at all. Slavery was not even considered a "necessary evil." It was, in fact, simply necessary since society could not exist without it. It is only in the last two hundred years that slavery was viewed as bad and, through war and revolution, legally abolished. Plato argues thusly: "Music has two functions—one the accompaniment of the noble words of the poets, the other the accompaniment of dances and other exercises of the limbs. If children are once accustomed to the sober and ordered Muse, when they hear the opposite kind of music, the sweet kind, they will think it only fit for slaves. On the other hand, if they have been habituated to the sweet Muse in early life, they will find true music cold and harsh."[12]

This then leads to another compelling point: slaves provided, by and large, the musicians who were, in turn, employed by society's ruling elites to produce the kind of music appropriate to the societies they ruled. There are many texts attesting to this. Africans, along with Slavs and other peoples were enslaved for thousands of years long before the Atlantic slave trade. These slaves provided labor but they also provided music both inside their own social life and to the courts and networks of their masters. The history of the Romany people (gypsies), while particular and specific, is not so peculiar or anomalous when seen from this musical perspective.[13] Further, the many "ethnic" or national styles that are classified by musicologists or historians are, in the main, variations based in the same social structure and coming from similar sources. Too long we have been misled by the view that there was music from "noble savages" living in harmony and producing music collectively, and then there was "the European Tradition." This is, in fact, utterly false. Anthropologists may have discovered people who remained untouched by conquest, until the 20th century. But the vast majority of the world's peoples and the music they made were conquered and enslaved long, long ago. The task was completed in the 16th century following the conquest of the western hemisphere and the advent of the African slave trade. But the features of this in terms of social structure and music were already well established.

This also helps us understand the ambivalent role of musicians themselves, past and present. For one thing, the vast majority of musicians have themselves been and continue to be among the poorest of the poor. The privileged position of the composer (or pop star) is rare and, though widely promoted as a "goal" towards which musicians should aspire, is an insidious illusion maintained to control musicians. Within the larger population of laboring people, there have always been those who played music especially well, who gained access to some kind of training or instruments. Also, even among the lowest social orders, there has been an ambivalence toward musicians. Exactly as music itself was valued above all other expression, the musician was viewed with distrust and derision. This was due, in part, to musicians' often mendicant, nomadic existence, the fuzzy line between inspiration and inebriation, between high spirits and low behaviors. As Hakim Bey noted, "Music is spiritual—the musician is corporeal. The spirituality of the musician is low but also ambiguous in its production of highness. (Drugs substitute for the priest's ritual highness to make the musician high enough to produce aesthetic highness.) The musician is not just low but uncanny—not just low but 'outside.' The power of the musician in society is like the power of the magician—the excluded shaman—in its relation to wildness."[14] This separateness works even within the context of music made for all by all. It underlies the tension that continues within the struggle for liberation of the oppressed, among whom are most musicians. Even when the slaves' demands for justice are voiced in popular revolt, this tension does not go away. It has, more often than not, been channeled into the general melee of political opposition. Musicians have often willingly joined in the struggle against Power. But there remains, within such emancipatory effort, the friction between the two kinds of power discussed earlier; between the power of music and the Power of politics. Thus, it is not only music that Power seeks to control. It is the musician as well. And this by those in Power as well as those fighting against it.

DuBois' view challenges those that have attempted to explain or make comprehensible the power of music by analyzing great works of great composers. *The Souls of Black Folk* was a resounding cry for the liberation of black people but it is also an "emancipation proclamation" for music. By celebrating the making of music in its living connection with the struggle of the slave, DuBois showed how music of great power could and did thrive apart from, and opposed to, the clutches of the client—be that client bourgeois, aristocrat or religious. Here the musician's role is different, too. While contradictory and complicated, it is a role played within the great body of struggling multitudes, nourishing and being nourished by the ongoing music making process.

All of this, however, operates within the world too long confused about this basic fact: music and slavery are inextricably bound. No discussion of music is complete without discussing slavery. No discussion of slavery is complete without discussing music. And no struggle for liberation can fail to make this connection. History is two dreams: that of the master and that of the slave. From Pharaoh to President the master claims his prize. From Exodus to Insurrection the slave dares to rise. To rule is right, dreams one. To rebel is justified, dreams the other. And the sound of music swells in both.

To begin with, between 1871 and 1968 the world was shaken by revolution of a new kind. The Paris Commune, celebrated in song by "The Internationale," was the first seizure of power by the laboring classes as such. Conscious of themselves as workers and participants in the struggle to emancipate the international working class. "Proletarians of all countries, unite." The quick demise (after 90 days) of the Paris Commune meant not the end of such struggle, but the beginning. And a relationship of music to politics was being defined. In two of the first revolutions of the 20th century, the Mexican and Irish, we see the connection between music made by the multitudes and their advancing political struggle. The world-renowned legacy of Irish Revolutionary Songs and Mexican Corridos are musical genres that continue to live. As will be discussed more fully later on, it was the words, the texts of this music that made it revolutionary. The music was a product of many centuries of music making by people within specific oppressed groups. It is important to note that even as these genres have definite characteristics, they are each characterized by hybridization as well. The musical elements that have come to be called "Irish," "Mexican" or "African-American" are themselves a synthesis of diverse influences resulting from conquest and migration; the intermingling of people thrust together in exile, enslavement and resistance. The fundamental characteristic, however, is that this is the music of the oppressed, made by, and for themselves. It is not music to be listened to as much as a concrete activity in which all are expected to participate. The corresponding relationship to the political struggles of these oppressed people was direct and inseparable.

By the time of the Russian revolution, there were already traditions in many parts of the world of music written and performed specifically for revolution. The new situation that revolutionary Russia presented was that liberation, in the form of a workers' republic, made it possible to legislate, or at least pronounce officially, what proletarian music is. In the life-and-death struggle that engulfed the world in the 20th century such a question was not abstract. In the United States it could be viewed as alien and foreign, given the peculiar history of the United States, its own revolutionary legacy and vibrant musical heritage. Nevertheless, within the international revolutionary movement a great debate was unleashed that involved artists and intellectuals from many countries, including the US. There were three major lines of thinking that profoundly affected political struggle, music made to serve it, and music in its own right.

The first was from Europe, specifically, the new Soviet Union and Germany. The second was from the US. The third came from the rising tide of national liberation struggles that were breaking out in Asia, Africa and Latin America: the former colonies of Britain, France, Spain, Portugal and the Netherlands. From the Soviet Union and Germany came the attempt to define music in accordance with European traditions of great composers and great works, along with the infusion of popular song with the aims of the proletarian revolution. From America came a rejection of the European classical tradition and an identification of the music of the rural workers as "folk music" that was, by its very nature, proletarian. Somewhat later, from Africa and the Caribbean, in particular, came the Negritude movement, which sought to establish the validity in theory and in practice of the music of colonized peoples, as opposed to that of their colonizers. On the one hand, there was a true flowering of revolutionary music, championing the revolutionary struggles of the workers and oppressed peoples that, in many places, had become a mass phenomenon, broadly influencing society and music at large. On the other, there were intense debates within the ranks of revolutionaries and artists over how to better define and propagate proletarian revolutionary ideals through music.

In hindsight, many of these issues were resolved by the music born of the Sixties. The towering popular image of a conscious social revolutionary, Bob Marley, makes this abundantly clear. Here was a musician from Jamaica whose breadth of influence was greater among the peoples of the "Third World" than any other. And his is only one example. Two songs by John Lennon, "Imagine" and "Working Class Hero," articulate, as clearly as any, the attitude and aspirations of millions throughout the world who seek justice and freedom. The Clash, Fela Kuti, Pubic Enemy, Rage Against the Machine, the Coup, Ozomatli, Michael Franti—the list is very long and spans many continents. The point is that whether it be a Bob Dylan, a Jimi Hendrix, a Manu Chao or a Lauryn Hill, music that is consciously designed to inspire the liberatory aspirations of the oppressed and their struggle to make real those aspirations is a major influence in music now and has been for a very long time.

It is not, however, sufficient to celebrate great music and musicians. Particularly not now when music of liberation has an especially important role in combating Anti-music and contributing to the health of music in general. It is necessary to examine key controversies of the not-so-distant past and attempt to bring clarity to their current unfolding. For one thing, since the collapse of the Soviet Union, there has been a renewed assault on music, part and parcel of the imperial designs of the US ruling elites and their counterparts throughout the world. For another, politics, for many, is something from which no good can come. It has no emancipatory promise. As the "art of the possible" it contains no possibility.

So what was that music all about, then? What were people thinking? Speaking from within a revolutionary movement, just prior to the outbreak of World War II, Walter Benjamin said, "Mankind, which in Homer's time was an object of contemplation for the Olympian gods, now is one for itself. Its self-alienation has reached such a degree that it can experience its own destruction as an aesthetic pleasure of the first order. This is the situation of politics which Fascism is rendering aesthetic. Communism responds by politicizing art."[15]

Here is where the problem lies in all its complexity. There is a real world-wide war between fascism, liberal democracy and the Soviet state, on the one hand, and the world-wide revolutionary struggles unleashed and inspired by the Russian revolution on the other. The close identification of liberation with the Soviet state was, I think, an inevitable consequence of the situation. However, it bred all the problems with which music and politics have had to deal ever since. First of all, the Soviet state, like its opponents, was determined to defend itself at the expense of the Commons. It was no longer concerned with the problem of emancipation. Not how the Commons will decide but how the Politburo and the State will decide. It was concerned with its survival as a state among states. Second, outside the Soviet Union, revolutionary struggle was against the states that were the instruments of their ruling elites. In a consciously internationalist struggle, however, there could not help but be an identification on the part of most of the struggling multitudes with what appeared to be a beacon of their own victory. This led directly to the conclusions that Benjamin expressed. The policies of the Soviet Union towards music (and art in general) were interpreted and employed by revolutionary activists throughout the world.

It would be easy to dismiss them as obviously wrong. But that would be a major mistake. The questions that were being debated were vital and remain alive. Indeed, the most damning criticism of the Soviet-influenced Left in the 20th century regarding music is the failure to recognize the music of the slave, specifically jazz and rock and roll, that by the Sixties had become the revolutionary music so long sought after in other places. How could political leaders fail to recognize what was happening? How could such an incredible blindness (or deafness) be possible? This was the central issue then and it is the central question now. As Anti-music proliferates, it does so at the expense, not of symphony halls, opera houses or conservatories, but by silencing and marginalizing the great legacy of the music of the slaves (from all countries). It is doing through the mechanisms of the free market what was done by the pronouncements of cultural commissars and radical theorists before. What was brought about by the musical revolution of the Sixties, affecting virtually all genres of music, was not the transformation of the proletarian multitudes into bourgeois audiences, but the elevation of music to a position of extraordinary importance in social life. It was not always greeted with "hushed reverence" but was certainly "lifted from its role as sheer entertainment." This meant that even under the conditions of urban, industrial, mass mediated alienation, music of all kinds penetrated the fabric of everyday interaction, opening ears and souls to the possibilities of sound, to the vast diversity of forms, and to the participation in the utopian Commons that music calls into being.

But, just as the Haitian revolution had been maligned and its significance underestimated, so too had the music of the slave. The model for proletarian music was sought in the European classical tradition or in folk songs with the explicit exclusion of jazz and rock and roll. Righting this wrong means two things for both the music of liberation and the liberation of music. First, the conflict between the musician as slave and the slave as musician is resolved within the processes of music making, not by ranking of superior and inferior types of music. Music demands that individuals be able to explore and experiment the farthest reaches of their imaginations at the same time as it demands that music making be a joy and inspiration for the Commons. Second, music serves liberation because it needs the Commons to exist not because it is harnessed by authorities into "proper" functions. Indeed, it is the "improper" functions of music that necessarily inspire the "festival of the oppressed" that is revolution.

## ADORNO, EISLER, SEEGER

Theodor Adorno wrote extensively on music, and was himself a musician and a politically engaged theorist. His musical training was classical, but he soon became an admirer of Schoenberg. His philosophical and political education was in Kant, Hegel and Marx. He was forced to flee Germany by the Nazis, first to England then to Los Angeles. In LA, he wrote many stunning and prescient works about the Culture Industry, specifically about how music was commodified and its emancipatory thrust diverted into serving the ever-extending tentacles of capitalism. Until his dying day, he was a committed adherent of both classical and avant-garde music expressed through the European model, namely, the orchestra or some smaller ensemble playing the works of a composer. This, as opposed to popular music, music of particular ethnic groups (Irish, African-Americans, etc.) or anything that did not fit into what he considered the highest expression of the musical force. It is not correct to view this as simply Eurocentric or elitist. Adorno's arguments are profound and insightful about music and capitalism. They are not simple, two dimensional rantings at the futility of musical effort or political struggle. They do, however, express a traumatic shock at the sudden, crashing demise of the German musical tradition, Bach to Schoenberg, and the brutality and banality of the Nazis. Moreover, they reflect his disillusionment with the hypocritical "freedom" of the US and the equally hypocritical "freedom" of the Soviet bloc, particularly East Germany after the war.

His engagement included an ongoing relationship with Hans Eisler, another student of Schoenberg, who, as a communist, actively pursued the composition of proletarian music in general accord with the theories of the Comintern. He worked in conjunction with Adorno, Bertolt Brecht and others in the thriving revolutionary milieu that extended from Moscow to Berlin to Los Angeles. (It should be noted that this milieu extended to Spain and China and other parts of the world engaged in revolutionary struggles). These were not armchair revolutionaries. Nor were they ivory tower intellectuals cut off from the masses of workers. Eisler's career is particularly noteworthy, as he not only produced a large number of compositions for many ensembles—from workers' choruses (a very large movement in Germany before Hitler) to classical orchestra, but he was a pivotal figure in many of the debates surrounding music and revolution. Indeed, it can be said that the dynamics of Adorno's and Eisler's work combined with a third to define the most important questions facing music and politics in the twentieth century.

The third element was the work of the Popular Front in the US, specifically that of Charles Seeger, who developed, against Adorno and Eisler but in direct association with them, the theories that led to the championing of "folk music" as the appropriate form for revolutionary workers music. Charles' son, Pete Seeger, went on to become one of America's most beloved musicians within folk music and outside it. Not only are numerous of his songs widely known but his influence as a banjo player, songwriter, music scholar and archivist continue to influence music and discussion about it to this day. Artists such as Woody Guthrie, Leadbelly, Paul Robeson and The Weavers represented this approach by engaging and enriching the musical traditions of poor whites and blacks, the bulk of the working classes in the US at that time.

This was part of a complicated debate that was raging among artists and intellectuals throughout the world. It was not, as some historians have erroneously stated, confined to the Communist Party of the US or the Comintern in Moscow. It is true that these organized parties played a key role in the debate. But the debate did not originate with them nor was it controlled by them. These questions arose from the political struggles in which all society was involved; discussion and action not confined to any specific party or group. It does a great injustice both to the individual musicians who made much great music as well as to the life and death questions that were being grappled with to ascribe them all to some shadowy Politburo meeting. It flies in the face of the concrete facts of the mass movements of the first half of the twentieth century in which all of society was embroiled. Further, it fails to explain the enduring musical influence of artists such as those mentioned above. Just because Woody Guthrie was a communist doesn't mean that he was not a mendicant musician, who wrote great songs that have become part of American culture in the best sense.

The relationship between Adorno, Eisler and Seeger and the practices they articulated in theory are a way to view a much larger constellation of contending viewpoints. Simply put, Adorno and Eisler differed from within their general agreement about the importance of the composer and defense of what was progressive, educational and musically universal about the European tradition. Seeger opposed this and, from what might be viewed as a typically American perspective, said that classical music was bourgeois, the masses didn't like it and it could not be very useful in practice. In its place should be music made by the masses themselves, not composed for them by others, and music that is practically useful in actual struggles (performed on picket lines, at union meetings, etc.). It might appear that Eisler's was somewhere between Adorno's and Seeger's position, but this oversimplifies the case. Eisler was determined to be a composer, but a composer of music performed both by the amateur and the professional. In practice, his view had much in common with that of Brecht and Weill and, in America, with numerous composers and musicians from Duke Ellington to Mark Blitzstein, from Teddy Wilson to Leonard Bernstein. But it was more than that. One can see in the differing positions represented by these three men the complex relationship of music making to political Power. Adorno was a leftist opponent of Soviet orthodoxy from Germany. Eisler shared many of Adorno's views about music but was a conscious supporter of the Soviet (and, later, the East German) state. Seeger was involved in the struggles of the workers and oppressed peoples in the United States and, therefore, in opposition to that state. These positions relative to "official" or state policy, on the one hand, and the composer versus the popular tradition on the other, more or less embody the range of disputes with which musicians the world over had to contend until the outbreak of the Sixties, and its rejection of Soviet orthodoxy and the Old Left.

Lines were drawn that were to produce startling results in the coming decades. While Eisler has been forgotten, his work buried in the rubble of the Berlin Wall, Adorno and Seeger continue to exert an influence. But today, it is possible to see how the errors in their thinking have contributed to great confusion among musicians and political activists, practitioners and theoreticians.

The legacy of Woody Guthrie was the immensely influential folk movement of the early Sixties and "the voice of a generation," Bob Dylan. It is said that Pete Seeger was in tears when Dylan brought out an electric guitar at the Newport Folk Festival in 1965. Yet, this was a signal of the ultimate unraveling of central tenets of both Adorno's and Seeger's theoretical positions. Eisler, who died in 1962, might have taken a different view. He returned to Berlin after World War II where, similarly to Brecht, he wrangled frequently and heatedly with party bosses while maintaining his allegiance to "really existing socialism." On the one hand, there was the ascendancy to mass popularity of a form of music ("folk") and a musical artist of great eloquence (Dylan) and, almost at the same moment, it exploded into something new, obedient to none of the formulas and theories of the past 100 years; simultaneously defying the authority of bourgeois America and the Old, Soviet-inspired Left. The Beatles, the ultimate "boy group," became politicized, twice being the subject of banning and burning (once after Lennon's famous comment about being more popular than Jesus, second over the famous "butcher" album cover). The Mothers Of Invention ridiculed everybody including themselves, and "Dancing in the Streets" written by Marvin Gaye was banned from the airwaves in many cities because it was thought that it might inspire black rioting! Nothing that had happened in Europe or America could have prepared anyone for musical impact such as this. People might have recalled the Nazis rioting at the opening of Brecht/Weill's "The Rise and Fall of the City of Mahogany." They might have faint memories of Paul Robeson's confrontation with the American Legion. But this was unprecedented controversy over a musical genre! Yes, some of the lyrics were radical, but it was obvious that the music itself was inciting the masses in the manner predicted by the Radical Right. Freak Out, indeed!

The problems with Adorno's views were exposed. His argument was that music reaches its apex with the transcendent work of the Great Composer. The music of the slave/multitudes is, at best, raw material for the composer, at worst a trivial distraction from either aesthetic or political concerns. Perhaps it must be tolerated but it cannot be emulated or encouraged. Put crudely, liberation means everyone enjoying what hither-to only the elites enjoyed; the worker being "elevated" to the level of bour-geois listener—educated, articulate, but still an audience. In spite of his trenchant critiques of Soviet orthodoxy and state repression, Adorno's views nonetheless coincided with the Comintern's on this point. And it was the prevailing "official" position throughout the world from Moscow to Beijing, from New York to Johannesburg. It led to bizarre consequences such as the Chinese Communists after victory in a national liberation struggle against western imperialism adopting the European classical orchestra as ultimate form along with classical ballet (with toe shoes, no less!) and downplaying their own rich musical tradition. (Anyone who has attended a Chinese funeral or a Peking Opera knows the wealth of noisy, dissonant sounds incorporated into music long ago.) Moreover, it led to the rejection of, at first, jazz and related forms of African-American music as hopelessly compromised by commercial cooptation and, later, rock and roll as the embodiment of licentiousness and vulgarity or bourgeois hedonism.

The problems with Seeger's views were similarly exposed. While rejecting the Beethoven model it erected another. This entailed the strict limiting of the technology of music (banjos, acoustic guitars, etc.) and con-demning that which was "tainted" by use in commercial music (horns, drum sets, amplified anything). Creating a specific genre "folk music" and anointing it (authentic, proletarian), may seem a noble effort to employ Tolstoy's criteria. It certainly rejected Adorno's and most theorists' views of the transcendent work of the Great Composer. But it was simply stand-ing the argument on its head. It sought to eliminate the composer alto-gether. It ossified musical development in a particular time period before electricity and situated it in the rural as opposed to the urban setting. While this corresponded to what a large number of agricultural workers made and listened to, it excluded the growing numbers that were living in cities, making and listening to jazz, show music, urban blues, country and western, etc. It could not accept the continuous exploration and experi-ment that is always going on among the multitudes themselves with what-ever tools are at hand.

Furthermore, it could not deal with the ambivalent role of the musi-cian within the laboring population. There always were, in fact, poor peo-ple who were musicians not factory workers or field hands, and among these were anomalous individuals; oddballs, freaks, crackpots and vision-aries. Not necessarily drug-addicted or alcoholic, but not entirely "ration-al" either. The model was useful to an extent and, it must not be forgot-ten—some great music was made under its direction. But amongst all the streams of folk musics from Irish to Flamenco, from Cuban Son to South

African Township Jive, there were key musicians whose great skill and force of personality contributed mightily to what was known to the world as "people's music." They were not Beethovens in the grand European/bourgeois tradition but neither were they anonymous primitives laboring in the fields by day and sitting around the campfire strumming guitars by night.

## IT'S NOT ABOUT NOTES ANYMORE

The world wide political revolution known as the Sixties contained within it the musical critique of both Adorno and Seeger's views. Among its results—perhaps its most enduring legacy—was the dethroning of European classical music as "highest form." The composer continues to be maintained, almost entirely, by the three institutions enumerated by Tolstoy: the music critic, the music school, and the music professional (who Tolstoy specifically named the well compensated professional). Without such supports the "composer" would survive only as works and lessons, among all other works and lessons of music the world over. Indeed, much of the hullabaloo that surrounded Stravinsky, Schoenberg, Varese, Cage, Stockhausen, and "new music" in general seems almost poignant in light of subsequent events. In place of the transcendent work is the immanent work; the ongoing creative effort of making music, participating in it, demanding from and contributing to its perpetual renewal. Musicians thus engaged are no less devoted but no longer allow the head to dominate the heart, the brain to be removed from the body, the intellect to tyrannize the emotion and the historical to enslave the imagination.

Folk music, on the other hand, is simply one more genre among many that are popular. The fact that it is an artificial creation of individuals and political movements (as opposed to the many folk musics in the world) does not render it any more or less valuable in terms of music making. Perhaps its most enduring characteristic is to promote a love and appreciation of a certain group of instruments, a certain repertoire of songs and a general attitude of disdain for the hype and hoopla of the music industry. It can obviously be credited for contributing to the popularity of blues and gospel among the parents of the children coming of age in the Sixties. This should not be overlooked.

Nevertheless, it never was more than a style of music or, in the minds of those who believed in it, a utopianism not unlike that of many "back to nature" movements. It was anti-commercial, egalitarian, agriculturally based. Even when its influence generated major hits and mass popularity (of The Weavers, for example) musicians continued to make music with any and all means available. From the ghettos have come "non-musicians" who have used advanced electronic devices to make music in a new way. At the same time, people have continued to be inspired by older instruments and styles, in and of themselves, or in new combinations with other instruments and styles.

The musician within the multitude continues to play the role he (and occasionally she) always has: different from, while part of. Egalitarianism in social and political terms does not directly equate with music at all. If anything, the "tribe" of musicians the world over shares a special relationship to itself insofar as the particular problems of making music are confronted by all, regardless of country, language or musical tradition.

With the dethroning of European classical music came the welcoming within music making, at least, of the vast reservoirs of equally sophisticated, equally rich musical traditions from all parts of the world, and from within Europe and America. Perhaps it should not be surprising that it was often popular musicians who popularized the works of artists whose country, language, or generation kept them from being heard. One has only to think of the Beatles and Indian music, specifically that of Ravi Shankar, to know this. But this is an effort that has continued with gathering force ever since. Peter Gabriel, Bill Laswell and David Byrne have launched ongoing efforts to record and promote the works of many wonderful musicians throughout the world.

Simultaneously, the most extreme musical experiments of the twilight years of the dominance of the European classical tradition were made by numerous groups and musicians in other genres. The most obvious example is the parallel developments that were taking place within what is commonly referred to as jazz. Artists such as Sun Ra, Ornette Coleman, John Coltrane and Albert Ayler were at least as adventurous and challenging as their "high art" counterparts. "It's not about notes anymore," as Ayler said, is as eloquent a theoretical statement as any uttered by Adorno or Cage. In fact, what was clearly in evidence from the Sixties forward, was that slavery and music could never be understood apart from each other. That included the music of the descendants of slaves being relegated to a subordinate position in society to that of the music of the slave master or, to put it more accurately, that music commissioned by the slave master. This entire subject had been evaded or ignored by the very theoreticians who, otherwise, were devoted to the struggle for liberation![16]

## THE LIBERATION OF MUSIC

All music makers I have ever known, ever heard of, or read about have experienced being "set free" by music. This special, uplifting connection to the muse has set poets versifying, philosophers pondering and theorists analyzing. Words abound, in every culture, around this phenomenon that music can produce this liberatory effect. Of course, it has its religious or ritual dimension. In church services, sacrificial rites, ceremonies marking birth, marriage and death, music is used to call forth the life-giving spirit that flows through the universe, invisibly seizing all in its perilous grip, inviting all to paradise.

This special quality, this resonance within the cathedral of the world is both sought after and visited upon us unexpectedly. We are toyed with by mystery and we are inventors of a cosmic compass. All our suffering, all our doubt, all our vanity, all our aloneness is challenged, mocked and swept away by timeless moments when imagination takes flight, worlds are born, fear disappears, and mind and body dissolve.

And yet, there is no expressing it in words. It is only music that makes this so. We can describe but we cannot do without music. This is the liberation effect. The liberation of music.

But this happens in a world. This experience begins and ends many times within a lifetime. We are all too aware that our joy, our jubilation, our indescribable freedom is momentary and fragmented by "real life." Yet this wondrous experience must be exalted. It must be cherished, it must be nurtured for the sake of music itself. Wherever it comes from, invention or discovery, it must be understood as real and, at the same time, beyond anyone's capacity to control. Even the master musician is a servant in this cause. Humbled before the tangible no science can explain, the magic no ratio can define, the infinity no numbers can measure, the master revels in the adventure of exploring eternity.

When the Enlightenment broke the shackles of superstition and religious dogma and, ultimately, gave rise to social revolutions that overthrew the ancient regimes, it posited Reason as its most powerful weapon. The victories won with it were indisputable. Nevertheless, as philosopher Alain Badiou has so strikingly demonstrated, there were "sutures" made within the realm of philosophy and its generic conditions that have produced the errors and catastrophes discussed above.[17] Such is the suture of politics and music. It might also be called the tyranny of science, since science has been used to replace both religion and philosophy. Capturing and controlling music (among other human endeavors) has been the special task of rationalists, whether they be scientists or political activists. Defending their efforts on the basis of "the greatest good for the greatest number" in opposition to the obscurantism and mystifications that have characterized reactionary, oppressive forces, liberals and revolutionaries alike have made the profound error that had the effect, not so much of hurting music, but of hurting the cause of political emancipation.

It is time now to thoroughly critique these errors by a radical de-suturing. As Badiou vigorously asserts, we need philosophy but not in the role of "ruler." We need science, art, politics and love. But in each of these categories of human endeavor that make philosophy possible there is struggle and production specific to each that defies dominance by the others. Thus, not only is music not politics, any emancipatory politics must learn what its own tasks are and not confuse them with those of music or music maker. The same holds true for the other categories and for philosophy itself. To lead is not to rule. To educate is not to dominate. To liberate is not to go crazy (except in the eyes of Power).

Feeling good is not opposed to knowing good (or, to be grammatically correct, knowing well). Feeling the Good is not opposed to knowing the Good. The liberation of music does not mean opposition to Thought. Quite the contrary. Particularly when music is thought of from the viewpoint of the maker, it enriches and emboldens thinking. We can better struggle past the tired categorizations and false oppositions that have plagued philosophy, science, art and politics for centuries. We can unleash the imagination and offer it shelter within the struggle for justice and truth. Instead of fearing it as disruptive, we can view it as eruptive: the moments when the infinite breaks through the barrier of the "being for death" that is the drudgery of capitalist social relations. Instead of viewing the musician as either genius or lunatic, we can all participate in the music-making process by joining consciously in the sustenance of its production as opposed to its "consumption." Even if everyone is not themselves a music maker, nonetheless, everyone can learn this relationship to music and come to appreciate more deeply what music does in order to protect it as such. This collective activity that produces active collectivities. Belonging to and deciding in the Commons.

# FOOTNOTES

1. Interview by Bob Marshall, October 22, 1988
http://www.science.uva.nl/~robbert/zappa/interviews/Bob_Marshall/index.html
The full exchange was:
Frank Zappa: The right would like to put you out of business and the left would like to hire you, and I'm not for hire. I don't think that anybody who has a truly individualistic way of evaluating the world of a creative urge to do unique stuff needs to be snuffed out or hired. You should be free to do what your abilities will allow you to do because it is only when you are free to do that, the benefits of what you can build will be distributed to those parts of the society who will find your work useful. Really creative people don't work good as employees.
Bob Marshall: But you're saying there is more of a threat in the right-wing environment.
Frank Zappa: Yeah, that's the threat of death.
2    Whitfield, Greg. "The Rebel Dread: Greg Whitfield interviews Don Letts." *3 A.M. Magazine.* June, 2003.
http://www.3ammagazine.com/musicarchives/2003/jun/interview_don_letts.html
3    Nigerian musician Fela Kuti created "Afro-Beat," a musical genre combining elements of American funk and jazz with African rhythmic and compositional structures. The lyrics were politically charged and corresponded closely with Fela's radical activism. His music, in turn, was among numerous hybrids that inspired World Beat.
       World Beat was a phrase originally used by musician Dan Del Santo in Austin, Texas. Without knowing about Del Santo, a group of musicians in San Francisco, of whom this author was a member, also coined the phrase. (Naturally, we soon found out about each other—even performing together at a World Beat festival in Berkeley, California.) Not long after, World Beat was appropriated by record labels to market music from many parts of the world that did not neatly fit into categories such as Reggae, Township Jive, Calypso, etc., yet was nonetheless rhythmic and popularly based. Inevitably, the term, originally intended by the musicians to express solidarity and an internationalist viewpoint, was emptied of its political content altogether.
4    Tyrangiel, Josh. "Can Bono Save The World?" *Time Magazine.* March 4, 2002.
Note the word substitution here. In the Sixties it was "Change the World." Now it's "Save the World." The world, however, does not need to be saved. With or without humanity, it will continue. There are no saviors anyway. This is designed to make us forget what we can and must do. Jesus Saves! It was Marx who famously declared: "The philosophers have only interpreted the world, in various ways; the point is to change it."
5    Rumson, Gordon. "I've Got The Music in Me." *Music and Vision.* October 25, 2002.
6    Attali, Jacques. *Noise: The Political Economy of Music.* University of Minnesota Press, 1985, p. 47.
7    Ibid. p. 145.
8    Cage, John "An Autobiographical Statement."
 http://www.newalbion.com/artists/cagej/autobiog.html
Cage ended his piece with this comment:
"Author's note: 'An Autobiographical Statement' was written for the Inamori Foundation and delivered in Kyoto as a commemorative lecture in response to having received the Kyoto Prize in November 1989. It is a work in progress."
9    Cage, John. *Silence.* Wesleyan University Press, 1961, p. 10.
10   DuBois, WEB. *The Souls of Black Folk.* Dover Publications, p. 155.
11   Tolstoy, Leo. *What Is Art?* Penguin Books, 1995, p. 156.

12    Burnet, John. *Greek Philosophy, Thales to Plato*. St. Martin's Press, 1961, p. 307.

13    "At first known as the Dom in India, they were a low caste and earned their living by singing and dancing. The Dom began migrating from India in the 9th century, first as minstrels in Persia and later to escape the havoc wreaked by a series of Muslim invasions. As they migrated through the Middle East, the D of Dom was replaced by an R. The Gypsies today refer to themselves as the Rom, meaning "married man" and also "ethnic group." Their language, Romany, is a mixture of Sanskrit and loanwords from various countries in which they have lived. All Gypsies speak Romany. Today there are an estimated 8 to 10 million Gypsies in more than 40 countries, an estimated 1 million of them in North America." *The Grollier Encyclopedia*, 1997.

14    Bey, Hakim. "The Utopian Blues," from Fred Ho and Ron Sakulsky, *Sounding Off! Music As Subversion/Resistance/Revolution*. Autonomedia, 1995, p. 29.

15    Benjamin, Walter. *Illuminations*. Schocken Books, 1969, p. 242.

16    Cage and Adorno, in particular, took a dim view of jazz. While this can be partially attributed to taste and personal inclination it, nonetheless, betrays a serious weakness in their otherwise illuminating theoretical work. Indeed, the 20th century is replete with iconoclastic composers who challenged European traditions without ever fully considering the implications. Thus, the more radical aspects of their work and thought were left to gather dust as they were being embraced by the very institutions against which they had rebelled! This has definitely not been the case with African-American musicians or, for that matter, most musicians whose inspiration comes from elsewhere than the European. In the main, such artists and movements remain "ghettoized" even when spoken of respectfully. The ideas and theoretical contributions to music of Ornette Coleman, for example, are not taught or explored in most institutions of higher learning.

17    Many works by Alain Badiou, including:

Badiou, Alain. *Manifesto For Philosophy*. State University of New York Press, 1992.

Badiou, Alain. *Ethics*. Verso Press, 2001.

Badiou, Alain. *Infinite Thought*. Continuum Books, 1998.

The concept of "sutures" is a central tenet of Badiou's critique and is referred to frequently in all the above works. The Marxist suture, for example, is one that collapsed all thought into politics. ("everything is political") This is due, not to Marx, but to the "dead end" that Philosophy reached in the 20th century. Other sutures include those that make science, art or love "transcendent" and dominant over the rest.

# From Lyre to Lyric and Back

## Words and Music

The lunatic, the lover, and the poet
Are of imagination all compact....
The poet's eye, in a fine frenzy rolling,
Doth glance from heaven to earth, from earth to heaven;
And as imagination bodies forth
The forms of things unknown, the poet's pen
Turns them to shapes, and gives to airy nothing
A local habitation and a name.

SHAKESPEARE, *A Midsummer Night's Dream*

Hip-hop don't have no fresh energy, none at all. It's money driven, everybody tryin' to make that check, nobody putting art in their albums any more.

ANDRE BENJAMIN OF OUTKAST

"In the beginning was the word," or so the Bible says. But ask any parent and they can tell you that before a child can walk or talk they dance and sing. In other words, they move their limbs in time to rhythm and they make tonal sounds akin to musical notes in response to music they hear. Furthermore, music and dance do not need to "make sense" in order to provide pleasure to those engaged in the process of doing them. Indeed, words contain ideas, concepts, narratives that can be absent from music and dance until they are spoken about.

Poetry, on the other hand, is not simply words. Etymologically, poetry is derived from the Greek word *poiein* (to make), and the poet is one who invents, or makes things up. Poetry disposes with knowledge in the sense of facts, figures, data, even narrative, in its production of truths. This is the art of it. Art that is not science, is not politics, is not love, is not philosophy. Although expressed in words, it is exactly the opposite of the logical, narrative, empirical, historical or pedagogic. The chasm between what words normally do in speech or writing and the radical disruption that is made by their poetic use. From the simplest nursery rhyme to the sophisticated imagery of a Rimbaud or a Hughes, a Ginsberg or a Baraka, there is at once a familiar sequence of meaningful sounds (or letters) and a door opening into that which is beyond symbolic representation. It is presentation itself. Here, Now, Is. The immediate and forever that confounds Reason with its power to evoke being. To be true and to truly be.

The use of language—the fundamental tool of Reason—for such a purpose makes poetry, more than dance or music, appear to be a paradox. Its function as speech (or writing) belies its function as art. This has made poetry the focus of attack and worship. It has been banished and sacralized, damned and praised in the most strident terms. Plato decided that even a poet like Homer should be banished from the ideal city. This because the poet misleeds the populace, using fascinating imagery and clever word play to divert people from the higher purpose of the cultivation of wisdom and the pursuit of the greatest Good. This was not, as a modern interpreter might infer, some sort of crude "censorship." It was a radical polarization between the functions of philosophy and the functions of art; an operation from which we can still learn a great deal. Plato proposed that philosophy is the discovery and enunciation of Truth by which humanity should guide its action, that it should articulate the principle of Justice to make it a manifest bond between living, breathing humans. Thus, philosophy defended rational thought as its ultimate tool and the study of mathematics as the supreme method of inquiry into the workings of Nature. In this work philosophy should surrender to no other—particularly the intoxicants of poetry and music. Better to have no poetry than a poetry that misleads. Better to have no music than a music that deludes.

Nietzsche, conversely, attacked Plato and aspired to elevate poetry above all else, including philosophy. Exemplified by *Thus Spake Zarathustra*, he named himself, not philosopher, but poet. His targets were both Reason and Faith which, as science and religion, had enslaved humanity. His anti-philosophy heralded an era in which Poetry was pitted against the tyranny of Christian dogma and bourgeois order. The poem became, to Nietzsche, the instrument of liberation from servility to the "Truth" that danced before the hapless gaze of the obsequious masses as they trudged to their duties at the furnaces of mediocrity. His influence was great and renewed repeatedly as the world faced the horrors wrought in the name of religion and technocratic scientism. The greater good was as dead as God.

But where is poetry now? Poets read to poets. It is published in small runs on small presses. It appears as addenda in magazines. Fragments are quoted here and there. Poetry slams and readings at night clubs have enjoyed a certain resurgence. Occasionally there is a political controversy unleashed when a poem succeeds in outraging reactionaries. Reference is made to the great names of earlier eras when poetry enjoyed pride of place in the pantheon of art. It is still taught in literature courses at universities. So poetry is not dead. But it is far, far away from what it once was and from what either Plato or Nietzsche had in mind.

Today, poetry is in music. It is in the lyrics to songs that poetry thrives and has its widest influence. This is not only a matter of popularity. It is, fundamentally, a matter of a mutually reinforcing exchange between two independent arts that together offer each other protection and sustenance. Given music's unparalleled social importance, this might seem an unequal exchange wherein poetry and poets are dependent for their daily bread on their musical benefactors. But this is not really the case. For one thing, music has always drawn inspiration from its creative interaction with lyrics. (Similarly with dance, it must be said.) For another, it is an essential component of the attack on music that lyrics must be made insipid, banal, trivial. Poetry's own demands make it a willing ally in music's defense. Indeed, as we shall see, this may be more true now than ever before.

## ROCK AND ROLL AS POETIC REVIVAL

While poetry appeared to be shrinking in relevance, it was being reinvented in association with popular song. Arguably the last great poetic moment was the Beats. This is not to underestimate the enormous importance of African-American and West Indian poets, from Amiri Baraka to Aime Cesaire, who were at the forefront of social movements that were to converge, during the Sixties, in the struggles for national liberation characteristic of that period. But the Beats—Ginsberg, Kerouac, et al, rose to fame as representatives of the continuity of a pre-television, pre-movie tradition of literary significance. Even so, this was at the high point in popularity of jazz and, to a large extent, they enjoyed their notoriety by basking in the glow of this "negro" art form. Already evident was the decline in influence of poetry in and of itself. "Howl" was as much a howl for the poem as poem as it was a denunciation of what had become of "the best minds of my generation."

Meanwhile, at the very moment the Beats were reaching the apex of their influence, another musical and lyrical eruption was underway. This came to be known as rock and roll. From its inception, its leading exponent and champion was Chuck Berry, an extraordinary lyricist. Amidst a flood of silly lyrics that, at one point, dominated the field, Berry's intelligence, wit and insight demonstrated the possibilities for poetic expression of the new musical genre. But it was two other poets who were also musicians that announced the coming of a poetic revival in the blossoming of rock and roll in the turbulent Sixties. These were Bob Dylan and Gil Scott-Heron. "The Times They Are A-Changin'" and "The Revolution Will Not Be Televised" announced the liberation of the popular song from the lyrical inhibitions it suffered at the time. Cars, girls and parties were not the only subjects permissable, now. Moreover, they presented the poet as poet in the context of the popular. Scott-Heron, in fact, spoke, rather than sang, many of his most famous and compelling compositions. This cut in two directions at once. While opening up new possiblities for poetry and music it reconnected with ancient traditions.[1]

For thousands of years, in many parts of the world, there was a close relationship between the singing of song and the recitation of poetry among the lower orders. To this day, in Basel, Switzerland, for example, at Fastnacht (Carnival) ribald, satirical rhymes, pointedly mocking authority, are read aloud and then posted on the door of the Burgermeister's office. Similarly, calypso, with its clever, socially-critical, word play wedded to dance rhythms is the "newspaper" or "editorial page" of the People's version of events. Indeed, virtually all folk tradition is characterized by this connection between text and music that is more than simply words being accompanied by music or melody needing words to have something to sing about.

Something happened in the 20th century, however, that separated the populace from the popular. As world war and revolution engulfed humanity, social groups vying for control sought to mobilize the masses using many techniques including popular song. This was not entirely unprecedented since the world had learned the powerful effect of great revolutionary anthems such as "La Marseillaise" and the "Internationale" in the preceding century. In keeping with such examples, poets like Bertolt Brecht scandalized the bourgeoisie and inspired popular struggle in works that gained worldwide influence. But whether it was bourgeoise critics or radical theoreticians, there was always a profound mistrust of what the populace would come up with on its own. There was, from Right and Left, a fear of the rabble whose ignorance and uncultured prejudices could destroy civilization. On the one hand, bourgeoise art critics mocked the triviality and vulgarity of popular art. On the other, theorists like Theodoro Adorno warned that the Culture Industry would turn anything the masses might produce into chains perpetuating their enslavement. Indeed, the Culture Industry is so comprehensive, so dominant that nothing the masses like can be authentically their own, let alone true art of artful truth.[2]

While the Sixties successfully blew much of that away, it came roaring back in the wake of the collapse of the Soviet Union and the "triumph" of capitalism. The evidence is everywhere of the betrayals that support Adorno's claims. Not only is much popular culture manufactured for consumption by the masses, but much of it is indistinguishable from advertising. Indeed, Allen Ginsberg shilled for the Gap. William Burroughs did adverts for Nike. Spike Lee sold beer. These are facts. But they conceal a more profound truth.

First of all, only social revolution can transform the social order completely, ending the suffering and injustice produced by this, capitalistic one. Whatever forms it takes, however it erupts, it will not be a social revolution if it leaves the current state of affairs intact. But this political truth cannot serve as an excuse for doing nothing until such a revolution magically appears, thus ensuring that it never will. This cannot be a justification for dismissing, on either artistic or political grounds, that which spontaneously emerges within what is broadly considered popular culture—especially music. In fact, there can only be a revolution if, in the course of all struggle, in all spheres of society, there is a constant effort to renew and revitalize precisely those qualities that have long exemplified the populace in opposition to the State. The targets, as always, are privilege and Power. The weapons, collective thought and action. The aim, justice and equality for a humanity still bitterly divided.

For poetry and music, these questions have renewed urgency, because the last years of the 20th century saw the emergence of a popular form that, more than any before, brought words into the foreground. Poetry came forth to establish itself, on its own terms, alongside the music that had been its shelter for the previous two generations. Rap music, in this sense, is the elevation of the text to preeminence over all other musical elements except one: rhythm. The beat remains the musical foundation upon which the poetry must depend but that's the only one. From here on out, melody, harmony, musical instruments, and musicians all play a clearly supportive role to the verbal statement that is the rhyme and reason for rap.

### HIP-HOP: HYSTERY AND HYSTERIA

Following its emergence on the streets of New York, rap music or hip-hop rapidly spread, first through the ghettos of North America, later throughout the world. Originally, artists such as Afrikka Bambatta, Kurtis Blow, Grandmaster Flash and KRS One were part of an "underground" that contained disparate musical and social influences, from live bands playing rock and funk to DJs and breakdancers.

Simultaneously, a dirty war was under way. What became known as the Iran/Contra scandal revealed the secret, illegal deals being cut by the CIA to sell guns to the Contras who were fighting the Sandanista-led Nicaraguan revolution. This was paid for by the vastly increased sale of crack cocaine to the ghettos of the US. Documentary evidence of this was compiled by, among others, a reporter for the San Jose Mercury News and submitted to Congressional Representative Maxine Waters for investigation.[3] It was subsequently buried in a cloud of "conspiracy theory," media dismissal and deliberate Congressional obstruction. But anyone living in a major American city knew something out of the ordinary was going on. "The White House is the Crack House," was a commonly voiced sentiment on the streets.

That the CIA was involved should be no surprise since they have manipulated the Mafia since World War II. In fact, it was the OSS (forerunner of the CIA) that was responsible for a deal with Lucky Luciano to ensure both the revival of the Mafia following the war (the Fascists had seriously constrained their activities) and the Mafia's dedicated effort in preventing the Communists from taking power. Since then, much evidence has come to light about how the CIA and other US government agencies have used drug trafficking and various criminal gangs to fight revolutionary and nationalist movements in different parts of the world, including southeast Asia, Africa and Latin America. That this same formula would be used on the black communities of the US is part of a well documented pattern.[4]

Its relevance to hip-hop is that by the mid '80s the black community was awash in crack. Only a few years before, cocaine in the powdered form was a recreational drug for mainly middle and upper class whites. Crack was the drug for impoverished blacks. The drug trade that burst upon the ghetto employed large numbers of young black men and large numbers of guns. The Crips and the Bloods, two LA gangs that began a generation previously, were transformed into gun and drug running business enterprises. Literal warfare, reminiscent of the prohibition-era gang wars, broke out in cities across the country as the business was systematically expanded and fought over by rivals vying for control.[5]

When, in 1988, two records were almost simultaneously released, a crossroads had been reached. And they would signal a widening divergence between two trends in Rap music: "conscious" and "gangsta" rap. NWA's "Straight Outta Compton" and Public Enemy's "It Takes A Nation of Millions to Hold Us Back" announced the arrival of a sound and fury that were far more than a musical phenomenon. This was the drumming of the slave amplified a thousand fold. Its backdrop was the nightly drive-bys and the terrorizing of entire neighborhoods by gun-wielding, drug-dealing gangsters. Big bucks went along with big guns. A way out of poverty was being dangled before the eyes of any kid desperate enough to try it. The seething anger of a generation of black and hispanic youth completely frustrated by what appeared to be the failures of the Sixties and certainly were the racist assaults of the Reagan regime exploded into a musical genre that leapt beyond its origins into new sonic and lyrical territory.

The music industry (whose ties to the Mafia, incidentally, went back decades) saw both an opportunity and a necessity.[6] At first, responding to the pressures of the "establishment"—Reagan's right wing social base as well as the PMRC—and wanting to appear to be "good citizens," the majors were uncertain about what to do with hip-hop. But they also had learned from the "golden age" of the indies—basically, 1977–1987—and the hip-hop phenomenon was becoming big business without them. In fact, many of the most popular artists were making and selling their records themselves, right out of the trunks of their cars! Very, very fast, the big boys dove into the fray, much more quickly than they had responded to the challenge posed by Punk Rock and other indie based musical genres. They poured millions into the signing, marketing and promotion of acts such as Ice Cube, Dr. Dre (both from NWA) and Snoop Dog all the way up to Eminem (the Elvis of hip-hop) and 50 Cent (whose album title *Get Rich or Die Trying*, says it all). Music videos, films, product endorsements (specifically malt liquor and shoes), awards shows, in a word, all the glamour and glitz of Hollywood in its heyday. The audience, by the early '90s, was overwhelmingly white. The sales of hip-hop CDs were far larger in the suburban malls of middle America than they were in the ghettoes from which the music originated. It was—and is—an extremely profitable business.

Initially, enormous controversy surrounded this music. First and foremost from within the black and hispanic communities themselves. While a great hue and cry was raised by "respectable" civic leaders over the horrific lyrical content, musicians and others were demanding to know why the same concern was not being expressed about the horrific conditions in which black and hispanic people lived. While politicians and church elders decried the moral decay of a generation, activists attacked the economic decay faced by people in the ghetto and the utter hypocrisy of a "free market" economy that made millions from the music they were denouncing.

Now, it's all a bit of yawn. Gangsta rap, full of self-loathing and misogyny is no more controversial than porn. In fact, it's less so now than internet downloading! While serious debate continues among musicians, music lovers and some critics, society at large, particularly the mainstream media, couldn't care less. For one thing, much hip-hop has degenerated into a sad parody of itself with scarcely the veneer of authenticity being applied any more. For another, the genuine article, including as it does, sophisticated and thought provoking socio-political critique, is simply not interesting to the attention-span-deprived. Exceptions are numerous (Dead Prez, for example) but they prove the rule. "Conscious" rappers and groups are not, in the main, to be found on MTV or BET, let alone CNN or FOX. Indeed, the music, its spirit, remains vital and full of promise. But, like rock and roll, it is increasingly defined by what specific creative artists do with it as opposed to a genre or sound which, in itself, conveys a rebellious attitude.

## THE STRATEGY OF REPLACEMENT

In the last twenty years, the means employed to make music a willing servant of capital have been adapted to new conditions. The specific task of purging music of the legacy of the revolutionary Sixties has been high on the agenda. To a greater and greater extent, suppression and replacement, rather than cooptation, have become the favored strategies. But this is suppression and replacement with an important twist. Suppression is favored by the Radical Right, replacement is favored by the neo-liberal establishment including the music industry. While, since the 80s organizations like the Parental Music Resource Center (PMRC) have made a lot of noise and real difficulties for certain artists, they have, in the main, been lightning rods for the mobilization of a specific right wing, racist constituency. Stickers on CDs, like bandaids for cancer, expose the fact that they have had little effect on music or lyrics overall.

Replacement, on the other hand, has been very effective. But this replacement is done in different ways. In addition to Anti-music in general, there is the special kind of replacement in hip-hop, a musical genre that has become one of the two or three most popular in the world and it is a truly global phenomenon, embraced by youth of many lands, in many languages. Within this genre, replacement has focused on the text, not the music. A systematic effort on the part of certain forces in the music industry has led to the proliferation of "gangsta" rap and the marginalizing of "conscious" rap. The latter is a loose category inclusive of overtly political texts along with discussions of spirituality, history and personal experience. "In the past, people maybe rapped and they did the music for the masses of the people," says Chuck D. of Public Enemy. "Rap was anti-elitist, and anti-establishment, it wasn't turning its nose up at the masses. Now it's a bit troubling to see that where rap was rap for the people, now it's become the elite, speaking against their people. Rap is rap for the companies, rap for the corporations."[7] In case there is any doubt about this or the extent to which it pervades the genre the overt use of brand names in songs has become an aspect of the marketing the music industry does with the music. For example:

> Compiled by the US marketing company LucJam Inc, in addition to listing the artists and their songs, it also references all the products plugged in their lyrics. American Brandstand, they call it, and it's quite cool. With an additional bit telling you which brand is doing best in a plugs-per-year running total (so far it's Mercedes, followed by Burberry and Timberland footwear), it also tells you that, out of the April 19 US Top 20, 10 songs have one (but usually more) plugs in them.
>
> Perhaps this shouldn't really be all that surprising. From Run DMC's "My Adidas" onwards, hip-hop (which effectively forms most of the US Top 20) has always been a genre of music that has been extremely brand-conscious, and you continue to be able to tell a lot about an artist by what they plug. 50 Cent only plugs Benz and Bacardi, which makes you think he's quite a real kind of guy. L'il Kim's "The Jump Off" references six different brands, which makes you think she's got a market stall where she sells stuff on.[8]

This is only a small indication of how a calculated move to remove and then replace the emergent rebel music of the ghetto actually functions. Let's recall, again, some of hip-hop's history:

It can be argued that rap music was born with a song called, "The Message" (released in 1982). This song was not without precedent. Gil Scott-Heron and Linton Kwezi Johnson were poets who successfully combined their texts with music in a sophisticated interplay that had wide influence. Calypsonians in Trinidad had been doing it for decades. But "The Message" broke through at a particular time when it seemed that black music had lost all contact with the streets of the ghettoes where a large part of the black population lives. Stars such as Whitney Houston and Luther Vandross embodied middle class aspirations utterly ignoring the large and growing majority of black people living in deepening poverty. hip-hop "overthrew" this aristocracy, indicting its irrelevance and reasserting the importance of rebel music to oppressed people. However, by the time rap had entered the mainstream (meaning a large audience of suburban white youth were buying what was an urban and ghetto-oriented sound) there was already a growing element within the genre that was deliberately apolitical, focusing more on partying, sexual escapades and the drug trade. By the early '90s this element took over.

> No new innovative artists are hired to balance out a roster of the porno-
> graphic genocide MC's. In their place, we're presented with yet more exam-
> ples of arrested development—the portrayal of grown men and women act-
> ing and dressing like 15 year olds. Balding insecure men in their mid 30's
> making entire songs about their sexual prowess and what shiny toys they have
> and you don't. The only hate I see is self-hate. The only love I see is self-love.
> As a DJ, it's hard: I pick up the instrumental version of records that peo-
> ple nod their head to… and mix it with the a cappella version of artists with
> something to say. It is expensive and frustrating. But I feel like the alternative
> is the musical equivalent to selling crack: spinning hits because it's easy, ignor-
> ing the fact that it's got us dancing to genocide.[9]

In a piece called "Hip Hop's Ten Commandments," writer Stephanie Mwandisi Gadlin argues persuasively that a calculated strategy has been employed whereby "success" is guaranteed the rapper/producer who scrupulously abides by certain rules.

> Commandment I: Thou must dis' black women.
> Commandment II: Thou must kill.
> Commandment III: Thou must covet. Thou must talk about lusting after
> things that do not belong to you.

Commandment IV: Thou must have a lot of sex.

Commandment V: Thou must celebrate the drug culture.

Commandment VI: Thou must rarely talk about God and spirituality.

Commandment VII: Thou must promote capitalism.

Commandment VIII: Thou cannot have a sense of history.

Commandment IX: Thou must not advocate. Thou art prohibited from advocacy of anything of social redeeming value.

Commandment X: Thou must promote all things ghetto.

And the reward:

By keeping the aforementioned commandments we, "the industry," guarantee the following:

1. Unlimited marketing success and cross-over appeal.
2. A guaranteed income.
3. Fame beyond your wildest dreams.
4. Unlimited (but recoupable) industry resources.
5. Several music awards, citations and honors.
6. Protection from community repercussions.[10]

Quite early on, the music industry was able to profit enormously by the selling of these images of sex and death, riches and fame, first and foremost to suburban white youth who saw in them the excitement and "authenticity" that has long been associated with the oppressed, particularly black people. Second, they discovered (surprise, surprise) that it was quite easy to manipulate these violent gangsters (who in some cases were literally killing each other). Control of the media (broadcast, print, distribution) and vast sums of money made the apparently "threatening," "countercultural" hip-hop "movement" the perfect vehicle for the diversion of the youth from a course of political opposition into self-destructive, self-enslaving behavior. The underlying fact that the great majority of black and hispanic youth in the US, UK, Europe, Africa and Latin America were suffering intensifying attacks on their economic and social well-being, that all the gains that had been made in the Sixties were being swept away and replaced by increased immiseration was easily disguised using the tried and true methods of "old style" colonialism. Thus, the alliance between Columbian drug lords and ghetto gangs was valorized at the street level while being condemned at the official level.

## DON'T BELIEVE THE HYPE

"Don't believe the hype," said Chuck D. This was directed at a number of targets. But, it contains a warning to all those who would be mesmerized by the media maze surrounding hip-hop. Much of the controversy is phony and deliberately designed to divert attention from both the larger social conflicts that rage unabated behind the smokescreen and the deeper, timeless truths that reside in the best music and words. A massive publicity machine swings into action behind each "important" (read: major label) hip-hop release. This inevitably includes well rehearsed objections by "concerned" critics to the anti-social lyrics, thereby ensuring that the widest possible audience is made aware of them. This formula has been repeated so often that it has become clear that what is ultimately at issue is not that rap songs (or heavy metal, punk or any form, including grand opera) are misogynist, violent, drug praising or crime extolling. It is that they are lies.

The so-called "authentic" is, what? That the speaker is black? Originates in the ghetto? Comes from a broken home? What guarantee is this that such a person will not lie? The President of the United States lies. Why shouldn't anyone else? It does no good to resort to the intellectual gymnastics many academics and critics do when confronted with this question. Their naive acceptance of race or economic status as credentials of credibility simply betrays their own isolation from the people about whom they theorize. Suffering does not bestow honor upon the sufferer. It certainly does not bestow Papal infallibility. While it provides a basis for understanding, suffering provides no guarantee that the sufferer will speak truth. A black 15 year old single mother on crack, by her very existence, may present a fact. From this we can decide that free market capitalism doesn't guarantee the greatest good for the greatest number. But this is by no means the only conclusion one might draw—let alone, is it automatic. Quite the contrary. In the face of innumerable such facts the big lie of "America, land of the Free" continues to be effective.

Misogyny, homophobia, murder, mayhem, dysfunctional families, drug addiction, organized crime—this is really happening. It is the sordid, sickening state of the oppressed. Of course, there are rappers who are macho assholes. Of course, there are lumpen hoods barfing bullshit by the bale. Of course, there are thugz and playaz and gangstaz spewing their ghetto version of free market capitalism. But this is the reality of the situation, not the lie. The lie is that this is black culture. The lie is that this is the prevailing attitude of the oppressed. The lie is that this is "just happening" and that it is not being consciously, systematically produced in the exact same fashion that pornography and fast food is. There is no longer any question of this being authentic. This is a calculated effort to eliminate what is.

So what's new? Doesn't this simply confirm Adorno's (and others') prognosis? Doesn't this prove that, in the end, popular culture always becomes "pop," is always, only a commodity, never an effective expression of people's yearnings to be free?

## OPPRESSION AND RESISTANCE, THE LIMITS OF COOPTATION

Suppression/replacement have become increasingly important as cooptation has approached a certain limit. The limit to cooptation is this: where there is oppression there is resistance. Music is among the most powerful means of rallying the oppressed to resist. Contrary to the views propounded by most theorists (post-Modernist or otherwise) there is a limit to what can be coopted. There is a dynamic in music-making itself, which, combined with the impulses of the oppressed to rebel against their oppression, constantly revitalizes the effort to escape co-optation. This dynamic is the conscious rejection, on an ongoing basis, of the very sounds, patterns, styles, etc. that have been coopted. They become the very targets at which the creative assault is directed. One might even call it the cooptation of cooptation. In other words, young music makers deliberately seek to break the rules that they themselves or, perhaps, the previous generation, created. What was considered the Good, the Beautiful or the True by one's parents or older sister is now ridiculed; rejected in the pursuit of, apparently, opposite qualities. The most obvious examples are the employment of noise, distortion, atonality, howls and shrieks in place of the elements music is "supposed" to be composed of. But, mainly, it is the invention or discovery of anything that cannot be "understood" according to criteria established by what the dominant culture defines as music, poetry or art in general.

This does not, however, culminate in one or any style, sound, composition, etc. that is, magically, "uncooptable." As Adorno demonstrated conclusively and has been borne out by successive cooptations—including the most radical sounding hip-hop beats—there is nothing that, in and of itself, cannot be coopted by capital.[11] However, contrary to Adorno and virtually all theorists since, music makers among the lower social orders repeatedly evacuate the very social spaces they create as soon as they are threatened by cooptation. This has become a well-established practice, particularly since the advent of punk rock in the late '70s. The vast networks of underground scenes that literally span the globe are testament to this fact. Hakim Bey's *Temporary Autonomous Zone* theorizes this social phenomenon which, in the face of all efforts to curb and corral, continues to spread, virus-like, throughout the social body and from generation to generation.[12] The Temporary Autonomous Zone is exactly what it says it is: it is a specific, limited, but very effective response to cooptation which evades suppression and replacement as well. It is the social site where the imagination is given voice in clear opposition to the forces that would capture and enslave it.

Indeed, the music industry is fully conscious of this phenomenon and pays its representatives to infiltrate these rapidly mutating scenes, scouring them for the "next big thing" that can be snapped up, repackaged and sold. These agents of corruption can be found snooping around wherever something appears to be "happening," no matter how deeply underground it is. They adorn themselves with the requisite attire and, armed with the magic wand of their business card, are certain to find young people susceptible to the temptations of riches and fame. In the last decade, however, this has become increasingly difficult and less and less profitable to do—in part, due to the widely disseminated lessons of the past twenty years and the speed with which music scenes, like guerrilla encampments, appear and dissolve. As social antagonisms intensify, musical expression amongst the dispossessed has now come to consciously include what might be called its own, anti-authoritarian model. This could be stated as: creation > cooptation > rejection > new creation. While this does not render the music industry inoperative, let alone lead directly to social revolution, it produces a seriously destabilizing effect. Nebulous and inarticulate as this may be, it nonetheless reinforces the growth of a counter-culture that enunciates and champions conscious opposition to the dominant culture. Cooptation is no longer an effective enough tool. It has failed to adequately control or profit from the threatening disquiet oppression inevitably produces.

For both political and economic reasons then, the preferred strategy of replacement has come to the fore. This is what "Pop Stars," MTV, the manufactured "Boy" and "Girl" groups, the Robbie Williamses and the Christina Aguileras are about. Anti-music. Displace and replace the real with the fake.

If you think this is only about hip-hop or pop music, think again. The world's most prestigious classical music label is Deutsche Gramophone. This is the "new" policy they describe in an interview with *The Independent*:

> As DG's chief talent-spotter, Martin Engstroem was frank about the way his priorities had shifted in "artists and repertoire." "Our releases are primarily linked to the artist, the star. People go to a concert, fall in love with the artist and buy their record. Yes, it's a big change, but it's one we have to live with. Ten years ago, you went purely for quality." But not now? "Of course, you still go for that, because we're still talking DG. But quality is no longer enough on its own. You have to listen to the market. We've recently

signed a lot of charismatic young artists like Lang Lang and Hilary Hahn, because we feel that's where the energy lies." He agreed this runs counter to the old assumption that age and wisdom make the best music. "But that is not what the public says. To keep our figures in the black, we have to listen to the market."[13]

Replacement, however, cannot work on its own. Its evil twin is suppression, without which it could not be successful. Behind the veneer of democratic rights, the offer of free choice, suppression goes on with a vengeance. There are two basic suppressive tactics, the first being banning and burning, the second, marginalizing and impoverishing. There is a long and continuous history of authorities banning and burning, which include the well known cases of The Beatles and The Dixie Chicks. Photographs of bonfires of Beatles records or trucks crushing piles of Dixie Chicks CDs are famous. The case of a Dead Kennedys record being hauled into court for its "obscene" album cover art is another example. Frank Zappa's hilarious account, in his autobiography, of his confrontation with British judges over song lyrics they could not even understand is yet another.[14] Outside the US, there is a long and bloody legacy of singers being jailed or killed. Latin America is full of them. Some of the most important artists in the last 50 years are included in this index of inquisition, Gilberto Gil and Victor Jara being only two notable examples. There are literally thousands of musicians world wide, who were murdered or incarcerated for their opposition to the authorities. But, here we are focusing on the period following the collapse of the Soviet Union and the rise to global hegemony of the US, which has culminated most recently in overt, governmental assaults such as shutting down Rage Against the Machine's website in the wake of 9/11 or the vindictive visa denials for Cuban musicians seeking to perform in the US.

Though many people still cling to the illusion of the US and other "democracies" being devoid of such censorship, rights deprival or other "fascistic" tactics, they are quite common. This excerpt from the website "Banned Music in the US" is revealing:

> Following the September 11th terrorist attacks, Clear Channel Communications, the largest owner of radio stations in the United States, releases a list of more than 150 "lyrically questionable" songs that stations may want to pull from their playlists. Few songs portray explicit violence, but most have metaphoric themes that ring a bit too close to the tragedies. The list, containing music from almost every genre in popular music, includes Sugar Ray's "Fly," "Jet Airliner" by Steve Miller, Nine Inch Nails' "Head Like a Hole," AC/DC's "Shoot to Thrill" and "Highway to Hell," Pat

Benatar's "Hit Me with Your Best Shot," "Dust in the Wind" by Kansas, Jerry Lee Lewis' "Great Balls of Fire," REM's "It's the End of the World as We Know It," "Only the Good Die Young" by Billy Joel, Dave Matthews Band's "Crash Into Me," "Nowhere to Run" by Martha & The Vandellas, and all songs by Rage Against The Machine.[15]

Reading this list is almost laughable. Were it not backed up by the Power of a crypto-fascist regime it would be. It is, however, only the most obvious form suppression takes.

Being marginalized and impoverished is a condition of life for most musicians, and so it is very difficult to prove that any particular song, performance or artist is being victimized for their specifically political or social-critical stance. Nonetheless, it is quite clear that for a very long time artists who posed a threat to the social order were ostracized, kept out of reach of the audiences for their work and thus, prevented from having any social effect. Since the outrages of the McCarthy era, this has been done in such a way as to keep the process hidden from public view. It usually means denying access to funds or resources necessary to produce or distribute works and can, thus, be disguised as the blind workings of the market. Nevertheless, explicitly anti-authoritarian or revolutionary works have been so frequently dismissed by the arbiters of taste (usually art/music critics or the talent scouts of corporate entertainment) that it scarcely needs mentioning. Two examples are sufficient: Warren Beatty's film *Bullworth* commented insightfully on racism in America and the impact of deindustrialization on the post-Sixties ghetto. Now, Beatty's a bankable star. "Important" was written all over this film. It sank like a stone weeks after its debut, never even appearing in Europe. The recent case of Steve Earle and his song "John Walker's Blues" is also representative. When, shortly after September 11, 2001, Earle wrote and recorded a song exploring the motives of an American, John Walker, found among the Taliban in Afghanistan, he was vilified by the country music establishment, with the specific comment that he was only seeking controversy to save his flagging career.

But suppression is a dangerous tactic for the powers that be. It has many potential uses, but at least as many potential drawbacks. To begin with, even when a particular artist or group of artists are banned, burned, blackballed and buried, others immediately spring up to say similar things and to make use of the allure that outlaw status confers. Further, it has become part of the complicated process of propaganda to employ this status as a selling point. Particularly in the music industry, it is well-established practice to exploit and even deliberately create the "bad boy" image since it has long proven effective in attracting consumers. Trouble with the law or other authorities makes an artist a symbolic representative of a segment of the population who will "cheer" for them. This has roots as deep as Robin Hood, Jesse James or Pretty Boy Floyd. It ties in with the mythopoetics of Dashiell Hammett's private eye or with Clint Eastwood's characters in Sergio Leone's films. The most outstanding example is that of Jimmy Cliff's character in *The Harder They Come*. That character and story provides a blueprint used with no greater effectiveness than in the world of hip-hop.

While the 20th century is replete with examples of the suppression of music this has, if anything, proven the ultimate futility of such tactics for those in Power. The Nazis tried. Franco tried. The Soviet Union tried. The Chinese government tried. Rock and roll was singled out in the latter two cases as a corrupting, foreign, bourgeois influence. In fact, in both places, music without words was scrutinized for its subversive content and, as in the famous case of Shostakovich, the artists pressured to mend their ways. But, certainly since the collapse of "communism," and most especially with the emergence of hip-hop, virtually all efforts to suppress a musical genre have proven ineffective. Instead, suppression is now focused on words (secondarily, and less significantly, on visual images). And it is always accompanied by replacement. There is always an antiseptic substitute (read: toxic potion) ready to shove into the slot left by what had to be removed.

## SHUT UP AND PLAY YOUR GUITAR

It can be argued that this only applies to the "political" or socially conscious artists. Musicians need not concern themselves with lyrics or poetry at all, let alone politics. That's why they got into music in the first place. Music produces its effects without reference to these contentious and tedious subjects. Besides, it takes enough energy and dedication to make good music without being bothered by all this "talk."

There is a serious objection in this that needs to be considered before going any further. I've already discussed the difference between music and politcs elsewhere in this book, but it is important to say that the intertwining of text and melody, of poetry and music, does not begin or end with politics. It does not begin or end with "meaning" of any kind. It is certainly not simply a matter of what is suppressed, replaced, coopted or otherwise abused. When someone resorts to a litany of song lyrics to prove a point, it is usually damning evidence of an unwillingness or inability to think about music or poetry; to confront the difficulties presented by art's ambivalent energy, its "suspicious" aspect.

When it comes to art the question is: "does it move me?" When it comes to being moved we are no longer speaking of data, styles, ethnic origin or market shares. We are speaking of emotions, feelings, loves, hates, angers, sorrows, desires, aspirations. Putting on a costume or a uniform may identify to some extent. Adopting a threatening posture may be a necessary introduction. Practicing certain rituals or customs may bring inclusion into a group. But being moved is something different. It requires an interaction between participants mutually engaged in an exchange, a collective activity. It requires a sensitivity, a vulnerability, that everything in the so-called "real world" is telling us to repress. It requires a determination to seek, an active pursuit of the connection that art and only art can produce.

This connection has two aspects. One is to the sacred or holy. The other is to the transformative Event. Regardless of the particular subject of a poem or song, its effect, its magic, results from creating a link to the infinite. Whether one is an atheist (as I am) or a religious person it is useful to call this the sacred. In my view, the sacred is the Void. The nothing that is the infinite omniverse of being. It matters little whether a work is comedic, tragic, angry, sad, political, sexual or anything else. The sacred is a power, a potential. It blasts through the humdrum, everyday "real" and carries us away to the infinite that is beyond sense. Non-sense. Not rational. Not knowledge. But true.

The transformative Event, on the other hand, is that which erupts in time, history, chronology, to completely break the grip of the ruling State. This State is not simply the government or ruling class (politics). It is the entire State of affairs, all social relations, the naming of things, the structures and symbols that, hitherto, were considered whole and inviolable, absolutely beyond question. Such eruptions occur within all spheres of human activity, including falling in love. Einstein's "Theory of Relativity" is one. The French revolution is another. The point is that such tranformative Events affect everything and everyone.[16] Long after they have passed some will oppose them. Others will remain faithful to them. So, for example, Public Enemy was faithful to the Event of the world wide revolution of 1968, specifically, the black liberation struggle symbolized by figures such as Malcolm X. It is not, however, because their songs speak of this in some literal, analytic fashion that they are powerful. It is because they capture the spirit and uphold a loyalty to that spirit. That they became enormously popular says something about how much young people in 1988 yearned for such a feeling. If, however, Public Enemy were not artists this would not have been possible. It was, above all, the artfulness of their work that made it powerful.

This is a complex question. It is made more difficult by words themselves since we must use them to speak about this which is not what words do in poetry. Meaning, in the sense of objects, actions, personalities, stories, is usually present in a song text or poem. But it is not the meaning that gives that text its power. It is precisely that which goes beyond meaning, escapes it and conveys wonder in its place that makes a work art, and a great work timeless. It is, in this sense, why "The Message", perhaps the founding work of rap, is timeless. Of course, the song is gritty, street smart, funky, real. But what makes it resonate as art is not these outward signs. The use of rhythm, of the sounds words make beside their meaning particularly in rhyme, the juxtaposition of pauses and non-verbal inflections all combine to deliver the hypnotic invitation of the Pied Piper. Follow me children, your townspeople are liars.

It should be noted that the technical virtuosity displayed by rappers, in particular, and poets in general, is only one component of the art. The craft, which demands mastery to achieve any noteworthy artistic result, is still not the guarantee of a great work. There is plenty of absolute crap in music and poetry that is technically impressive and displays great skill. The difference returns us to the issue of proximity to the sacred. While the transformative Event will shape all the names, all the symbols, all the methods with which we connect with each other, only timeless art can break through the mask of the real into the Void from which every singularity, every individual springs.

## WHO CARES?

"Who gives a fuck? is one of the first questions a kid will ask himself growing up in the ghetto. He'll look around at the broken-down buildings, the shabby projects, the cracked schoolyard playgrounds, and it doesn't look like anybody gives a fuck."—Ice T, *Ice Opinion: Who Gives A Fuck?*

There is another angle from which this can be viewed: the audience. How does one conceive the audience to which a work is directed. Who is Ice T speaking to? Precisely because a work must confront the sacred and the Event it must be addressed to everyone. All human beings. Contrary to the claims of "identity politics" or post-modernist deconstructions, art speaks to a generic audience, exclusive of no one. The anonymous crowd. The generic multitude. The amorphous mass. The point is not that everyone will "understand." In fact, understanding is not the main objective of great art, anyway. The fact that a particular song may be in one language or musical genre does not mean that it is only addressed to those who speak that language or enjoy that genre. "I Speak the Same to Everyone" is the title of a song that clearly expresses what this implies.[14] In a world of difference, the "same" is honesty. It is the pursuit of what is true or just. What is truth unless it is true for all? Opinion. What is just unless it is just for all? Domination.

It is the fundamental characteristic of hierarchical rule to elevate "difference" above the "same." To oppose truth with opinion. To oppose justice with rule. Kicking over the wall, removing the blinders, a panorama unfolds. Difference is simply the way the world is. It means no more or less than being, existing. What art seeks to approach and present to view is the "same." Not what differentiates or ranks, but what presents the audience to itself and evokes the sacred from which it comes.

Who gives a fuck? Who doesn't? The song hurls back a challenge and an invitation. Into the babel of tongues humanity sings of humanity. There is a Great Divide. Haves and have nots. Masters and Slaves. But division confronts its nemesis in the bard and the balladeer. The audience gathers to hear what it has known all along. The Message announcing the possibility: All this must change.

# FOOTNOTES

1    Berry was not alone. Notable for their wit and craftsmanship were Mike Lieber and Jerry Stoller. They penned many songs for acts like The Coasters that were comic, intelligent and socially aware. Moreover, there was always an underlying reservoir of the deep poetics of blues and country that occasionally surfaced on the top of the charts.

Similarly, Dylan and Scott-Heron are representative and, by no means, unusual. In fact, in widely disparate subgenres of popular music the Sixties firmly re-established the place of the artful lyric. The Black Poets, Bob Marley, Leonard Cohen, Tom Waits, Joni Mitchell all spring to mind as poets in song.

2    Adorno's complex analysis led him to a pessimistic conclusion regarding the effectiveness of any resistance to oppression and injustice expressed through the popular arts. Every outburst of true popular feeling would be coopted and turned into yet another link in the chains binding the masses to their masters.

He was a determined opponent of capitalism, however, and wrote scathing attacks that exposed the connections and underlying similarities between Nazi Germany and the USA. While describing the mechanisms by which "choice" is made under the dominance of the Culture Industry Adorno, and his partner Max Horkheimer wrote:

"We are closer to the facts if we explain these phenomena as inherent in the technical and personnel apparatus which, down to its last cog, itself forms part of the economic mechanism of selection. In addition there is the agreement—or at least the determination —of all executive authorities not to produce or sanction anything that in any way differs from their own rules, their own ideas about consumers, or above all themselves."
Adorno, Theodor and Max Horkheimer, "The Culture Industry: Enlightenment as Mass Deception." *Dialectic of Enlightenment.* 1944.
http://www.marxists.org/reference/subject/philosophy/works/ge/adorno.htm

3    Gary Webb was the investigative journalist who broke this story. Subsequently many others have corroborated and expanded on his initial disclocures. Among them is Alexander Cockburn whose book *Whiteout* offers extensive documentation of the CIA's drug trafficking.

4.    "During WWII, America needed new allies to advance its invasion of Sicily, and Luciano was a perfect choice— imprisoned but with good connections in the Italian Mafia, which had been severely persecuted under the Fascists in Italy. A patriot and devoted to Sicily, the Mafia and the USA alike, he helped tremendously and was duly rewarded. In 1946, he was paroled on the condition that he leave the United States and return to Italy (at his pandering trial, however, he had maintained that he was born in New York City on 11 November 1896, and was therefore not subject to deportation upon completing his imprisonment if convicted). He accepted the deal, but was deeply hurt about having to leave the USA, a country he had considered his own ever since he arrived there at the age of ten. Later that year, he flew to Cuba, from where he began to lead the American syndicate and ordered the execution of Bugsy Siegel, who had cost the mafia millions in opening the casinos at the city of Las Vegas, which were losing money at the time. But the USA government learned of his presence in the Caribbean island, and soon he had to fly back to Italy."—*Wikipedia.* "Lucky Luciano."
http://en.wikipedia.org/wiki/lucky_luciano

5    Gary Webb's investigation carefully documented how this actually evolved. In an interview Webb summarized:

"There was a CIA cable from I believe 1984, which called him (Norman Menenses) the 'kingpin of narcotics trafficking' in Central America. He was sort of like the Al Capone of Nicaragua. So after getting these fundraising instructions from this CIA agent, these two men go back to California, and they begin selling cocaine. This time not exclusively for themselves—this time in furtherance of U.S. foreign policy. And they began selling it in Los Angeles, and they began selling it in San Francisco.

"Sometime in 1982, Danilo Blandón, who had been given the LA market, started selling his cocaine to a young drug dealer named Ricky Ross, who later became known as 'Freeway' Rick. In 1994, the LA Times would describe him as the master marketer most responsible for flooding the streets of Los Angeles with cocaine. In 1979, he was nothing. He was nothing before he met these Nicaraguans. He was a high school dropout. He was a kid who wanted to be a tennis star, who was trying to get a tennis scholarship, but he found out that in order to get a scholarship you needed to read and write, and he couldn't. So he drifted out of school and wound up selling stolen car parts, and then he met these Nicaraguans, who had this cheap cocaine that they wanted to unload. And he proved to be very good at that.

"Now, he lived in South Central Los Angeles, which was home to some street gangs known as the Crips and the Bloods. And back in 1981–82, hardly anybody knew who they were. They were mainly neighborhood kids—they'd beat each other up, they'd steal leather coats, they'd steal cars, but they were really nothing back then. But what they gained through this organization, and what they gained through Ricky Ross, was a built-in distribution network throughout the neighborhood. The Crips and the Bloods were already selling marijuana, they were already selling PCP, so it wasn't much of a stretch for them to sell something new, which is what these Nicaraguans were bringing in, which was cocaine.

"This is where these forces of history come out of nowhere and collide. Right about the time the contras got to South Central Los Angeles, hooked up with 'Freeway' Rick, and started selling powder cocaine, the people Rick was selling his powder to started asking him if he knew how to make it into this stuff called "rock" that they were hearing about. This obviously was crack cocaine, and it was already on its way to the United States by then—it started in Peru in '74 and was working its way upward, and it was bound to get here sooner or later. In 1981 it got to Los Angeles, and people started figuring out how to take this very expensive powdered cocaine and cook it up on the stove and turn it into stuff you could smoke.

"When Ricky went out and he started talking to his customers, and they started asking him how to make this stuff, you know, Rick was a smart guy—he still is a smart guy—and he figured, this is something new. This is customer demand. If I want to progress in this business, I better meet this demand. So he started switching from selling powder to making rock himself, and selling it already made. He called this new invention his 'Ready Rock.' And he told me the scenario, he said it was a situation where he'd go to a guy's house, he would say, 'Oh man, I want to get high, I'm on my way to work, I don't have time to go into the kitchen and cook this stuff up. Can't you cook it up for me and just bring it to me already made?' And he said, 'Yeah, I can do that.' So he started doing it.

"So by the time crack got ahold of South Central, which took a couple of years, Rick had positioned himself on top of the crack market in South Central. And by 1984, crack sales had supplanted marijuana and PCP sales as sources of income for the gangs and drug dealers of South Central. And suddenly these guys had more money than they knew what to do with. Because what happened with crack, it democratized the drug. When you were buying it in powdered form, you were having to lay out a hundred bucks for a gram, or a hundred and fifty bucks for a gram. Now all you needed was ten bucks, or five bucks, or a dollar—they were selling 'dollar rocks' at one point. So anybody who had money and wanted to get high could get some of this stuff. You didn't need to be a middle-class or wealthy drug user anymore.

"Suddenly the market for this very expensive drug expanded geometrically. And now these dealers, who were making a hundred bucks a day on a good day, were now making five or six thousand dollars a day on a good day. And the gangs started setting up franchises—they started franchising rock houses in South Central, just like McDonald's. And you'd go on the streets, and there'd be five or six rock houses owned by one guy, and five or six rock houses owned by another guy, and suddenly they started making even more money.

"And now they've got all this money, and they felt nervous. You get $100,000 or $200,000 in cash in your house, and you start getting kind of antsy about it. So now they wanted weapons to guard their money with, and to guard their rock houses, which other people were starting to knock off. And lo and behold, you had weapons. The contras. They were selling weapons. They were buying weapons. And they started selling weapons to the gangs in Los Angeles. They started selling them AR-15s, they started selling them Uzis, they started selling them Israeli-made pistols with laser sights, just about anything. Because that was part of the process here. They were not just drug dealers, they were taking the drug money and buying weapons with it to send down to Central America with the assistance of a great number of spooky CIA folks, who were getting them [audio glitch—'across the border'?] and that sort of thing, so they could get weapons in and out of the country. So, not only does South Central suddenly have a drug problem, they have a weapons problem that they never had before. And you started seeing things like drive-by shootings and gang bangers with Uzis.

"By 1985, the LA crack market had become saturated. There was so much dope going into South Central, dope that the CIA, we now know, knew of, and they knew the origins of—the FBI knew the origins of it; the DEA knew the origins of it; and nobody did anything about it. (We'll get into that in a bit.)

"But what happened was, there were so many people selling crack that the dealers were jostling each other on the corners. And the smaller ones decided, we're going to take this show on the road. So they started going to other cities. They started going to Bakersfield, they started going to Fresno, they started going to San Francisco and Oakland, where they didn't have crack markets, and nobody knew what this stuff was, and they had wide open markets for themselves. And suddenly crack started showing up in city after city after city, and oftentimes it was Crips and Bloods from Los Angeles who were starting these markets. By 1986, it was all up and down the east coast, and by 1989, it was nationwide."
http://www.parascope.com/mx/articles/garyWebb/garyWebbSpeaks.htm

6    In Frederic Dannen's book *Hit Men*, there are numerous references to this well known link. Indeed, indie promotion—which is the main focus of *Hit Men*—has long had a strong mob presence with the likes of Joe Isgro and Morris Levy being notorious examples. Dannen, Fredric. *Hit Men*. Vintage Books, 1991.

7    Barton, Laura. "Rap Is Elitist." *The Guardian*. May 7, 2003.

8    Robinson, John. "Pull the plug." *The Guardian*. April 19, 2003.

9    Bennu, Pierre. "FUCK HIP HOP A Eulogy to Hip Hop." originally posted November 2002: http://www.exittheapple.com/apple/index.html

10    Reprinted from Davey D's *FNV Newsletter*: www.blackcommentator.com

11    "All are free to dance and enjoy themselves, just as they have been free, since the historical neutralisation of religion, to join any of the innumerable sects. But freedom to choose an ideology—since ideology always reflects economic coercion—everywhere proves to be freedom to choose what is always the same."
Adorno, Theodor and Max Horkheimer, "The Culture Industry: Enlightenment as Mass Deception." *Dialectic of Enlightenment*. 1944.
http://www.marxists.org/reference/subject/philosophy/works/ge/adorno.htm

12    Bey, Hakim. *T.A.Z.: The Temporary Autonomous Zone, Ontological Anarchy, Poetic Terrorism.* Autonomedia, 1991.

13. Church, Michael and Martin Engstroem. "This game is almost over." *The Independent.* September 15, 2003.

14    A famous example is furnished by Eric Nuzum in his book (online):

   "Three months before releasing *Yesterday and Today*, John Lennon was widely mis-quoted when he offered his observations regarding the decrease in Christianity's popularity with teens. He said, 'We're more popular now than Jesus.' His statement led to numerous protests, boycotts, and public burnings of Beatle records and merchandise; there were threats of violence; the band was denounced from the pulpit and the editorial page; and parents, politicos, and school officials rallied against deteriorating moral values. People felt that the Lads from Liverpool encouraged and personified moral decline. The Reverend Thurman H. Babbs, pastor at the New Haven Baptist Church in Cleveland, vowed to excommunicate any church member who listened to Beatles records or attended a Beatles concert. The Ku Klux Klan even nailed Beatles albums to burning crosses in South Carolina."

http://ericnuzum.com/banned/incidents/00s.html

or in print: Nuzum, Eric D. *Parental Advisory: Music Censorship In America.* Perennial Books, 2001.

15    Eric Nuzum's website: http://ericnuzum.com/banned/incidents/00s.html

16    Philosopher Alain Badiou has identified four generic conditions of philosophy: love, art, science and politics. He has further emphasized the transformative Event as the most useful way to describe the intersection between language (more specifically, naming) and ontology—the study of being. This goes beyond history, narratives or social custom. It provides a means of grappling with the phenomenon of revolution within a boundless universe.

Badiou, Alain. *Manifesto For Philosophy.* State University of New York Press, 1989.

17    Yerkey, Stephen. *I Speak The Same To Everyone.*

# NETS, WEBS, CHAINS AND DOMAINS

## MUSIC AND OWNERSHIP

The first man who, having enclosed a piece of land, thought of saying, "This is mine" and found people simple enough to believe him, was the true founder of civil society. How many crimes, wars, murders, how much misery and horror the human race would have been spared if someone had pulled up the stakes and filled in the ditch and cried out to his fellow men: 'Beware of listening to this impostor. You are lost if you forget that the fruits of the earth belong to everyone and that the earth itself belongs to no one!'

ROUSSEAU, *THE DISCOURSE ON INEQUALITY*

**M**uch is being deliberately obscured in the current debate about internet file sharing. In fact, calling it a debate is being generous. It would be more accurate to describe it as a well orchestrated propaganda offensive. We are being asked to uncritically accept that people, particularly teenagers, are engaged in illegal activity. They are stealing, and stealing is a crime. Moreover, the victims of this crime, we are told, are composers and musicians. These victims are having their ideas taken from them without compensation and without their consent. The inevitable outcome of this activity, if left unchecked, is that music will have no value and, therefore, will cease to be made since it can no longer be profitably sold.

OK. Let's assume that the earth is flat and the sun circles around it. Let's assume that music industry moguls have become paragons of virtue. Let's assume that they have descended from their mountains of money to deliver the commandment "Thou Shalt Not Steal." Whether this sudden moral rectitude is a result of technology's inexorable advance or a collective pang of guilt for past crimes, we can all breathe easier now. After all, we don't know how much they've invested so that we can have music. What would we do without them? Can you imagine?

Ten million kids are stealing music. Soon the record companies will go out of business. There will be no one making money from music because it is free. Gee. This could get interesting. What if the only people who made music were those who loved to do it? What if the only people who listened to music were those who loved to listen to it? What if MTV went off the air, the radios went silent and all that was left were people organizing their own concerts and playing the music they loved? What if the only recordings that were made were those of musicians who had something important enough to say that it justified their own investment in it? What if the only way to find and hear this music was PAYING ATTENTION?!

Actually, it sounds pretty damn good to me. Too bad it ain't gonna happen.

As anyone associated with it must admit, the music business is a cesspool of deceit. This is well documented. One book, *Hit Men*, by Fredric Dannen, provides enough compelling evidence of systematic fraud, theft, bribery and corruption to convince anyone that the people running it are generally despicable.[1] Particularly in the last 20 years such activity has characterized operating procedure at the highest levels of the major labels. Among the leading lights have been the likes of convicted gangster Morris Levy, self admitted degenerates like Walter Yetnikoff[2] and shyster lawyers such as Allen Grubman. Even after Yetnikoff's "fall" from the top of Columbia Records, he walked away with $20 million in severance pay. But beyond the loathsome personalities and psychotic behavior is the true depravity. These individuals and the corporations they serve have made billions of dollars from the brutal exploitation of music, musicians, and audiences—the dumb masses—they view with utter contempt. If a generation of young people are consciously targeting this price-gouging, extortionist cabal, perhaps a little street justice is being done. Let's not forget that the targets of the original "Pirates of the Caribbean" were the galleons bringing gold and silver mined by enslaved Indians back to Spain. While it's unlikely that the great majority of downloaders are consciously striking a blow at corporate criminals there are certainly some who know they've been manipulated long enough and are taking advantage of easier access to what they might like to listen to. As Prince recently wrote:

> It simply appears that the instinctive reaction of the lover of art (b it music, TV shows, movies, or other 4ms of art) is such that, if the industry has no respect 4 his or her identity as an appreciator of art, then he or she has no reason 2 have any respect 4 the industry as a purveyor of art. By making digital copies of so-called cultural products, many people r not demonstrating their lack of respect 4 art and 4 artists, but r xpressing—consciously or not—their frustration with the way the entertainment industry profits from art at the xpense of both art makers and art lovers.
>
> The consumers of the commercial products of the entertainment industry r only as cynical as the industry has deliberately made them, by dumbing down their products, by xploiting artists, by making profit-driven choices and decisions, and by providing their own kind with obscene compensations and legal impunity that r completely out of touch with the real world of ordinary people.[3]

Music will continue to be made whether we get it on an iPod or a vinyl record, at a live concert or on the radio, at a church service or on the street. And we'll have to pay for it, too. Anyone with any doubt about that is ignoring the obvious fact that under the current economic system we always pay for everything so that a tiny minority can remain rich. As the old song said: "Them that got are them that get and I ain't seen nothing yet."[4]

What is being deliberately obscured by the file sharing issue is something far more significant—the assault on the Commons. What the corporate "masters of the universe" are after is the total enclosure of the Commons and the privatization of every public good and function. Music is not even that important. Not when compared with the patenting of the human genome, genetically modified foods, corporate ownership of water and drug company monopoly on medicine. But it is useful to divert public attention from their own massive theft of public resources by focusing it on teenagers "stealing" music. What the RIAA is doing is only one component of a larger effort to make all uses of the internet profitable to the telecommunications industry, in particular, and capital, in general. This goes along with the erosion of public education, public libraries, public health and public lands. All of the resources that currently reside in the "common wealth" from the airwaves to the national forests are being plundered by these giant entities under the protection of copyright, patent and trademark law supported by the fundamental legal premise of capitalist governance: private property.

Fortunately, music is part of what can defend us from these insatiable gluttons. Not only will music not be killed it will thrive—precisely in opposition to the rich and powerful who want to "pave paradise and put up a parking lot." It will do this because it has always done this and, even if music ceased being a commodity—which is highly unlikely under present circumstances—it would continue to play this function since it can and will be made by millions outside of any market and for no other reason than the pleasure it brings. In fact, it is useful to gaining an understanding of the larger issues confronting us to examine more closely how music became a commodity. Not, however, to become trapped in the quicksand of endless pontificating or circular argument over technology and business. What is far more fruitful is to seek out music's origins in the Commons and its constant renewal of the Commons.

## WORK SONGS

Muscles straining, sweat pouring, twenty men become one as their hammers rise and fall to the rhythm and melody of the work song. Ancient as work itself, and as universal, it finds no better expression than in the cadences of the chain gang.

> Why don't you ring old hammer
> Hammer ring
> Ring-ho, ring-ho
> Hammer ring

Whether laying rails or hoeing rows, picking cotton or felling oaks, time and toil were made endurable by music.

I'm gonna preach to my diamond
Hammer ring
If you walk, I'll ride yuh
Hammer ring
And if you ride, I'll drive yuh
Hammer ring
'Cause I'm a number one driver
Hammer ring.

If the heart is work then the blood is song; one of the fundamental components of all music making. Woven together with songs of worship and festival in the fabric of human social life the work song can never be forgotten since work produces life and life requires work.

But work produces something else: Profit. Depending on one's point of view this may be god or it may be satan. For the slave bent over the black earth under a blazing sun it meant singing:

Go down, Ol Hannah, dontcha rise no mo,
If you rise in the mornin'
Set the world on fire, set the world on fire.

For the owner of the slave and all the slave produced it meant singing the praises of rising cotton prices.[5]

The tons of cotton thus amassed stood as testament to the labor that produced them and as a symbol of the power over the laborer. In this way, the work of the slave reproduced his servitude by increasing the might of the master against whom he would have to fight to be free.

## SONGS AS WORKS

Built on the basis of centuries of song and countless composers' efforts, the Music Industry presents a massive edifice to every aspiring songwriter or musician today. Just as the cotton that slaves produced mocked their servile status, music in the hands of the Music Industry lords it over the musician. Music is an ephemeral, passing disturbance of the air. It can only become a commodity by two means: 1. contracts that ensure its performance and, 2. mechanical reproduction. That's how this vaporous, joy-filled nothing is transformed: by constructing labor relations between music makers and their employers, and by separating THE WORK from work. In other words, either musicians are hired to perform by someone profiting from the sale of that performance, or the labor required to manifest an idea is cut off, completely severed, from its product, henceforth known as THE WORK.

This object—THE WORK—is frozen in a piece of paper, a piano roll, a vinyl record, a CD or a computer file. As an object it takes on another function. It can be copied. In fact, it is this transformation from a unique event, never repeatable, into a work that can be endlessly repeated and copied limitless times that enables the investment of capital in its production for profit. But, once again, the profit, like THE WORK, stands apart from and dominant over the labor and the laborer that originally produced it. The big record company or publisher can control the production or distribution of Works by dangling the carrot of employment before the music maker and wielding the stick of promoting or not promoting the Work. This appropriation and exploitation began with—in fact was necessary to—the rise of capitalism itself. From the outset it included three essential procedures taking centuries to accomplish:

1. The enclosure of the Commons.
2. The separation of the individual from the community.
3. The elevation of the right to private property above all other rights.

## ENCLOSURE

Enclosure was the process by which common land, owned by no one and used by many for planting crops and grazing animals, was turned into units to be owned by individual lords. This process began during the late Middle Ages but became a great wave across Europe in the 18th and 19th centuries. Its function was to make private property of once ownerless space and to drive the peasantry off of it and into rapidly expanding industrial production. That it met with stiff resistance is attested to by the innumerable peasant wars that broke out in many parts of Europe. Naturally, there were songs. Not only those sung in the fields or workshops but in the tavern or public square where current events were transmitted by the bard and the balladeer.

> The law locks up the man or woman
> Who steals the goose from off the common
> But leaves the greater villain loose
> Who steals the common from off the goose.
> The law demands that we atone
> When we take things we do not own
> But leaves the lords and ladies fine
> Who take things that are yours and mine.

The poor and wretched don't escape
If they conspire the law to break;
This must be so but they endure
Those who conspire to make the law.
The law locks up the man or woman
Who steals the goose from off the common
And geese will still a common lack
Till they go and steal it back.
—Anonymous [6]

The suffering inflicted by the Enclosures is both the stuff of legend and at the heart of contemporary debate concerning what is in the best interests of society. History, written by the victors, has twisted this story into one we still hear today: "it was the necessary and inevitable price to be paid for society's advance. How wasteful and inefficient were the peasants. How much better it is now that we can all be more productively employed. Besides, you can't stop progress." A more accurate account was offered by Peter Kropotkin:

> In short, to speak of the natural death of the village communities in virtue of economical laws is as grim a joke as to speak of the natural death of soldiers slaughtered on a battlefield. The fact was simply this: The village communities had lived for over a thousand years; and where and when the peasants were not ruined by wars and exactions they steadily improved their methods of culture. But as the value of land was increasing, in consequence of the growth of industries, and the nobility had acquired, under the State organization, a power which it never had had under the feudal system, it took possession of the best parts of the communal lands, and did its best to destroy the communal institutions[7]

Proponents of Enclosure used exactly the same arguments then as do the proponents of privatization do now. In fact, they are the arguments driving the policies of "globalization"—the system formerly known as imperialism.

What does this have to do with music?

## MUSIC HAS NO VALUE

While ostensibly defending the right of the author of a work to just compensation for its uses the real purpose of copyright was to provide a state sanctioned guarantee for the investment of capital. In other words, by defining an object in an idea—and in the case of music, a substanceless activity producing an intangible result—it was possible to generate profit from capital invested in its production. Unless this was enforceable law, ideas, and particularly musical ideas, would always remain part of the commons. Moreover, music, in particular, would remain a cost to be borne by wealthy patrons or society at large, never to produce either a market or a profit. This is because music has no value.

We may value music because it has emotional power that is, literally, priceless. We may hold certain values such as trustworthiness, honesty, responsibility and self-sacrifice to be those we aspire to and teach our children. But value, in economic terms, is simply this: the measure of equivalence in the process of exchange. In other words, what is an object or service worth? Using this definition it is clear that food, clothing, shelter, energy, land and other objects necessary to life can be measured and given value for exchange. A price. Moreover, a price for the labor necessary to make these things useable by people can also be determined. In fact, labor is the true "bottom line" since labor is what transforms the resources of nature into sustenance for human beings.

There is, however, more than one kind of labor. Indeed, philosopher Adam Smith went to great lengths to differentiate two principal kinds. He identified that labor which produces value and that which consumes it. In other words, that which is necessary for the material sustenance of our species, and that which is supported by it. The first category he named productive labor, the second, unproductive labor. The first category generates surplus and wealth in society. The second spends it.

Smith wrote:

> The labour of some of the most respectable orders in the society is, like that of menial servants, unproductive of any value... The sovereign, for example, with all the officers both of justice and war who serve under him, the whole army and navy, are unproductive labourers. They are the servants of the public, and are maintained by a part of the annual produce of the industry of other people... In the same class must be ranked.., churchmen, lawyers, physicians, men of letter s of all kinds; players, buffoons, musicians, opera-singers, opera-dancers, etc.[8]

This analysis was developed further by Marx who put it succinctly: "A writer is a productive labourer not in so far as he produces ideas, but in so far as he enriches the publisher who publishes his works, or if he is a wage-labourer for a capitalist"[9]

The music composer is in the same predicament as Marx's author. Within the capitalist market system, the productivity of his labor is not in the artistic creation, per se, but in the profit it generates for the record company or publisher through mass production, promotion and sales.

Since some composers did gain independence through compensation for the use of their works, in a few cases becoming rich and famous, it could be said that creativity was being rewarded and society benefited. There was, therefore, no contradiction between private gain and public good. Today, the RIAA claims it is protecting songwriters by prosecuting teenage pirates who, left to their own devices, will rob, not only particular individuals, but society as a whole of creative effort.

This turns reality on its head. An already abundant creativity, already benefiting society—albeit, without profiting anyone financially—was taken from society and put into the hands of individuals. Music that was already being composed and performed was turned into a commodity enriching a few and impoverishing a multitude. It is worthy of note that in the ferment of revolution that led to the formation of the United States and the French republic, the contradiction between private gain and public good was explicitly confronted. Thomas Jefferson was opposed to copyright in principle and contemptuous of the rationale for them:

> ....it is better to establish trials by jury, the right of Habeas corpus, freedom of the press and freedom of religion in all cases, and to abolish standing armies in time of peace, and monopolies, in all cases, than not to do it in any... The saying there shall be no monopolies lessens the incitements to ingenuity, which is spurred on by the hope of a monopoly for a limited time, as of 14 years; but the benefit even of limited monopolies is too doubtful to be opposed to that of their general suppression.[10]

In any event, copyright was established but was specifically defined and narrowly limited. Its stated purpose was not to profit middlemen such as publishers, but to ensure that authors, inventors and composers derived income from their ideas. Moreover, another category was named that stood in opposition to and as a limit to copyright: The Public Domain. (this designation was originally made in the British "Statute of Queen Anne" of 1710, the first "modern" copyright law.) We will return to the subject of the Public Domain.

Here, though, it is important to show how music is a prime example of Jefferson's often quoted argument:

> If nature has made any one thing less susceptible than all others of exclusive property, it is the action of the thinking power called an idea, which an individual may exclusively possess as long as he keeps it to himself; but the moment it is divulged, it forces itself into the possession of every one, and the receiver cannot dispossess himself of it. Its peculiar character, too, is that no one possesses the less, because every other possesses the whole of it. He who

receives an idea from me, receives instruction himself without lessening mine; as he who lights his taper at mine, receives light without darkening me....

Inventions then cannot, in nature, be a subject of property. Society may give an exclusive right to the profits arising from them, as an encouragement to men to pursue ideas which may produce utility, but this may or may not be done, according to the will and convenience of the society, without claim or complaint from anybody.[11]

The obvious stares us in the face: How much is one note worth? How can any equivalence be established between one song and another? How can price be fair when comparison between two musical pieces is only possible in aesthetic, not economic, terms? And, why, after centuries of such shenanigans, are so many musicians so poor?[12]

## MUSIC IS NOT PROPERTY

Music arises from and gives expression to relations between people. Feelings of love, hate, joy, sorrow or any yearnings of the human spirit are not abstract concepts. They are felt in real life. Music evokes these emotions and elevates them beyond the mundane, individual experience of them so that they can be experienced as they truly are—the links connecting all in the universal human struggle. No longer isolated in loneliness and obscurity, music maker and audience are united in an appreciation of the human condition. Any beauty, truth or nobility of purpose that has ever been expressed has been a product of human evolution in nature and in community. Music is, above all, a social product expressing social relations. It never was and can never be the solitary expression of one person alone.

And yet, this is the monumental hoax upon which the entire edifice of copyright and, indeed, the private appropriation of thought is based. We have been deluded for the last three hundred years into believing that without the incentive of private gain, none would make the effort to create or to share their creation with the world. This fiction, in turn, requires more mental gymnastics. To be coherent it depends on making an apple equal to a song. This denies the obvious difference between a limited supply of food, for example, and the limitless supply of an idea as Jefferson noted. Indeed, the purpose a house serves is diametrically opposed to that of a song. A house can only be used by a certain number of people at any given time. But a song serves its purpose being used by an unlimited number over unlimited time without diminishing its potential use. In spite of such twisted thinking we have many wonderful songs.

The fact is that the vast majority of all music, literature and art ever made was made without copyright "protection." The greatest scientific discoveries—mathematical, medicinal, agricultural, cosmological—were made without being appropriated or being patented by anyone. From the dawn of print—and with it the invention of copyright—the publication dates of earthshaking discoveries mark their entry into the world. 1543, 1632, 1687, 1789, 1859 and 1905. These correspond to Copernicus' *De Revolutionibus*, Galileo's *Dialogo*, Newton's *Principia*, Lavoisier's *Traite Elementaire de Chimie*, Darwin's *The Origin of Species*, and Einstein's *Special Theory of Relativity.*[13] No matter who owns the books or profited from their sale, no one owns the ideas contained in them. Indeed, the truth claims made in them could not, by definition, be truths unless universal—true for all time and all people. Aspiring to such a category necessitated that they be open to being tested, and possibly found wanting by anyone, forever. Can one seriously entertain the thought that such effort is motivated solely by greed? Can anyone seriously argue that the basic functionality of thought is "ownable?" Yet narrow self interest is the only basis in legal, historical or economic terms for the defense of copyright. This invention has always and will always serve those who would plunder nature and the community from which humanity has evolved.

It is a fact that a few amongst composers have profited handsomely while enriching their employers even more. Even if the numbers are tens of thousands, they are paltry compared to the tens of millions of musicians who have never gotten a dime for royalties. It is a bitter irony that one pillar supporting music industry domination is African-American music. Even though in recent years a number of black artists have become wealthy individuals this cannot obscure the fact that since Africans were first brought to America in chains, countless songs were composed by them for which no compensation was ever paid. Indeed, the music industry has viciously exploited black musicians destroying many lives in the process. Of course, this is not confined to black people. White, hispanic, native and asian musicians have been similarly exploited. But the idea that the "Idea," the creative effort, that is contained in a song belongs to someone is exposed as the fraud it is when one considers the legacy of a people. All music can be traced to common origins such as these. This in no way diminishes the contribution individuals of talent and insight make through particular compositions. In fact, it ennobles it.

There can be little doubt that virtually all composers want their works to be as widely enjoyed as possible. The greatest reward anyone can receive is knowing that their work has entered the common culture. What higher honor can there be? When one's music is loved by a large enough audience to be no one's property, instead becoming part of the shared experience of many, one has truly "made it." Naturally, all musicians want to be compensated fairly—and we'll go into that more in a moment. But the basic motivation for music making—composition in particular—is enjoyment not employment. Writing jingles for Coca Cola is a job, work for hire. Writing music for its own sake, however, is a quest for truth, for emotional intensity, for soul satisfaction, for connection with an audience—not for riches and fame.

The labyrinthine web of copyright law testifies to the ludicrous lengths people have had to go to circumvent the obvious: justifying plunder is ultimately impossible. Its foundation is force and fraud. This argument finally comes to rest on a fallacious reading of Darwin's theory of evolution. "Nature red in tooth and claw," Tennyson's famous phrase, summarizes this distortion. It's a dog eat dog world, a war of all against all. This is far from Darwin's own conclusions. Nevertheless, it is widely believed. It provides the modern, "scientific" gloss put on the ancient argument of Might makes Right which has been poisoning human relations for millennia. (Generally speaking, art and science have developed by struggling against this way of thinking.) It has gathered momentum in the early years of the 21st century in the massive propaganda effort to dupe the masses into supporting "intellectual property rights." Since the vast majority of humans own little or no property of any kind, the IP issue may seem a bit arcane. Hence, vast sums are expended attempting to link our common future to that of Monsanto, GlaxoSmithKlein, Archer Daniels Midland, in other words: Metropolitan Corporate Life.

In the context of this effort which seeks to make the human genome private property and genetically modified food a substitute for food organically grown, the question of composer's copyright is small potatoes. It fits into the larger scheme, however, since it appears to define a community of interests between poor musicians and giant corporations. Since I might, maybe, if I'm lucky, get a few shekels for my songs I'm supposed to enthusiastically support the very corporations that are immiserating millions. Since I might, possibly, some day, hypothetically, perhaps, get some royalties for music I write, I'm supposed to sign on to the destruction of the planet.

Of course, part and parcel of this mass deception is the genetically modified music that permeates the air today. Anti-music is the soundtrack for the intellectual property crusade and must be opposed as such. Not only are we being submitted to a massive bombardment by sonic fast food we are being recruited in a war on our very existence as social beings. We are being asked to join in a campaign to abolish what is left of the commons. Instead, we should abolish copyright.

Now, in calling for the abolition of copyright I am not calling for the abolition of credit for authorship. On the contrary, credit for creative endeavor must be defended since it is in everyone's interest to know history and to understand the process by which ideas are developed. Moreover, it is precisely because we want to learn, to share knowledge and find wisdom that we must know who among our fellow humans is responsible for what thought and deed. In fact, copyright ensures that credit will not be given to the many contributors to a particular musical expression. One example of this is portrayed in the film *Standing in the Shadow of Motown*. This film is about the musicians who played on the hundreds of hits produced by Motown in its heyday. These musicians may not have written the melodies and lyrics that are the basis for the songs. These, in most cases, were written by Holland, Dozier, Smokey Robinson and others among a talent rich pool employed by Berry Gordy. But the Funk Brothers (the name they gave themselves) made the music; often spontaneously arranged, always soulfully performed. And herein lies the bizarre artifice that comes from private property in the musical process. These musicians got no credit whatsoever even though, in many cases, their ideas were the instrumental hooks by which songs became memorable. A famous example is the guitar riff that opens "My Girl" by the Temptations. Everyone who's ever heard this—millions, no doubt—immediately recognizes the song to come. Did the writer of this hook get credit? Do you know his name?[14]

It is indisputable that individuals have written great music and deserve credit for their creativity. It is equally indisputable that in the great majority of cases this involved extensive collaborative effort that was never credited publicly. Moreover, the process by which a creative idea becomes a performance is always a collaborative one, since even with a completely written score a composer is dependent on myriad interpretations by individual musicians within whatever ensemble is called upon to perform the work. Clearly, the guiding light of inspiration deserves to be honored by acknowledging the individual who felt it and brought it into being. Furthermore, the perspiration expended in labor and time by such a person should be given our utmost respect. But music requires groups to create and perform. In this process the contributions of each individual is a necessary component, and credit must be given to all who have earned it.

It must be added that credit, in most cases, really means future employment. It's not about copyrights or royalties at all. Why a musician, producer or technician wants to be credited on a CD, in interviews or other publicity is because this is an important way those who might seek that person's services will find out about him or her. In this regard, file sharing can only spread the word more widely about an individual's efforts. It can take away nothing if credit is correctly assigned by the producers of the music in the first place. (Something, incidentally, Berry Gordy did not do.)

## WHAT'S PROPER ABOUT PROPERTY?

What could be more personal, more private than one's own name? And yet, your name is not your property. Many people share the same names. So how is individuality, uniqueness, identity embodied in property? In fact, it is not. Property reduces the individual, unique identity to a transferable quantity measurable by exchange with other equivalent things. It is precisely the function of property to extract from, to make an abstraction of, actually lived relationships between human beings. This abstraction, then, takes on a mystical quality that infuses pursuit of it with a religious zeal. The quest for property as the meaning of life makes all actions, all experiences, living itself, subservient to it. They are worthless unless they can be made into property.

This is a perversion of the motives one has to own a home or a farm, a workshop, a restaurant or an inn. Ultimately, one's uses of such privately owned places or enterprises is self-sustenance and enjoyment. And it is to offer them to one's friends, family and community. Furthermore, such ownership is a responsibility for maintenance. This inevitably extends outward into the social and natural environment in which one lives. Broadly speaking, everyone in the world is entitled to such ownership and responsibility by virtue of being born. Not because of property rights. But because we are human. A stunning refutation of the anti-social notion of "every man for himself" is the self-evident fact that we live in mutual dependence, sharing common assumptions about basic needs. In fact, this is so obvious that it is often overlooked. But it is this fundamental cooperation upon which all human activity depends—including protection of our individual rights and belongings. It is no surprise that among the vast majority of common people—in every culture—customs abound that uphold and defend the common interest. These are not sanctioned by laws or police. They are the fabric of social life. An example is the nearly universal custom of hospitality for the traveling stranger. The welcoming into one's home and social circle of the person needing food and shelter. That this spontaneous impulse must be regimented by fear leading to the abandonment of public space for the "privacy" of one's own home is one powerful indictment of capitalist property relations. It is mirrored by another: what is valued most by ordinary people are experiences and shared wonders such as love, friendship, games, celebrations, honor, music and art. Moreover, the wild places of the heart and nature are sacred exactly to the extent they cannot be owned.

As Thomas Powell recently wrote: "What's proper about property?" John Locke tried to justify it on the basis of labor. Recognizing that no possible claim could be made by anyone to the Earth or to Nature's bountiful fruit, he could only find one act that leant credence to a person's claim of ownership: the labor one invested. If someone picks fruit from a tree, that fruit, through the effort expended, belongs to he who expended the effort. Now, Locke was a radical critic of Monarchy and all divine right. His contribution to the Enlightenment in general and the US Constitution in particular is significant. But one can readily see the strain put upon his argument in these passages of his work. Because the question remains unanswered: Why not do away with this whole line of reasoning and come to the more sensible and pleasant conclusion that what is needed is a system of mutual aid by which the fruits of nature and the labor of people could be equitably distributed? Why does there have to be such a thing as property at all?

In fact, Locke, Jean-Jacques Rousseau, Thomas Paine and Thomas Jefferson were among the radicals struggling to reconcile universal principles with the actual social organizations Europeans encountered among the Natives of North America. They were speaking on behalf of humanity and yet here were humans whose large, complex societies did not have concepts such as property. Iroquois democracy was an inspiration to Paine, in particular, and survives as a lesson from which we still have much to learn. Furthermore, while they fought against the oppression of Monarchy, they were expropriating the land of the inhabitants of America and defining other human beings as property—namely the African slaves who labored on rapidly expanding plantations. This posed grave problems since the power of Enlightenment ideals lay in their universality. This universality was founded in Natural Philosophy (science) and the sovereignty of the People, theoretically inclusive of all humans subservient to none.

Even Locke, in his defense of property rights, acknowledged this.

"Where there is no property there is no injustice," is a proposition as certain as any demonstration in Euclid: for the idea of property being a right to anything, and the idea to which the name 'injustice' is given being the invasion or violation of that right, it is evident that these ideas, being thus established, and these names annexed to them, I can as certainly know this proposition to be true, as that a triangle has three angles equal to two right ones."[15]

Rousseau, went beyond Locke showing that property could not be logically defended. Its origins needed to be explained but its existence was neither natural nor just. Instead it was the result of theft and its inevitable consequence was injustice. Rousseau boldly exposed the scam:

> ...whatever disguises they [the rich] might put upon their usurpations, they knew well enough that they were founded on precarious and bogus rights and that force could take away from them what force alone had acquired without their having any reason for complaint....the rich man, under pressure of necessity conceived in the end the most cunning project that ever entered the human mind: to employ in his favour the very forces of those who attacked him, to make his adversaries his defenders, to inspire them with new maxims and give them new institutions as advantageous to him as natural right was disadvantageous...
>
> "Let us unite", he says, "to protect the weak from oppression, to restrain the ambitious, and ensure for each the possession of what belongs to him; let us institute rules of justice and peace to which all shall be obliged to conform, without exception, rules which compensate in a way for the caprice of fortune by subjecting equally the powerful and the weak to reciprocal duties."

Deluded by such promising words the people,

> All ran to their chains believing that they were securing their liberty...even the wisest saw that men must resolve to sacrifice one part of their freedom in order to preserve the other, even as a wounded man has his arm cut off to save the rest of his body.
>
> Such was, or must have been, the origin of society and of laws, which put new fetters on the weak and gave new powers to the rich, which irretrievably destroyed natural liberty, established for all time the law of property and inequality, transformed adroit usurpation into irrevocable right, and for the benefit of a few ambitious men subjected the human race thenceforth to labour, servitude and misery.[16]

Justice, on the other hand, demands the equality of all.

> The principle of justice is mutuality and equality, through which, in a way most nearly approximating union of body and soul, all men become cooperative, and distinguish the mine from the thine, as is also testified by Plato who learned this from Pythagoras. Pythagoras effected this in the best possible manner by erasing from common life everything private, while increasing everything held in common, so far as ultimate possessions, which after all are the causes of tumult and sedition."[7]

To paraphrase Pete Seeger: "When will we ever learn?"

# CREATIVITY IS PUBLIC DOMAIN

There is no clearer example of the benefits of creativity in the Public Domain than the World Wide Web. It was the brainchild of Tim Berners-Lee. "While the component ideas of the World Wide Web are simple, Berners-Lee's insight was to combine them in a way which is still exploring its full potential. Perhaps his greatest single contribution, though, was to make his idea available freely, with no patent and no royalties due. In 1994 he founded World Wide Web Consortium (W3C) at the MIT Laboratory for Computer Science in Cambridge, Massachusetts, and in 2003, the organization decided that all standards must contain royalty-free technology, so they can be easily adopted by anyone."

Now, Berners-Lee has professed a certain altruism about his effort. He was motivated by the desire to employ his thoughts in the service of society. But he has also willingly admitted that it could only have been as successful as it has been if it were free. "It was simply that had the technology been proprietary, and in my total control, it would probably not have taken off. The decision to make the Web an open system was necessary for it to be universal. You can't propose that something be a universal space and at the same time keep control of it."

It is not surprising that the internet was first populated by academics, anarchists, anti-authoritarians, artists, musicians and assorted freaks and weirdos. Here was an opportunity to develop and explore the potential of a new commons. Autonomous self-organization based on the free exchange of information was the operating principle. That this would inspire the World Wide Web, the Linux operating system and the open source software movement is an exciting example of how creativity flourishes best. It demonstrates how mutual aid as a factor in evolution manifests itself.

But, once the ways by which the technologic potential could best be unleashed had been charted, once the exploratory work had proven effective, computer manufacturers and the Telecommunications Industry began their drive to transform the Information Superhighway into an Information Supermarket. All the hyperbole about cyberspace and virtual reality aside, capitalism retains its dominance on the most mundane, terrestrial level. Indeed, almost all media are under the control of a few corporations. In the United States, the FCC has given away what remained of the publicly owned airwaves. Corporate dominance of everything previously considered public or in the "common wealth" is steadily being extended.

Opposing this are legal scholars such as James Boyle, Lawrence Lessig, and Yochai Benkler who have developed a critique of intellectual property legislation and the premises on which it rests. Moreover, they have offered many thoughtful alternatives to existing law that would, above all, reassert the primacy of the Commons. In fact, Lessig has been a pioneer of The Creative Commons, one of numerous attempts to effectively balance individual creator's needs with the public interest. Boyle has advanced the notion that the Environmental Movement (which did not exist 40 years ago,) has successfully influenced public consciousness, and has raised in new ways old questions of the planetary common good (and should inspire similar efforts on behalf of the Public Domain.) Boyle argues that,

> In the broader sense, though, it is not merely the word "environment" that catalyses attention. Rather, there were two very important ideas behind the environmental movement. The first was the idea of ecology—the fragile, complex, and unpredictable interconnections between living systems. The second was the idea of welfare economics—the ways in which markets can fail to make activities internalize their full costs. The combination of the two ideas yielded a powerful and disturbing conclusion: Markets would routinely fail to make activities internalize their own costs, particularly their environmental costs. This failure would routinely disrupt or destroy fragile ecological systems, with unpredictable, ugly, dangerous, and possibly irreparable consequences.[18]

This helps to illuminate far more than the legal ramifications of current disputes. It has direct and profound implications for music. Two connected issues become urgent. First is the role and cost of propaganda. This includes how the enormous promotional efforts expended by the music industry are actually responsible for the "crisis of file sharing"—not the other way round. The second is that beneath all the ranting and raving of "special interests"—meaning the rich and powerful—a Commons continues to reassert itself, even if it is constantly forced to retreat and mutate to survive.

## THE REAL REASON FOR THE "CRASH"

The "failure of markets to internalize their costs" is nowhere better exemplified than in the music industry. Like Dow Chemical polluting rivers to make trash bags, the music industry has dumped the costs of turning music into a commodity onto the public that both makes and uses it. In a vicious circle, promoting the sale of stars and hits has spiraled out of control to the point where advertising costs far more than the production of the music it is selling. In fact, the expenditure for promotion is so out of whack that it has consumed the profit generated by the sale of the commodity, "music," and regurgitated it into the "environment" of the broad-cast media and other channels of music distribution, thus necessitating extortionate prices from the public to cover these costs that have nothing to do with the product being purchased. We are forced to pay for the pollution of public space by the promotional onslaught of record companies. This is not a conspiracy. This is the way capitalism functions.

In the case of music, it takes on a peculiar shape since music, in and of itself, produces no economic wealth. Musicians may be paid for their performances or compositions. A promoter may derive a profit from the sale of tickets. But, as Adam Smith explained, this is revenue taken from the wealth produced by other people, in other pursuits and expended on music. Music does not produce food, clothing, shelter, transportation, energy or any other of the fundamental components of organic or social life. Regardless of how important its spiritual value may be this is not self-sustaining—except in the sense of the work songs with which this chapter began. Necessary costs of its production have always been absorbed by society.

The costs of turning it into a commodity, however, are not necessary to music or to the people who enjoy it. They are, literally, stealing resources from music production and squandering them on hype. Moreover, the vast sums wasted in this manner have made it necessary to sell ridiculous numbers of CDs to approach profitability. While nothing compels anyone to purchase music (as opposed to food, for example) we are being asked to pay more and consume more—regardless of its quality, regardless of its value, regardless, even, of our capacity to listen to it! And not because of what it costs to produce music, but what it costs to sell it.

This, then, is the real "crash" that the industry has created itself. This is the crisis that confronts them and that they would have us believe was caused by file sharing. The fact that there is much confusion about this is partly the result of deliberate obfuscation. But it is also the result of contradictory forces at work that are often overlooked because attention is focused solely on file sharing. Two such forces both mitigate and exacerbate the effects of this crisis. On the one hand, corporations like Sony continue to make enormous profits by using music to sell other products (the Walkman, for example). This is true, to one degree or another, of all the Majors. None are actually record companies. All are part of large conglomerates that use the music they own in various ways whereby music's marketing cost can generate profit elsewhere (film, advertising, computers, iPods, etc.).[19]

The other force at work is the Commons itself. Music is made by the people. As this book has been dedicated to showing, this is ultimately an ungovernable force that can only be controlled through constant and costly supervision. These costs are not only economic, however. Increasingly, they are political. They involve the government, its courts and police. The necessity to cow the masses into submission must be prepared for by propaganda and enforced by armed might. This is a dodgy business when it comes to music. In the end, the Powers That Be need the creativity of the masses to produce the music. Yet, it must be music that will both be consumable as authentic by these very masses and, at the same time, contrary to their interests. This will never work. Its chaotic unraveling is underway. Therefore, the repressive apparatus of the State must be brought from behind the veil of democratic rhetoric and imposed on the recalcitrant masses. This, though, threatens to expose the sham that democracy under corporate rule actually is. It also threatens to incite popular uprising against injustice.

In this context, the controversy over file sharing can be seen as a smokescreen. Many people are passionate about music. Its role in the lives of millions is both deeply personal and that of a social bond . It is relatively easy to focus people's attention on the "plight" of their heroes who are, supposedly, being shamelessly ripped off by uncaring, selfish teens. Attention can thus be diverted from the far more significant events taking place. We can be convinced that we are supporting music and musicians by giving away the public space offered by the internet and, at the same time, ignore the fact that far more is being stolen from us in the process.

## LABOR, CREATIVITY AND JUST COMPENSATION

It has been said that art is ten per cent inspiration and ninety per cent perspiration. It has also been said that a composer does not invent but discovers. These thoughts open a line of inquiry into the origins and measurements of creativity. They also demonstrate the limits of our capacity to define what is, ultimately, a mysterious process.

Undoubtedly, there is a good deal of labor in the creative process. But labor alone does not determine the quality of a work. Indeed, there can never be any equation between the quantity of labor or time expended and the quality of the artistic result. If Bach spent two hours composing "Art of the Fugue" and John Coltrane spent one hour composing "A Love Supreme" does that make Coltrane's work worth half as much as Bach's? There is simply no way to measure the immeasurable that is timeless music. Indeed, the origin of an idea is impossible to locate in space and time even if its birth is loudly announced. One can describe the processes leading up to a flash of inspiration but, like the famous "Eureka, I have found it!" of Archimedes, the moment itself erupts without warning defying attempts to explain or reproduce it. Visits by the Muse may be sought after, conditions favorable to her appearance may be prepared, we may perform exercises or practice rituals to call her forth. But as everyone involved in creative effort will attest, we know she is there, we love her presence but she can be frustratingly hard to pin down.

Simultaneously, the joys of creativity are their own reward. In the last analysis, ends and means merge in a process that brings a depth of satisfaction matched by few other human pursuits. Just compensation has no meaning here. Gratitude to whatever god, muse or cosmic energy one chooses to address might be in order. Giving thanks to all who made the effort possible might be what a creative person feels like doing. But establishing equivalent values denigrates our contact with the infinite. Like an insurance company assigning a monetary value to a lost arm or leg, it degrades the very nature of life.

Nevertheless, it is to protect the creative from rapacious corporate plunder that a new system needs to be devised. A home for the Public Domain must be constructed so that credit can be given and public access guaranteed. Theoretically, this already exists in institutions such as the Library of Congress in the US and its equivalent in many countries. But this principle must be extended to its logical conclusion to include all products of human intellectual effort. Here the concept of "the Creative Commons" could be practically employed guaranteeing the protection of the integrity of an individual's effort as well as its defense from exploitation. This must be maintained by the public itself, at its cost and in its own interest. What belongs to all must be preserved by all.

What necessarily follows is the means by which creative effort can be supported economically. It is in the common interest that equivalencies be established using labor input and common standards of living. The rich rock star is no model for music or society. If the RIAA were concerned with justly compensating songwriters they would be demanding a tax on the ridiculous salaries of the CEOs of the major record companies to be distributed to the songwriters who've made them rich. Obviously, they want to protect an inequitable and iniquitous system that prevents just compensation categorically while protecting and expanding its opposite. Musicians, composers, engineers, and instrument builders should enjoy the same standard of living as do their audiences: factory workers, teachers, health care providers and all the rest of those contributing to society's health and welfare. It follows that musicians should support the struggles of working people generally for improvements in everyone's standard of living—universal health care, for example. Moreover, in an exchange of this kind, directly between music makers and their audiences lies the best hope for both. An organic relationship between providers of music and providers of material sustenance should replace the artificial one most prevalent today. That is, either the parasitism of the star or the begging of the pauper. Neither dignifies music, musician or audience. Instead, a principal of fairness should guide negotiations over payment. Partnership between mutually dependent people and groups should take the place of the adversarial, rip-off contest that characterizes the music business now.

This is not a fantasy. To a great extent, such practices and systems already exist in the world. Though partial and inadequate, they suggest alternatives that must be explored. Contrary to what "Knowledge Economy" propagandists would have us believe most music, particularly popular music, still relies on live performance for its development. Throughout the world small venues present live music on a nightly basis. Some are straightforward business ventures, some are non-profit cooperatives, some are publicly subsidized, some are a mix of all three. This is where the basis already exists for establishing an open exchange for the benefit of music, musicians and audiences. Regardless of all the complexities involved in myriad local situations, the underlying economic principles are clear: costs of production, including musician's income, equipment maintenance, transportation and accommodations must be born by the public. This can either be in the price of admission or some form of subsidy. Needless to say, musicians depend on this vast network for survival. The public does, too. Whatever can be done to improve relations between the three parties—music makers, venue operators and audiences—must be on the basis of mutual benefit as opposed to mutual exploitation.

The same principles apply to recordings. There are many necessary functions in the production and distribution of recorded music whose costs must be born by society whether this happens in the market place or in a publicly subsidized manner. What is not needed is the massive hype and machinery of the music industry. This is an enormous waste of resources. The public and music makers are already bearing these costs. Where else does the money come from? If file sharing wiped out the profitability of music (which it will not) the costs for producing and distributing music would be much, much lower. But there would still be costs—including the necessity of paying composers for their creative effort. In this sense, what belongs to a composer or music maker is the means to continue the work that an audience has decided it needs. This is obvious. But it has long been obscured by the delusions of the star system; the deliberately manufactured division between audiences and music makers that prevents a healthy, human exchange. This barrier must be torn down.

The internet is full of reasonable proposals for compensating composers that should be widely read and debated. There are already many among educators, legal scholars and political economists who recognize that alternatives to copyright and corporate power must be developed in the public interest. But any discussion can only begin if we reject the arguments of the music industry and rally the public to join in an effort to defend and expand the Public Domain. Fortunately, musicians are among those already exposing the hypocrisy.

To quote Prince again:

So are most citizens really being completely disrespectful of the value of art and the need 2 provide appropriate compensation 2 the artists 4 their works? We've said it b4 and we'll say it again: the rise of digital technology and peer-2-peer file sharing has little 2 do with people's intrinsic respect 4 art and artists, and everything 2 do with the cynical attitude of big industry conglomerates, which have consistently pushed 4 more and more commercial, highly profitable products at the xpense of authentic art and respect 4 artists.[20]

This is one of many eloquent statements by musicians on this subject. It voices what can safely be called a gathering consensus among music makers, that wholesale changes in the current order are necessary and desirable. That this is a crisis is widely expressed. That the interests of music maker and audience coincide and must be united in common cause is a rising chorus. And virtually everyone views the RIAA and the music industry as defending old, outmoded practices.

Most important is that thousands of musicians are already actively pursuing the alternatives and organizing resistance on a grass roots level. Artists such as Michael Franti and Ani Difranco are exemplary of what can be called a great revival of popular spirit amongst the disenfranchised. Sharing, whether it be files or friendship, is what this is all about. We share music, we share life and we share the planet earth.

## ROUSSEAU, DARWIN AND KROPOTKIN VS. "SURVIVAL OF THE FITTEST"

"There is, of course, no more dangerous illusion than that of novelty, which often reflects nothing more than an ignorance of history. While history does not aim to prove that 'nothing is new', it should indicate that not everything is as new as contemporary opinion believes."—Pierre Vilar, *A History of Gold and Money*

For a very long time the privileged have sought to justify their social position on two bases: "that's the way God planned it" and "without rule (meaning ours) life would be nasty, brutish and short." This has been elaborated again and again in succeeding generations by various "authorities" from monarchs and priests to lawyers and scientists.

This is where the works of Rousseau, Darwin and Kropotkin can help us. Because the spontaneous impulses of people are not only, as constant indoctrination would have us believe, selfish, egocentric, acquisitive. In fact, Rousseau argued that people are born good, it is civil society that turns us into brutes. He waged a relentless struggle against those thinkers, such as Hobbes, who saw human development in exactly opposite terms. But Rousseau drew lessons from European contact with the Native Americans and other "savage" people that exposed the weaknesses in much of the argument of his time and put the lie to the concepts that had long upheld power and privilege. Thus his writings played a major role in the revolutionary storms that shook America and France. That he was persecuted, vilified and marginalized goes without saying. That he must be studied anew deserves to be frequently repeated.

With Darwin's articulation of the workings of evolution, Rousseau's thinking was given greater depth and wider range. The evidence Darwin gathered demonstrated beyond any doubt that humans were a part of nature—not apart from it—and that we have evolved collectively, as a species among other species. His ideas were distorted beyond recognition when among his defenders were those who championed the idea of "survival of the fittest" as the essential truth contained in the theory of evolution. This is a lie that has been promulgated by the powerful ever since. It continues to permeate thought from the halls of Academe to the ghetto streets. Interestingly, Peter Kropotkin, a revolutionary who was also a student of evolution, wrote a stunning refutation of this line of thinking in 1902, *Mutual Aid: A Factor in Evolution*. His learned discourse was buried in obscurity until paleoanthropologist, Stephen J. Gould, resurrected it and showed its great scientific merit.[21]

In essence, what Kropotkin argued is that crucial to understanding Darwin's discoveries was that mutual aid was as important an element in species survival as was self assertion. It is not one or the other. It is the continuous struggle of both together for the survival of the fittest species—not individual. Of course, part of what led to his evidence being dismissed was Kropotkin's political activities as an anarcho-communist. But, as Gould pointed out, the science in Kropotkin's book is beyond reproach. The data he gathered over years of personal observation and copious research were substantial contributions that supported Darwin's conclusions. They were not simply add ons. They were original developments, but in a direction completely consistent with Darwin's own thought. In fact, it can now be said with reasonable certainty that Kropotkin is "the real" Darwin. There is nothing in Darwin that can plausibly support capitalism, laissez-faire or otherwise. If anything, the opposite is true.[22]

Human evolution is a product of mutual aid as much as individual self-assertion. The commons is the actual site of our survival as a species. Our future depends on us grasping this, illuminating our thought and deed with its wisdom and resisting those who would turn every living cell into dead labor to be hoarded by a few.

# FOOTNOTES

1    Dannen, Fredric. *Hit Men*. Vintage Books, 1991.

2    Yetnikoff recently wrote his autobiography, *Howling at the Moon: The Odyssey of a Monstrous Music Mogul in an Age of Excess*. Random House, 2003.
The publisher's promotional statement concludes with:
"Seemingly, the more Yetnikoff feeds his cravings for power, sex, liquor and cocaine, the more profitable CBS becomes—from $485 million to well over $2 billion—until he finally succumbs, ironically, not to substances, but to a corporate coup. Reflecting on the sinister cycle that left his career in tatters and CBS flush with cash, Yetnikoff emerges with a hunger for redemption and a new reverence for his working-class Brooklyn roots."

3    Snyder, John and Ben Snyder, "Embrace file-sharing, or die: A record executive and his son make a formal case for freely downloading music. The gist: 50 million Americans can't be wrong."

4    Charles, Ray and Ricci Harper, *Them That Got*.

5    Lyrics collected by Alan Lomax and presented in the book: *The Land Where the Blues Began*. Pantheon Books, 1993.

6    Quoted by James Boyle in an article: "The Second Enclosure Movement and the Construction of the Public Domain." This article is made available by the author under a Creative Commons License at: http://www.creativecommons.org/licenses/by-sa/1.0 It is also available at: http://www.law.duke.edu/journals/66LCPBoyle.

7    Peter Kropotkin, *Mutual Aid: A Factor of Evolution*. 1902.
http://www.calresco.org/texts/mutaid.ht

8    Smith, Adam. *The Wealth of Nations*. p. 94–95.
Smith extrapolates further:
"There is one sort of labour which adds to the value of the subject upon which it is bestowed: there is another which has no such effect. The former, as it produces a value, may be called productive; the latter, unproductive labour. Thus the labour of a manufacturer adds, generally, to the value of the materials which he works upon, that of his own maintenance, and of his master's profit. The labour of a menial servant, on the contrary, adds to the value of nothing. Though the manufacturer has his wages advanced to him by his master, he, in reality, costs him no expense, the value of those wages being generally restored, together with a profit, in the improved value of the subject upon which his labour is bestowed. But the maintenance of a menial servant never is restored. A man grows rich by employing a multitude of manufacturers: he grows poor, by maintaining a multitude of menial servants."
Smith, Adam. *An Inquiry into the Nature and Causes of the Wealth of Nations*. b. II, ch. III, Vol. II, ed. McCulloch, p. 93–94

9    Marx, Karl. "Theories of Surplus-Value" [Volume IV of *Capital*]. 1863.
http://www.marxists.org/reference/subject/philosophy/index.htm
Marx continues:
"An actor, for example, or even a clown, according to this definition, is a productive labourer if he works in the service of a capitalist (an entrepreneur) to whom he returns more labour than he receives from him in the form of wages; while a jobbing tailor who comes to the capitalist's house and patches his trousers for him, producing a mere use—value for him, is an unproductive labourer. The former's labour is exchanged with capital, the latter's with revenue. The former's labour produces a surplus-value; in the latter's, revenue is consumed."

10   From a review of Jefferson's and Madison's views on copyright by Timothy Phillips.

Phillips explains: "Here Jefferson considers freedom from copyright and patent laws and other monopolies to be of similar importance to freedom of speech, religion, and the press. He repeated this view in his letter to Madison dated July 31, 1788.". https://mail2.cni.org/lists/cni-copyright/message/2113800.html

11    Jefferson, Thomas (letter to Isaac MacPherson). August, 13, 1813. *The Jefferson Digital Archive*, University of Virginia.

http://etext.Virginia.EDU/jefferson/quotations/foley/

12    No sooner had I completed this chapter than an article appeared illustrating the conundrum this thinking produces: "'Paid by the note? Don't be ridiculous' A group of German violinists are demanding more money—because they do more work than the brass. What do our musicians make of their pleas?" *The Guardian*, March 25, 2004.

13    This sequence of titles and the dates of publication were supplied by Adrian Johns in his excellent book *The Nature of the Book*. University of Chicago Press, 1998.

Johns presents an enormous amount of material about publishing, printing, copyright and piracy. While he does not explicitly draw the conclusion I do about copyright, the evidence he presents begs the question. A telling example: The first available German translation of *The Holy Bible* by Martin Luther was a pirated copy!

14    His name was Robert White. Perhaps even more notorious is the story of James Jamerson whose bass playing is legendary among musicians while his name is hardly known by the public at large.

15    Locke, John. "Essay Concerning Human Understanding." 1690.

http://weber.ucsd.edu/~dmckiern/locke.htm

16    Rousseau, Jean-Jacques. *A Discourse on Inequality*. Penguin Classics, 1981, pp.120–122.

17    Guthrie, Keneth Sylvan. *The Pythagorean Sourcebook and Library*. Phanes Press, 1987, p.99.

18    Boyle, James. "The Second Enclosure Movement and the Construction of the Public Domain." 2001.

Essays and papers were submitted to a conference on the Public Domain held by Duke University Law School, November 9–11, 2001:

http://www.law.duke.edu/pd/papers.html

There are many useful ideas presented. These include alternatives to both individual ownership and state ownership. Examples such as universities, cooperatives, communities (of inhabitants or crafts people) abound. The illusion that there are no other choices except individual private ownership and state ownership is exposed as the fraud it is.

Moreover, practical solutions for the replacement of current copyright and patent law with real protections and just compensation for the artist or inventor are plentiful and need serious discussion.

More resources and discussion are available from the Electronic Frontier Foundation (EFF): https://www.eff.org/share/

They suggest a few ways to pay artists without breaking P2P and criminalizing its users:

* Ad Revenue Sharing: http://www.iuma.com/About/pagePressRelease_10.html
* Bandwidth Levies: http://cyber.law.harvard.edu/people/tfisher/PTKChapter6.pdf
* Digital Patronage: http://www.musiclink.com/
* Media Tariffs: http://www.utexas.edu/law/faculty/nnetanel/Levies_chapter.pdf
* Microrefunds: http://www.templetons.com/brad/dontpay.html
* P2P Subscriptions: http://news.zdnet.co.uk/story/0,,t269-s2084029,00.html
* Tip Jars/Micropayments: http://www.mediagora.com/

19    "Sony is also the largest manufacturer of writeable CD drives. It, along with Philips, co-developed the CD and collects royalties from various CD patents. All CDs, whether used by commercial replicators or bought by the general public, are subject to these royal-

ties, which currently stand at $0.033 per disc. There were over 500 million blank CDs sold last year. The advantage of being a multinational corporation is the ability to use one asset to create another asset. Sony may make less money on music but is using it to make money elsewhere."

Snyder, John and Ben Snyder, "Embrace file-sharing, or die: A record executive and his son make a formal case for freely downloading music. The gist: 50 million Americans can't be wrong."—*Salon*. http://www.salon.com/tech/feature/2003/0201/file_trading_manifesto

20   Ibid.

21   Gould, Stephen Jay. "Kropotkin Was No Crackpot." *Bully For Brontosaurus*. W.W.Norton & Company, 1991.

22   "The old 'Darwinian' theory and story of 'survival of the fittest' and 'the celebration of selfishness'—by now fixed in our minds like the programming for robots driving our species toward destruction? Or the new Darwinian theory and story based on the fact that in *The Descent of Man* Darwin wrote only twice about survival of the fittest—but 95 times about love and 92 times about moral sensitivity!" From a new website called *The Darwin Project*: http://www.darwinproject.com. This was inspired by David Loye. Dr. Loye is a social psychologist who has also written a book: *Darwin's Lost Theory of Love*, iUniverse, 2000. In this book, Dr. Loye presents material drawn from Darwin's notebooks and *The Descent of Man* that has been overlooked/deliberately buried for more than one hundred years! It completely contradicts prevailing views of Darwin's ideas as it puts forward Darwin's own position which concurs on fundamental points with Kropotkin's. Moreover, it presents profound insights into the function of love and morality in the evolution of human beings.

A new, updated version should be available now in paper form. It is to be called: *Darwin's Unfolding Revolution*.

# CONCLUSIONS AND SOLUTIONS

I f we awoke tomorrow to find that the music industry had disappeared would it make any difference to music? If, as industry
mouthpieces continually warn, the entire enterprise is threatened
with extinction by internet downloading, should music lovers care?

Let's compare some statistics. According to the International
Federation of the Phonograph Industry:

London, April 9, 2003
World sales of recorded music fell by 7% in value and by 8% in units in 2002.
Recorded music sales worldwide fell to US $ 32 billion in 2002. Compared
to 2001, sales of CD albums fell globally by 6%, and there were continued
declines in sales of singles (-16%) and cassettes (-36%).

London, October 1, 2003
World sales of recorded music fell by 10.9% in value and by 10.7% in units
in the first half of 2003. Interim sales of all audio and music video formats
were worth US $12.7 billion, compared to US $14.2 billion in the same period of 2002.

Now let's look at sales of guitars in the same period. *The Guardian* posted this report:

Saturday November 29, 2003
According to a body of instrument suppliers called the Music Industries
Association, in the last 12 months the British people bought no less than
700,000 acoustic or electric guitars.

This staggering figure represents a 46% increase on 2000 sales figures.

Furthermore, sales of sheet music—an essential for any budding Jimmy Page
or Jack White—are experiencing a dramatic increase. Virgin's Oxford Street
megastore has turned part of itself into a colossal guitar warehouse.

Consider the following figures provided by *The Music Trades* magazine for
the US market:

Guitars
A Breakdown By Price Point And Product
Change From 1999
Acoustics
Under $800 Retail 491,643 +11.0%
Over $800 Retail 73,588 +9.6%
Acoustics With Pickups
Under $800 Retail 129,368 +14.6%
Over $800 Retail 38,658 +7.9%
Classical Guitars 79,718 +30.0%
Total Acoustic Guitars
812,975
+12.9%

Electrics
Under $800 Retail 515,561 +40.7%
Over $800 Retail 113,095 +26.3%
Hollow Body 28,550 +18.6%
Bass Guitars 178,414 +30.0%
Total Electrics
835,620
+35.4.%[1]

What do these numbers tell us? At the very same time that sales of recorded music are falling, sales of guitars are going up. Figures for the sale of pianos, organs, drums, violins and many other musical instruments show similar upward trends. People may be buying less recorded music but they're buying more musical instruments with which to make their own. People want to play!

It is also important to note that small workshops of one or a few individuals making all kinds of musical instruments continue to thrive all over the world. This is not "big business." It is not reported in industry publications. This is crafts people, artisans, employing ancient skills and proving, beyond a doubt, that the making of music is in no danger of extinction. In fact, it attests to the fundamental fact that music is a collective activity that produces active collectivities. It is not only—or even mainly—a commodity to be consumed.

## DOWNLOADS OF DOOM

Yet we are bombarded daily with reports declaring that digital downloading spells doom for music. An article appeared in the July, 2003 issue of *The New Yorker* magazine decrying a "vast, illegal, anarchic economy" that will destroy the livelihoods of musicians. "With no visible means of support many artists would be forced to stop working and a cultural dark age would ensue."[2] Meanwhile, the RIAA has launched its campaign to criminalize and punish this increasingly common practice. They support their arguments with statistics they claim establish a causal link between declining sales and downloading. They also spend large amounts of money lobbying lawmakers to pass legislation that will stiffen penalties and increase police powers to pursue and apprehend the millions of kids they label "playground pirates." What, one might ask, is going on?

Behind the pretense of protecting composers, defending the rights of artists, of "saving music," the RIAA and other trade groups have bigger fish to fry. The real battle is for control of the internet. Music is a sensational target but this has little to do with music, per se. It is, however, useful to line up celebrity musicians to, wittingly or not, become publicists for this devious purpose. The Information Superhighway is gone the way of the Peace Dividend and the dodo bird. (Does anyone even remember these glorious promises?) E-commerce is the equivalent of the enclosure of the commons that presaged the Industrial Revolution in Europe. In order to drive peasants into the factories they had to be driven off the land. The land they could live off, however meagerly, had to be enclosed, first by law then by force. The internet promised to be a commons for the free exchange of ideas. This is being steadily and more and more forcibly enclosed.

After the notorious dot com fiasco it became urgent for capitalism that exploitation of this medium be intensified. Huge losses had to be recouped. Mass markets had to be constructed out of what was "free space." This requires enclosure. People must be forced to pay for all uses of the internet. This is the real goal and purpose of the attack on file sharing. How this will be accomplished is being debated now. But rest assured, Microsoft, the telecommunications industry and manufacturers of hardware such as Sony and Phillips will work out deals amongst themselves for increasing the profits they can extract from every conceivable use of the internet and attendant technology. Governments will comply with their wishes and then enforce the laws devised. Music is the stalking horse but it is, ultimately, only a part of the potential profits to be gained by extorting money from every single exchange that takes place over the fiber optic cables that have been laid at considerable expense. As a spokesman for AT&T has said, "we didn't spend 56 billion on a cable system to have the blood sucked from our veins."[3] There was a time when the thought of paying to watch TV appeared to be crazy. And now?

Most of what is being heatedly debated by music lovers and industry hacks is utter nonsense. For a tiny handful of musicians there may be a small loss of income. For the vast majority of musicians there is the potential that more people will hear their music and, perhaps, become fans. It is patently absurd to view a few highly paid rock stars and the labels that have profited handsomely from their "hits" as having anything in common with the rest of world. The hue and cry over copyright presumes that we are all equal in the eyes of the law. In practice, however, the purpose of copyright is to enable profit to be made from an otherwise valueless product. It is not to protect anyone—except the wealthy. The idea that because I own the copyright to a song I will get compensated for its use means very little unless I have the means to create a very large demand for its use. This requires large sums of money to accomplish. But the myth persists. It is the same myth that makes people believe in the American Dream. One guy gets rich and a 100 million think they will. Think again, folks. One guy gets rich because a 100 million are poor. Without the vast majority slaving for peanuts there wouldn't be any riches at all. This is especially true for musicians.

What downloading has done is to expose the inequities inherent in the current system of music distribution. It has laid bare the way the music industry has functioned since recorded music became a profitable commodity. Fundamentally, this is not a question of the majors being slow to adapt to a new technology. It is not about technology at all. It is about a commodity—music—which actually has no value unless access to it is limited. Without walls and doors concert halls would be open to the pubic. Charging admission depends on the ability to block admission. What most of us who make music realize is that this state of things is diametrically opposed to why we make music in the first place. We do not do it to limit access at all. We want everyone to hear it, bar none. We should enjoy a level of material existence equivalent to that of our audience but we have to earn that directly from that audience. It is the financier, the businessman, who seeks to profit from this relationship between artist and audience that is responsible for turning it into an exploitative one. We become producers of things, and audiences become markets for them. This has nothing to do with music and why music does what it does.

The only thing new about the current situation is that the industry does not completely control the new media—yet. The internet still provides an outlet that, once upon a time, was available through radio (most recently college radio). Radio except for the pirate stations is now completely dominated by the corporations of which the major labels are a component. It is only natural that the millions of musicians who want to develop an audience use alternative means to do so. That that entails the public having free access to music is necessitated by two things: 1. People must hear music before choosing to purchase it. And, 2. musicians must be providing for a felt need in order to expect compensation. Playing or writing music does not automatically entitle one to payment.

## PIRACY AND PIRACY

No one is suggesting we invade China or Russia to stop piracy. Yet in these vast countries most CDs are bootlegs. Further west, in Italy, millions of pirated CDs are manufactured and sold daily. The EU has loudly proclaimed its intention of bringing these outlaws to heel. But aside from a few high profile busts, nothing is done. In fact, the Mafia continues to profit handsomely from this business as it has from all of its other nefarious operations. The IFPI announces on its website the "progress" that is being made in the battle against piracy. It gives a country by country accounting of the efforts authorities are undertaking to stop such practices. But visit any Italian beach and you will be approached by men selling CDs illegally manufactured in factories outside of Naples.

Similarly, piracy on the high seas is not a thing of the past. It continues unabated in the waters of the South China Sea, the Caribbean and elsewhere. The illusion that the modern State has control of "everything" is widely promoted. It is, nonetheless, a lie. As with the drug trade, prostitution and the porn industry, capitalism produces piracy as a matter of course. It has only been able to control it in certain zones where the majority of the population is more or less well housed, fed and educated. This is not the condition of the vast majority of the world's population. Therefore, there are large reservoirs of willing people with nothing to lose who will take any opportunity to escape the misery that engulfs them. The only surprise is that anyone is surprised.

Yet we are inundated with loud denunciations of such practices. Politicians and regulators solemnly announce new efforts that will finally rid the world of the scourge. How many times do we have to watch this story unfold to realize that the faces change but the plot is always the same? The real pirates are called CEOs. They run corporations called Enron and Exxon and GlaxoSmithKlein. They make deals for diamonds that fuel the genocide in Rwanda. They refuse the medicines needed by the sick and defend their right to do so on the basis of copyright! This is the context in which the whole charade of busting teens for downloading is taking place. Everyone knows that Ken Lay will not be punished for ripping off billions. Kids may not know all the details but they can smell the hypocrisy. Bullshit stinks.

After examining piles of statistics the evidence is contradictory. There is a relationship between downloading and the purchase of music, but it cuts both ways. Some sales are lost and others are gained. Some people decide they won't purchase a CD on the basis of hearing a downloaded copy. Others decide they will. The implications are far from cut and dried since the variables are manifold, and the competition for people's disposable income is coming from video games, films and other entertainments besides music.

The real reasons for the decline in sales is something else entirely. First, there is the underlying fact of economic downturn which affects most industries. Bust follows boom under capitalism. When a boom is fueled largely by financial manipulation and blatant swindling (as was that of the '90s) the inevitable bust is all the more precipitous. This has a great deal to do with how people guard their disposable income and will, obviously, be reflected in purchases of "non-essential" items. But there's more to it in the case of music. It is now commonly understood that, as drum 'n' bass producer Jonny L recently stated, "The majors have forgotten an important factor in any market—quality. People have had enough of all the manufactured bands," he says. "Now they want real musicians. That has had a big effect on the singles market. If you look at the records real musicians like Eminem are making—they're not suffering."

And the industry should also take a look at the salaries of pop's fat cats, says Jonny L. "They should put the price of CDs down. Big artists like Robbie Williams are ridiculously overpaid. If they were paid a bit less, the majors could cut the costs of CDs."[4]

To this must be added: the music business is not interested in quality. It is only interested in profit. In other words, larger and larger amounts of money derived from the exploitation of musicians and copyrights. The only people concerned with quality are music makers and music lovers. There are millions of us. Our talents are not in short supply. There is as much or more great music being made today as at any time. But that does not make it profitable. On the contrary, it is because such quality is relatively plentiful that it is viewed uneasily by those who seek to profit from it. In order to extract more profit from the coffee bean for which farmers are paid very meagerly, if at all, Starbucks was invented.

In the case of music it goes a step further. Quality is increasingly viewed as a threat to the main product the music industry sells, i.e.: celebrity. It is imperative that consumers be created who will not be able to distinguish quality from celebrity. Thus it actively seeks to have quality replaced. It must be drowned out by Anti-music.

## ANTI-MUSIC

Perhaps there are those readers who, while agreeing with some of the arguments made thus far still consider the existence of Anti-music as, at best, a rhetorical twist, at worst, a paranoid delusion. I must reemphasize the point that Anti-music is a real category of sound. Moreover, we hear it all the time. If it is not always easy to distinguish it from the genuine article then it is even more important that the criteria be reviewed (see "Speaking of Music").

Anti-music is composed and performed on commission by record companies and producers to monopolize an existing market according to specific criteria. It cannot, by definition, express the personal experiences or feelings of the people involved, but must instead, propagate sugary sentimentality, loveless sexual fantasy, idiotic boasting or lamenting and "Hallmark Card" philosophizing, accompanied by easily memorized but utterly forgettable tunes. It may borrow fragments or phrases from real music but it must do so only by repeating them until they, like advertising jingles, enter the subconscious of the listener and once installed, replace genuine emotion and thought.

One need deviate only slightly from normal routine to perform the following experiment: Stop and actually listen carefully to what you hear randomly where ever you happen to be—other than at a place and time when you consciously choose to listen to music. If this process is completed five or six times, it is likely that at least four or five examples of Anti-music will be in evidence. I exclude from this the happenstance encounter with street musicians (more later). Music played live can be Anti-music, but it is not likely to be—although it might be bad music. In fact, the main form Anti-music takes is the recording. It's mainly on the radio, on TV and in public space, those venues most easily dominated by sheer economic or political force.

It is to increase our awareness of this phenomenon and our ability to differentiate it from music that this book has been dedicated. It is vitally important that we prevent the insidious proliferation of this sonic garbage from going unchallenged. We must vigorously defend ourselves from its invasive entry into everyday life. Give me music or give me silence! But don't tell me it's harmless. Anti-music poisons just as air pollution does. In fact, it is air pollution!

Above all, we need to oppose the view that this is a matter of opinion or taste. Criteria must be debated and refined. I have suggested certain standards based on many years of discussion with musicians and technicians that hopefully, will contribute to this effort. What Tolstoy wrote 100 years ago is a vital source. So is the work of WEB DuBois. But it is beyond doubt that actual effects can be observed and measured. There is far too much evidence to ignore. By insisting that real music requires the lived experience, the actual emotion of its makers in order to exist, we can readily identify in the process itself what makes Anti-music and what it does.

## TIMELESS MUSIC

Equally important is the defense and celebration of Timelessness as the key characteristic of great music. That this requires time—to listen attentively, to reflect on, to participate in—is at the heart of an organic, mutually inspiring exchange between musicians and audiences. It opposes "killing time"—distraction from boredom—with the experience of being moved. Regardless of genre, style or cultural origin, there are great works from the distant past to the present day that, given a devoted ear, will provide this experience. One needs only the willingness to find and cherish them.

Of course, there is a wide range of quality even in the work of great artists. All music is not great. Much is not even good. There are certainly compositions or performers who satisfy on a temporary basis, but when we later return to listen again, prove to be shallow, dated, or just poorly made. But Timelessness is created out of an endless effort by a virtually infinite number of musicians trying, and often failing, to make great music. It is not, fundamentally, the work of the lone genius or solitary talent that produces this quality of experience as important as such exceptions are. Instead, it is the ongoing, continuous application of talent, skill and hard work to the "raw materials" of inspiration, experience, emotion and thought. This is a social process involving many "all at once." In other words, every performance of every song contains the input of those directly involved, such as fellow musicians, technicians, and audiences. But it also includes all the influences, musical or otherwise, that have made up the life of the person who wrote and/or will sing that song.

This is, of course, best exemplified in the anonymous music of all cultures. No one invented flamenco. No one invented blues. The composers of most music ever made will never be known. This is not simply because no records were kept or there were no outstanding individuals with whom to identify particular compositions. It is because the soil from which all music grows is the suffering, struggling and rejoicing of the people. It is not, at root, a question of authorship or copyright at all. What beats in the heart of Timeless music is humanity, a generic multitude, not the individual or any One. It is the connection between people, the Commons, that is called forth by the herald of music for which music, itself, exists. It is, in turn, this Commons on which music depends for its existence.

This is vitally important since for a couple hundred years we have been indoctrinated to think of music in terms of great composers meaning people who own copyrights and can get rich from the sale of their works. This has led to the confusion of the "star" system. It has led to the denigration of the music of the slave which, in fact, is the basis of most music ever made. While great compositions by great composers are many and wondrous and need to be savored, shared and studied, it is nonetheless more important that the pursuit of the Timeless in music be consciously directed to its anonymous origin. Not one great man, but an enormous number of unknown people.

It is this that will enable us to break the grip of "stars" and "hits." Indeed, it will enable us to see beyond the quicksand of copyright; in fact, the ownership of music altogether. Timelessness and its origins among the laboring masses proves that, in the end, music need not be property at all. This is an artificial construction that has been parasitically attached to an organic process in which all can fully participate without the aid or interference of "official" or "authorized" institutions. While we must support and give sustenance to those with special gifts for music making—whose work we love and respect, it is not because they own a product whose sale they control. Very few musicians even among the most famous actually control their own works, anyway. This is what the music industry is founded on. The expropriation and exploitation of the work of composers.

Timelessness belongs to no one.

## THE COMMONS

When James Brown announces, "The Groove is here," it is a naming of an event, a moment erupting within chronology, warping it. It invites comparisons but submits to none. It is not "like" anything else except other such timeless moments with which it is the same. And yet, with the absolute assurance of a master, Brown knows he is calling forth the Commons as musicians and audience become one under the sign of the Groove. While one particular event was immortalized in a recording (*James Brown: Live At The Apollo*[5]) it need not have been because it is immortality itself. When we pay homage to a particular musician we are savoring this momentary experience of the Timeless. But it must not end there. Instead, we must pay homage to the nameless musicians who, down the ages, made music so this particular moment could exist.

Who were those drummers that disturbed the peace of the slave master? We will never know their names. But they are the unnamed that produced the unnamable in music. As John Lennon once said of rock and roll, "You might as well call it Chuck Berry." A fitting tribute, to be sure. But more significant is that Chuck Berry combined his talent with the new instrument of the electric guitar to bring that slave drumming into a new Commons. The naming goes on but it is transitory, impermanent. What is forever is presented to us by us. It is the infinite we make ourselves. "Hail, Hail, Rock and Roll!"

Music is born of community and calls community into being. It evokes the yearning for a humanity united in common purpose. While it does not make this happen politically—music is not politics—it does demonstrate such possibility. Not in some distant future but right now. Immediately.

For ten thousand years, humankind has been at war with itself. A tiny number of privileged potentates have enslaved vast numbers of their fellow humans. Music, now more than ever, displays the traces, the birthmarks of this tortuous passage. Slavery and music cannot be separated. The Great Divide of wealth and poverty pulses through all music, everywhere, from the oldest lament to the latest popular trend. That suffering and injustice may one day be overcome, that this legacy may, at long last, be left behind, is what music inspires us to imagine.

## THE PUBLIC DOMAIN

This is another name for the Commons. It was specifically created to distinguish the free exchange of creative work from that which is traded for profit and, most importantly, to designate those works attributable to no one but which are, nevertheless, in use by many. For music it is obvious that limitless quantities of wonderful compositions exist in this category. Indeed, the Public Domain houses the Timeless. The songs that carry the legacy of every history, every narrative, every struggle, in every language known to humans are here.

Musician Richard Thompson recently launched a performance series called, *1000 Years of Popular Song*. He wrote:

> Thinking about all these songs has led me to wonder: has anything changed in 1,000 years? Probably not. The themes seem fairly consistent throughout—boy meets girl, girl meets boy, boy loses girl, girl loses boy, boy repines, girl repines, boy dies, girl dies. At the early end of things, what survives of the secular is mostly moralizing:
>
> The joy of the world does not last
> It fritters away soon enough

The longer a man knows pleasure,
The less satisfaction he finds in it.

The age in which song was the entertainment, the news and the bedtime story offered a wide range of topics: nobles committing adultery and murder, heroic battles, political scandals and social dissent; the ploughboy putting one over on his employers, the beggar putting one over on the farmer; the usual wooings, weddings and deportations. Politics and social comment are still big themes in rap today, but most popular song in the 20th century has been concerned with that old love thing.[6]

Another example was the album entitled *Public Domain* by Dave Alvin. Alvin's liner notes open with the remark: "Old folk songs are Spirits." He concludes with: "They are in the public domain. They belong to nobody. They belong to all of us."

Riches and fame have absolutely nothing to do with this. In fact, they oppose it with the sharp rattle of the idiot. Moneychangers in the Temple. There is more great music on the streets of the City, any city, than there is on the radio or television, now. There is more variety, more lived history, more devotion, more craft. There, I see an aged Romany (gypsy) man playing Mazurkas on his violin. There, I see a group of Senagalese, pounding out the rhythms played for centuries. There, I see a young Spaniard playing sonatas on tuned pitchers of water. There, I see a Swiss playing Vivaldi on an accordion. Peruvian pipers, Bronx Doo Woppers, a Kentuckian one-man-band, all in one day, on one street in one City. The audience gathers, dissolves, gathers, dissolves. Money falls into hats, instrument cases and cigar boxes. The public does not know the names of these musicians. The musicians are not playing for a "scientifically selected" demographic. The music is played, an audience is gathered: a generic multitude. Some money is donated. It happens again. Over and over. Will this end if the music industry collapses? Will this stop if pirates download Warner Brothers to death?

"Now, if 6 turned up to be 9," sang Jimi Hendrix, "I don't mind, I don't mind."

# SOUL

For centuries philosophers and theologians sought the seat of the soul. Bitter argument could not resolve the issue. By the 20th century it had become common to dismiss the quest entirely as the pursuit of a phantom that could better be understood in scientific terms. The border between organic and inorganic matter could be defined and measured chemically. It was no longer fruitful to inquire as to what the soul is or where it might reside. It was simply a word used to describe a phenomenon which we could now study without reference to supernatural causes. But the quest persisted because people's experience included everyday encounters with something that was both inside and all around them.

It was the genius of African-Americans to solve this conundrum once and for all. This was done by a two part operation: First, the article was dropped. Not "the" soul. Just soul. Second, it was identified with music. Music regularly presented the evidence. It was the "clinical trial," the double blind test, the repeatable experiment that proved conclusively the existence of a quality, soul, with which music could be full. Since music was made by people it was obvious that this was a quality people have in themselves that was brought out in the music they played. Identifying it enabled defining it. Soul is an immanent quality to be nurtured not a transcendent entity outside lived life. "You don't have to die before you live," as Sly Stone said.

Defining it also exposed why it had been so elusive before. The importance of number to both science and music had confused the search. Measurements—sizes, shapes, durations, weights, etc.—were vital to an understanding of how musical instruments functioned, how they had to be constructed in order to sound good. Furthermore, it was clear that patterns, in the orbits of planets, the seasons of terrestrial motion, the period of gestation of new life, could be measured to more effectively predict the outcome of human interaction with Nature. More specifically, these patterns could be given corresponding expression in music and dance. But this was not the whole story and people knew it. While much could be learned and used to improve human understanding, numbers, taken by themselves, obscured the causes for an essential human experience.

In the hands of music makers numbers play a vital role. But it is the innumerable of rhythm, melody, harmonization and timbre that makes music out of sound. Music transforms the mundane unit into the experience of forever. This is where soul comes in to name and define precisely that quality without which music cannot produce its truth. Without which music becomes a disposable unit produced for distraction and sale.

Soul came into being as the Civil Rights movement was turning into the Black Liberation Struggle. In the work of Ray Charles, Sam Cooke, James Brown and Aretha Franklin we see how this process unfolded. The merging of specifically musical elements that represented more than music. Techniques and vocabularies arising from gospel and blues were systematically combined to heighten emotional intensity without any specific religious reference. In fact, it was through the political conflict of the descendants of slaves to assert their humanity, to demand equality and justice that their music was given this name: soul. It is epitomized in Sam Cooke's song, "A Change Is Gonna Come," with its powerful expression of the universal longings of the oppressed.[7]

Nothing is sacred. Capitalism has seen to that. In this state of things, soul burns laser-like through the gathering gloom. It is the defining characteristic of the undefinable that is, nevertheless, entirely real. It is the demand of each of us made upon each other, of the music we make and listen to: to be "for real," to have soul. The demand for an expression of true feeling in opposition to the prevailing social norm that sanctions brutal oppression while observing proper manners at the dinner table! The demand for a faithfulness to the act of making soulful music in opposition to the Act that is performed for the privileged who proclaim their superiority by being uptight, stiff, graceless and cold while committing the most heinous crimes. The demand for a decision when faced with impossible odds. A commitment to carry on. To refuse to surrender.

As Jimi Hendrix sang,

> White-collar conservatives flashing down the street
> Pointing their plastic finger at me.
> They're hoping soon my kind will drop and die,
> But I'm gonna wave my freak flag high . . . HIGH!

And everyone has this capacity. For it is a capacity and not our property. Not a possession but that which possesses us. When we make ourselves the vessels for the groove, for the connection to each other and to all who have given themselves to music—ever. We become the vibrating string attuned to the Music of the Spheres resonating throughout the cosmos. The sound old Pythagoras said we hear at our birth but cannot distinguish, since there is no silence with which it can be compared.

## MASTERY AND IMAGINATION

"A spirit and a vision are not, as the modern philosophy supposes, a cloudy vapour, or a nothing; they are organized and minutely articulated beyond all that the mortal and perishing nature can produce. He who does not imagine in stronger and better lineaments, and in stronger and better light, than his perishing mortal eye can see, does not imagine at all. The painter of this work asserts that all his imaginations appear to him infinitely more perfect and more minutely organized than anything seen by his mortal eye. Spirits are organized men."—William Blake[8]

The most important tool for approaching the infinite, as Blake so eloquently taught, is the imagination. Far from the manipulations of power and avarice, far from the fetters of quantity and measurement of any kind, the imagination is what penetrates the veil of mortal existence and discovers Timelessness in artistic (and scientific) expression. This is, according to Blake, the only worthwhile pursuit of the creative force which, ultimately, resides in every human breast. Without this, all our strivings are futile, doomed. His lifelong labors were devoted to the apprehension and application of this faculty against all the pomposity of the so-called "great" particularly the famous artists of his day. Since he was, himself, the living embodiment of his own ideals, he was scorned in his time and rediscovered only later by, among others, the radical Irish poet, WB Yeats. Blake, in this sense, was untainted by celebrity; his motives unimpeachable. He has, therefore, become for many artists a spokesperson for the most radical break with the values of capital, the most uncompromising defense of those qualities that cannot be bought and sold. He is a champion of all that music makers must strive for in order to sustain themselves.

But Blake is another often misunderstood thinker. The imagination he praises is not supernatural. It is not a visitation of angels no matter how often he used such terms, poetically, to describe the process. Rather, Blake combines his demand for freedom of the imagination with the demand for the most rigorous discipline. "The great and golden rule of art, as well as of life, is this: That the more distinct, sharp, and wiry the bounding line, the more perfect the work of art: and the less keen and sharp, the greater is the evidence of weak imitation, plagiarism and bungling." And further, "Without Unceasing Practice nothing can be done. Practice is Art. If you leave off you are Lost." And further still, "Invention depends Altogether upon Execution or Organization; as that is right or wrong so is the Invention perfect or imperfect. Whoever is set to undermine the Execution of Art is set to destroy Art. Michael Angelo's Art depends on Michael Angelo's execution Altogether."

Thus, the mystic Blake can be seen as the master he truly was. And the relevance of this man and his work to all I have been trying to say in this book becomes obvious. For if homage is to be paid it must be first and foremost to those unknown, who did what they did because they knew it to be true and not for fame or gain. Second, to those whose work, though now known to us as being of their design, was nevertheless made without reward or recognition in their own time. Their dedication, their commitment must be our beacon now. Our inspiration may include the expressions of those among us who have become famous. But that fame must be held at a critical distance when evaluating the work itself. Moreover, it is that fame that proves an obstacle to appreciating the mastery that is most to be learned from. Precisely because we become uncritical of all that is contained in the works themselves. It is an encouragement to laziness. We find ourselves surrendering any criteria of judgment instead saying to ourselves, "it must be great, he's a star!" Or, "Who am I to say? 'So and so' is famous." This is why Blake is so useful. Both for what he teaches and for the example he set.

Returning to the problems with which this book began: Anti-music, media control, the plight of music makers and the marginalization of music itself, it should be clear that we have tools with which to master the craft of music making and we have the masters to teach us how to use them if we are willing and determined to join in the struggle. This, then becomes the principle question of the present day. Are we able to make the commitment that music requires? Are we able to break with the illusions and temptations constantly being dangled before us like a hypnotist's watch? Are we able to see through the mountains of media hype and seize the criteria with which to judge our own and others' efforts?

I am stubbornly optimistic that these tasks will be undertaken by enough people to insure that music will continue to thrive. Perhaps more importantly, that music will continue to inspire the struggle against the Power of the Lie and for the untiring quest for Truth. The fulfillment that making music brings is its own reward. The joy that it brings to others is our assurance that we are doing well at doing good. Whatever sacrifices are required, whatever dues must be paid, these are but fuel for the fire that burns in the hearts of those for whom the love of music is the love of life.

1    http://www.musictrades.com/index.html
The Music Trades, 80 West Street , Englewood, NJ 07631
Other data from sources already cited.

2    This article was originally cited by *Guardian* critic Alex Patridis. He ridiculed its presentation and conclusions. Alexis Petridis, "Let the playground pirates rule," *The Guardian*. July 5, 2003.

3    quotation cited by Lawrence Lessig in his essay, "The Architecture of Innovation." http://www.law.duke.edu/pd/papers/lessig.pdf
In this essay Lessig states, "Cable companies make a great deal of money streaming video to television sets. That is the core of their legacy monopoly power. Some think it would be useful to stream video to computers. Cable companies are not eager to see this form of competition. So they imposed rules on broadband users—no more than 10 minutes of streaming video could be contracted for at any time. When they are smart, they said they were worried about congestion. But when they were honest they said something different. Said Somers, of AT&T, 'we didn't spend 56 billion on a cable system to have the blood sucked from our veins'."

4    Dennis, Jon. "Chart attack." *The Guardian*. August 5, 2003.

5    Brown, James. *Live at the Apollo*. 1962.
"The first million-selling r'n'b album, and a dynamic snapshot of the greatest soul act ever to tread the boards. Brown's influence on modern music is immeasurable, beginning with his impact on Sixties Mod groups and continuing apace with his presence in contemporary urban music."
O'Hagan, Sean. "Fifty years of pop." *The Observer*. May 2, 2004.

6    Thompson, Richard. "My favourite songs of the past 1,000 years." *The Guardian*. September 16, 2003.

7    Sam Cooke was among the greatest gospel singers of the 20th century and among its biggest stars. Lead singer of the famous group, The Soul Stirrers, it is no accident that he was a pioneer of the category of music, "Soul." After making the transition from exlusively religious music to rhythm and blues/rock and roll he achieved even broader popularity outside of the almost exclusively black milieu of the black church/gospel music. His song "A Change Is Gonna Come" was released shortly after his untimely death on December 11, 1964. The song expressed profound doubts:

> it's been too hard livin'
> But I'm afraid to die
> I might not be if I knew
> What was up there beyond the sky.

This agnosticism was widely shared and yet was embedded in the bulwark of determination and resilience through struggle that is the hallmark of popular music in general and African-American music in particular.

8    From a description Blake wrote of his painting, "The Bard, from Gray." It first appeared in an 1809 catalog for an exhibition of Blake's work, now reprinted in *The Complete Poetry and Prose of William Blake*. David Erdman (ed). Anchor Books, 1982. p. 541.

# BIBLIOGRAPHY

The books listed below all contributed to my research and informed the positions I have taken. It is with gratitude and respect that I present them here. For those interested in further reading or research I have included some "relevance indicators." In other words, the books are listed alphabetically by author, but I will intrude with comments where I consider them necessary to explain how they related to my themes. This is not a book review, though. I will confine my comments to what I hope may direct the reader to the material most useful to their purposes.

Adorno, Theodor. *Essays on Music*. University of California Press, 2002.

Adorno, Theodor and Max Horkheimer. "The Culture Industry: Enlightenment as Mass Deception." *Dialectic of Enlightenment*. 1944.
http://www.marxists.org/reference/subject/philosophy/works/ge/adorno.htm
    (theory, polemic; important for historical data and broadly influential analyses-particularly of music)

Attali, Jacques. *Noise: The Political Economy of Music*. University of Minnesota Press, Minneapolis, 1985.
    (theory, polemic with invaluable historical information about music)

Badiou, Alain. *Manifesto For Philosophy*. State University of New York Press, 1999.

Badiou, Alain. *Infinite Thought*. Continuum Books, 2003.

Badiou, Alain. *Ethics: An Essay on the Understanding of Evil*. Verso Books, 2001.

Badiou, Alain. *Deleuze: The Clamor of Being*. University of Minnesota Press, 2000.
    (revolutionary and profound, nothing short of a philosophical call to arms)

Bakhtin, Mikhail. *The Dialogic Imagination*. University of Texas Press, 1996.

Bakhtin, Mikhail. *Rabelais and His World*. Indiana Univeristy Press, 1984.

Bakhtin, Mikhail. *Toward a Philosophy of the Act*. University of Texas Press, 1995.
    (radical intervention on behalf of carnival, laughter and the common people. The "missing link" in revolutionary theory.)

Barrow, John D. *Pi In the Sky: Counting, Thinking, and Being*. Oxford University Press, 1992.
    (good explanation of mathematics for people who want to know but lack the formal training)

Benjamin, Walter. *Illuminations*. Shocken Books, 1969.
    (theory, polemic and true art criticism-the most poetic of the Frankfurt School theorists: Adorno, Habermas, Horkheimer, Marcuse, etc.)

Bennett, Jr. Lerone. *Before the Mayflower: A History of the Negro in America 1619–1964*. Penguin Books, 1968.
(important African American history).

Bernays, Edward L. *Propaganda*. Horace Liveright Inc., 1928.
(it's all here! How they lie and why...)

Bey, Hakim. *T.A.Z.: The Temporary Autonomous Zone, Ontological Anarchy, Poetic Terrorism*. Autonomedia, 1991.

Bey, Hakim. "The Utopian Blues." included in Ron Sakulsky and Fred Ho, eds., *Sounding Off!* Autonomedia, 1995.
(theory, polemic, unusual and vital historical information about music).

Blake, William. *The Portable Blake*. Viking Press, 1969.

Yeats, W.B., ed. *William Blake: Collected Poems*. Routledge, 2002.

Bloch, Ariel and Chana Bloch. *The Song of Songs (a new translation)*. Random House, 1995.

Burnet, John. *Greek Philosophy*. MacMillan & Co. 1961 (originally 1914).
(important background for reading Adorno, Badiou, Bakhtin, etc.)

Cage, John. *Silence*. Wesleyan University Press, 1961.

Chomsky, Noam. *New Horizons in the Study of Language and Mind*. Cambridge University Press, 2000.

Dannen, Fredric. *Hit Men*. Vintage Books, 1991.
(must read for musicians!)

Darwin, Charles. *The Origin of Species*. Penguin Books, 1985.

Denisoff, R. Serge. *Great Day Coming*. Penguin Books, 1971.
(a somewhat skewed view of folk music and the 1960s; included here since it provides useful data).

Denning, Michael. *The Cultural Front*. Verso Books, 1997.
(crucial information and analysis on how 'American Culture' really came to be. Documents the period 1935–55 characterized by working class struggles and their musical and artistic expression. Must read for anyone concerned with popular music as it relates to popular struggle.)

DuBois, WEB. *The Souls of Black Folk*. Dover Publications, 1994 (originally published 1903).
(one of the two books that guided my entire project—must read!)

Ersasmus, Desiderius. *The Praise of Folly*. Yale University Press, 1979.

Ewen, Frederic. *Bertolt Brecht: His Life, His Art, His Times*. Citadel Press, 1992.

Gould, Stephen Jay. *Bully For Brontosaurus*. W.W.Norton & Company, 1991.

Greenway, John. *American Folk Songs of Protest*. A.S.Barnes and Company, Inc, 1960.

Guthrie, Kenneth Sylvan. *The Pythagorean Sourcebook and Library*. Phanes Press, 1998.

Guthrie, Woody. *Born To Win*. Collier Books, 1967.

Guthrie, Woody. *Bound For Glory*. New American Library, 1967.

Hallward, Peter. *Badiou: A Subject to Truth*. University of Minnesota Press, 2003.
(explanatory with background material on Badiou).

Hart, Mickey and Jay Stevens. *Planet Drum*. Harper San Francisco, 1991.

Hirshey, Gerri. *Nowhere To Run*. Da Capo Press, 1994.
(good source of information on Soul music).

Hobsbawm, Eric. *The Age of Extremes:A History of the World 1914–1991*. Vintage Books, 1996.

Hofstadter, Douglas R. *Gödel, Escher, Bach*. Vintage Books, 1980.
(further exploration of the close connection between mathematics and music opening chapter on Bach is worth the price of the book).

Ice-T, *The Ice Opinion*. Pan Books, 1994.

James, C.L.R. *The Black Jacobins*. Vintage Books, 1989.
(understand Haiti then and now, crucial analysis with far reaching implications.)

Johns, Adrian. *The Nature of the Book*. The University of Chicago Press, 1998.

Kostelanetz, Richard. *John Cage (ex)plain(ed)*. Schirmer Books, 1996.

Kropotkin, Peter. *Mutual Aid: A Factor in Evolution*. 1902:
http://socserv.mcmaster.ca/~econ/ugcm/3ll3/kropotkin/mutaid.txt
(Kropotkin's reasearch is essential to an understanding of Evolution. Buried for almost a century, still a must read for scientific, political and philosophical study)

Litwack, Leon F. *Trouble In Mind: Black Southerners in the Age of Jim Crow*. Alfred A. Knopf, 1998.

Locke, John. "Essay Concerning Humane Understanding".
http://www.rbjones.com/rbjpub/philos/classics/locke/

Locke, John. *Second Treatise of Government*.
http://libertyonline.hypermall.com/Locke/second/second-frame.html

Lomax, Alan. *The Land Where The Blues Began*. Pantheon Press, 1993.

Lomax, Alan. *Folk Songs of North America*. Doubleday Books, 1960.

Lomax, Alan, Woody Guthrie and Pete Seeger. *Hard Hitting Songs For Hard Hit People*. Oak Publications, 1967.

Marx, Karl and Friedrich Engels. *The Communist Manifesto*. Oxford University Press, 1998 (originally 1848).

Marx, Karl. *Capital Vol.1*. Charles H. Kerr, 1906.

Marx, Karl. *Introduction to the Critique of Political Economy*. Prometheus Books, 1998.

Marx, Karl. *Theses On Feuerbach*. Prometheus Books, 1998.

Marx, Karl. "Theories of Surplus Value" (Volume IV of *Capital*). Progress Publishers, 1863.

Negri, Antonio. *A Time For Revolution*. Continuum Books, 2003.

Nietzche, Friedrich. *The Case of Wagner*. Vintage Books, 1967

Nietzsche, Friedrich. *Thus Spoke Zarathustra*. Dover Publications, 1965.

Nietzsche, Friedrich. *Beyond Good and Evil: Prelude to a Philosophy of the Future*. Vintage Books, 1967.

Paine, Thomas. *The Age Of Reason*. Willey Book Company, 1942.

Plato, *Complete Works*. Hackett Publishing Company, 1997.

Rousseau, Jean-Jacques. *A Discourse On Inequality*. Penguin Books, 1984.

Smith, Adam. *An Inquiry into the Nature and Causes of the Wealth of Nations*. Random House, 1976.

Sydenham, M.J. *The French Revolution*. Capricorn Books, 1966.

Thomas, Hugh. *The Slave Trade*. Simon and Schuster, 1997.
  (important data about the trade in slaves and its ending—disputes Eric William's conclusions (see below). Read both book for a comprehensive grasp of this subject).

Tolstoy, Leo. *What Is Art?* Penguin Books, 1995.
  (central to my thesis and important to any discussion of art and society, this book can not be neglected by anyone intending honest inquiry into this theme.)

Vilar, Pierre. *A History of Gold and Money*. Verso Books, 1976.
  (important information about the "mystification" of precious metals, specifically, the rise and fall of the Spanish and Portugese empires and the role of gold and silver).

Vincent, Rickey. *Funk, The Music, the People and the Rhythm of the One*. St. Martin's Griffin, 1996.

Williams, Eric. *Capitalism and Slavery*. University of North Carolina Press, 1998.
(crucial analysis of slavery and its economic impact, disputes the Thomas book metioned above. Read both)

Wright, Charles H. *Robeson: Labor's Forgotten Champion*. Balamp Publishing, 1975.

Zappa, Frank (with Peter Occhiogrosso). *The Real Frank Zappa Book*. Poseidon Press, 1989.
(must read for musicians).

Zizek, Slavoj and Mladen Dolar. *Opera's Second Death*. Routledge, 2002.

Zizek, Slavoj. *On Belief*. Routledge, 2002.

Zizek, Slavoj. *The Ticklish Subject*. Verso Books, 2000.

Zizek, Slavoj. *Welcome To The Desert of the Real*. Verso Books, 2002.

Zizek, Slavoj. *Did Somebody Say Totalitarianism?* Verso Books, 2001.
(theory, polemic; dense with important information and insight on the development of philosophy, politics and psychoanalysis).

# Additional AK Press Titles

## Online at:

www.akpress.org / www.akuk.com